On February 24, a three-man Special Forces reconnaissance team two hundred miles inside Iraq was compromised and taken under fire by Iraqi reaction forces. The team requested a daylight "hot" extraction. Although Air Force Special Operations Command doctrine stated daylight extractions were too dangerous for helicopters, its commander made a guts-ball decision, alerting the 160th to fly the mission anyhow.

"Lady Godiva," piloted by Chief Warrant Officer Jim Crisafulli and CWO Randy Stephens, was launched for a two-hundred-mile run through Iraqi air defenses in the middle of the day.

"We never had direct contact with the team," Crisafulli pointed out, "but they were somehow communicating with the F-16 overhead. He was dropping ordnance all around them, trying to keep the Iraqis off. Finally, I remember the pilot telling us if we weren't there in ten minutes, there'd be no team to recover."

Lady Godiva's crew put the pedal to the metal.

AT THE HURRICANE'S EYE

U.S. Special Forces

from Vietnam to Desert Storm

Greg Walker

IVY BOOKS • NEW YORK

Ivy Books
Published by Ballantine Books
Copyright © 1994 by Greg Walker

Library of Congress Catalog Card Number: 93-91729

ISBN 0-8041-0955-9

Manufactured in the United States of America

First Edition: February 1994

DEDICATION

For the operators, whom a wise commander uses with great
skill and forethought, and
whom the fool throws away in ignorance and contempt.

CONTENTS

ACKNOWLEDGMENTS

This book would not have been possible without the support and assistance of a number of individuals and organizations. In no special order, the author would like to thank these sources/resources for their contributions and encouragement.

Jim Morris, former Green Beret and noted author, who posed the question to me about whether such a book could be written and if I thought I could do it. I trust this effort meets his high standards and expectations.

Robert K. Brown, publisher of *Soldier of Fortune* magazine. Without RKB's support, much of my research could not have been funded. In addition, *Soldier of Fortune* allowed me full control over the miniseries which previewed the formal publication of *Special Reconnaissance*, a privilege not often enjoyed by a contributor.

Mr. George Grimes and Maj. Craig Barta (U.S. Special Operations Command), Maj. John Marlin (Special Warfare Center), and Lt. Comdr. Bob Pritchard (Naval Special Warfare) from the public affairs offices of USSOCOM/SWC/NAVSPECWAR. Without the support of the special operations forces (SOF) community, it would have been impossible to access the information necessary to present SOF's role in the Gulf. The U.S. Special Operations Command's public affairs personnel were exceptionally helpful to this project.

Mr. Fred Fuller, whose expertise, judgment, and friendship were critical throughout the writing process.

Mr. Dan Pitzer, who as a POW during Vietnam, brought back the human tools and techniques with which to combat the horrors of being a prisoner of war, and then taught them to those who might need them in America's future conflicts. His insight, grace, and hospitality were much appreciated.

Mr. Ethan Ellenberg, who as my agent ensured the best publisher was approached and convinced of this book's worth. And Mr. Owen Lock, who as my editor allowed me the time and space necessary to present the story on its own terms. Both men have my gratitude.

Col. Kenneth Bowra, 5th Special Forces Group commander, who opened the doors to his command for my benefit. In addition, my respect and gratitude is extended to Gen. Jack Singlaub (USASF), Gen. Donald Blackburn (USASF), Lieutenant Colonel Bargewell (USASF), Lieutenant Colonel Brownlee (5th Grp), Lieutenant Colonel Davis (5th Grp), Colonel Fucci (160th Special Operations Air Regiment), Colonel Stankovich (3d Grp), Colonel (Ret.) Britton (USAF), Colonel (Ret.) Montrem (USAF), Lieutenant Commander Walsh (USN), and Adm. George Worthington (USN) for their time and recollections of events past and projected.

Those operators past and present who offered insights, photographs, recollections, after-action reports, personal notebooks, recommendations, and above all, encouragement. Most prefer their names not be mentioned; they only want their stories told by someone whom they trust.

Those authors and writers whose work I immersed myself in. Their superb works were necessary in order to understand the history, concepts, and future of special reconnaissance/special forces/special reconnaissance.

My wife, Carol, and our four sons. All of whom allowed me to divert time and energy away from our family life so this book could become a reality.

Finally, and most important, to my Lord and Savior, Jesus Christ. Without whom I could never have accomplished the challenges of life, not to mention those presented by Special Forces and its demands.

CHAPTER
ONE

The American Flag was still flying over the embassy. For some reason the Iraqis never lowered it during the occupation. After bomb disposal experts checked the building and grounds for mines and booby traps, Ambassador Edward Gnehm arrived by helicopter to reopen the embassy.
CNN Special Report: War in the Gulf

We'd already been in the embassy for two days and we literally had to evacuate it so they [Special Operations Command Central] could assault it.
Lt. Col. D. BROWNLEE, Operations
5th Special Forces Group (A)

On December 14, U.S. Ambassador Nathaniel Howell ruefully locked the doors of the embassy in Kuwait City. Shortly after Iraq's successful invasion of Kuwait on August 2, 1990, the embassy and a bare-bones staff began defying the Iraqi army by continuing to fly the American flag despite orders from Saddam Hussein that it should be lowered and the embassy closed. Living on meager rations and getting their drinking water from the outdoor pool, the staff took comfort in knowing that the British and the French embassies were engaged in similar psychological combat with the invaders. The decision to authorize the use of force (Resolution 678) by the United Nations influenced Hussein to offer the release of over 565 foreign hostages, including those holed up in the American embassy. Howell, whose courage and leadership qualities were demonstrated throughout the siege, did what any American ambassador would be expected to do under the circumstances. He closed up shop, destroyed classified documents and sensitive equipment, then ushered his staff out the gate, locking it behind him.

He also lowered the flag which had been flying since the invasion. The ambassador then raised the largest American flag his staff could find at the embassy and left it flying over the compound. A State Department source confirms that Ambassador Howell presented the original embassy flag to President George Bush upon the ambassador's return to the United States. This flag was then used to swear in Howell's successor, Edward Gnehm, in early January 1991. Ambassador Gnehm would return the flag to Kuwait, raising it on March 1 to commemorate the reopening of the embassy in Kuwait City.

American embassies have long been the targets of political terrorists and revolutionary factions. In 1979, Special Forces operators entered Nicaragua under false passports to prepare a classified summary on the American embassy in Managua. Because of Nicaragua's impending fall to the Sandinistas, the military wanted the most up-to-date information possible as to how a rescue attempt of embassy personnel might be made. Fortunately, no such operation became necessary.

On November 4, 1979, the embassy staff in Tehran was going about its business despite the increasing political tension in the streets. By noon, a large crowd had gathered outside the embassy's walls. As Iranian police stood aside and watched, militants clambered over the gates and rushed the compound. Ordered not to fire upon the angry crowd, Marine guards watched as the compound was ransacked, its occupants taken hostage. One of the most dramatic political dramas in American history had begun, one which would trigger events and reactions around the world for years to come.

On April 18, 1983, the American embassy in Beirut was preparing for the lunch hour when a van loaded with explosives was driven directly into the building. Among the dead were seventeen Americans, including the first Delta Force operator killed in an enemy attack. Again, an American embassy was selected as a specific target with which to make a political statement.

The reasoning behind such violent acts has to do with the role an embassy plays. It is the formal residence and place of business for whichever country it represents. Its personnel are protected under international law, its grounds are considered to be territorial extensions of the guest nation. To attack an embassy is to attack the country in question, and in the past, gunboats have been sent to put such matters in order.

There is a more subtle reason for assaulting a foreign embassy. If successful, the operation demonstrates a country's inability to defend its citizens and interests in the region. If hostages should be taken, long and complicated negotiations result, and political concessions are often sought in exchange for their release. In short, embassy bashing has proved a viable tactic in the past, especially if the embassy belongs to the United States.

The signal sent by the flag in Kuwait was simple and direct: The United States did not recognize Iraq's claim of legitimate control over Kuwait and, therefore, would not bow to demands made by Hussein. Iraq's ruler was forced to seek an alternative to storming the embassy, a move which would have provided a legitimate excuse for an immediate military response from the United States. Unlike the debacles in Iran and Lebanon, in Kuwait, U.S. forces were far better prepared to mount conventional and unconventional actions. In addition, Hussein was still attempting to convince the world that his invasion of Kuwait should be viewed as solely an Arab matter. In a diplomatic feint, Iraq released its foreign hostages in Kuwait, allowing that foreign embassy grounds were off-limits, at least for the time being.

There were sound economic reasons for assuming this posture. Iraq knew it needed to pacify the West in order to resume increased petroleum sales once Kuwait had been successfully annexed. This meant showing some fashion of restraint where diplomatic concerns lay. Iraq would not want to deal with formal complaints regarding the wanton destruction of embassy grounds and property by its troops, should these incidents occur. By ordering the embassies safeguarded rather than looted, Hussein felt he would be in a better bargaining position with those world powers Iraq was ultimately dependent upon in terms of both economic and military support.

Kuwaiti resistance cells operating inside the city reported that the Iraqis entered the shuttered embassy shortly after Howell's departure, but only "to look around." They never occupied the grounds, nor did they appear to damage any of the buildings or offices. Contrary to widespread reports, they did lower and remove Howell's second flag. Special Forces operators involved in the clearing of the embassy on February 28 would tell of blowing open locked doors. If the Iraqis had ravished the compound as they had the rest of the city, there would not have been a door left hanging on its hinges. Kuwaiti resistance fighters observed the Iraqi forces complete their cursory search, resecuring the embassy gates and leaving the compound abandoned. It would remain so until the wee hours of February 26.

At 0400 hours on February 24, a SEAL deception mission having already been conducted with great success, the 1st Marine Expeditionary Force was scheduled to begin its second-division breaching operation, which was to draw the Iraqis' attention to the southern portions of Kuwait. In truth, the Marines had jumped off fully twenty-four hours early and were within eyesight of what was supposed to be their final objective of the war. "The Marines were ahead of schedule regarding their assigned objectives," recalled one senior army officer. "In fact, they'd breached the lines twenty-four hours prior to the designated time and were already entering the third obstacle belt by the time General Schwarzkopf's Central Command (CENTCOM) realized what was happening." This "off-side" penalty committed by the Marines was the result of Gen. Norman Schwarzkopf's permission for Marine Central Command (MARCENT) to probe forward as the ground war's H hour loomed closer. The farther the Marines probed, the more obvious it became that they faced no opposition. Soon the probing action became a rush for Kuwait City, without Central Command's being advised until the Marines were over thirty miles inside Kuwait. "This posed a serious political problem to the Bush administration," offered the same officer. "The president had given Saddam until midnight on the twenty-fourth to withdraw his forces. The Marines were already nearing the city by the time the president's deadline for a peaceful settlement was reached." In Baghdad, well before the government of Saddam Hussein expected to give any kind of a response regarding the Bush ultimatum, it had been receiving reports of U.S. forces moving toward Kuwait City. For Hussein, the war was on.

Reports of faint Iraqi resistance were passed to Central Command where Schwarzkopf, somewhat astonished by the Marines' liberal interpretation of his original order, launched the general offensive so as to catch up with the Marines. Already moving were both the VII and XVIII Corps, which had been monitoring the MARCENT's radio communications since they'd breached the first obstacle belt the day before. For Special Forces, whose advisers were assigned to Joint Forces

North and East, the order to get their Arab commands moving came nearly twenty-four hours early. "The Arabs weren't supposed to go through the berms until the morning of the twenty-fifth," one operator recalls. "But the order to get them moving reached us by 1500 hours on the afternoon of the twenty-fourth." When Group commander Col. Jim Kraus informed his Arab counterpart of the change, the Arab commander laughed. "They thought it was a joke," says Lieutenant Colonel Brownlee, Kraus's operations officer (S-3). "It took some time to convince them we were not at all being funny."

By the time Kraus did convince the Arabs that it was time to move, American ground forces were twenty miles into Kuwait and moving fast. There simply was no resistance to be found anywhere. The air war, which had targeted the Iraqi artillery concentrations, had destroyed the core of the Iraqi defense. Despite superb obstacle belts made up of fire trenches, mine fields, fighting positions, and bunkers, without artillery to lay down a massive wall of steel, the Iraqi defensive system became impotent. "There was an attitude which was tangible in the air around the American units," one veteran remembers. "They wanted to engage the enemy, to shoot anything that showed opposition. You could feel it all around you."

The Kuwaiti 35th "Al-Shahid" Armored Brigade was the first unit to pierce the sand berm to the north. Their war plans were written for them by senior special operations forces (SOF) officers, each Arab force was to be accompanied by Green Beret advisers, many of whom had been living with the Arabs for months. By mid-December 1990, Central Command approached the SOF advisers about Arab intentions regarding their participation in a ground war. "They [Central Command] couldn't get a straight answer from the Arabs about this," says one officer who was privy to the somewhat awkward development. "But we'd become part of the Arab Coalition because we'd been eating goat with them for six months straight, and were considered close." Egypt was all for war and was ready to roll across the border in an instant. The Syrians said "no," playing a political game which would continue until Coalition forces were reaching Kuwait City. Saudi Arabia said it would not go to war for Kuwait and would only fight if she herself was attacked by Iraq. With this information gathered for them by SOF operators, Central Command and the State Department went to work to convince each nation involved that it would be in its best interests to get on the same sheet of music. "The

Arabs would never give Schwarzkopf a simple answer about their intentions. But they'd talk to us, knowing we'd pass their thinking up through the channels."

By January 13, 1991, Special Forces could confirm that all the Arab forces were located on the border, each in its assigned position and with the proper Command. Linkup with the Allied forces was complete. Informed that the ground war would begin sometime between January 23 and 27, 5th Group advisers began writing the Arab's plan for crossing the berm into Kuwait. On the ground, operators were assembling equipment like mine detectors and plows which would be bolted onto the heavy tanks assigned to breach the high sand walls. "The Arabs had no idea of what to do," said one Green Beret. "It was all they could do to stand around and watch us demonstrate each piece of equipment for them." Now, forced to get their Coalition forces moving nearly a full day early, the advisers took matters into their own hands.

Special Forces Humm-Vs led the way toward the imposing berms. Sixteen lanes had been planned for Joint Forces Command North (JFC-N), whose units included the Egyptian, Syrian, and Kuwaiti forces. Three lanes were to be prepared for JFC-East, which was comprised primarily of Saudi and Omani forces. In accordance with Schwarzkopf's explicit orders, no breaching activity was to have occurred until the early hours of the twenty-fifth. Now those orders had been changed. "The Egyptians were totally at a loss," says one SOF officer on the scene that afternoon. "In fact, everyone was in a state of confusion." Special Forces soldiers jumped into Arab tanks, aiming the heavy steel plows at the berm. Other Green Berets rushed forward and began cutting down the heavy barbed-wire fences, while demolition specialists placed the charges which would blow open the initial gaps for the tanks. JFC-North would get three of its sixteen lanes, courtesy of the United States Army's Special Forces; JFC-East's operators opened up just one. The attack was on . . . kind of.

Colonel Kraus, watching the Egyptians attempting to move their forces into their one lane, finally moved down to where the Kuwaitis had gotten impatient and made their own breach through which to pass. Driving through, the 5th Group commander made a sharp turn and drove several kilometers down to where he could watch the Egyptians still working away at their somewhat enlarged gap. But now he was on the Kuwaiti side of the berm, waiting patiently for his Egyptian counterpart to join him. Meanwhile, back at the berm, Saudi forces were milling about the entrance into Kuwait, their soldiers gently probing the sands for Iraqi mines. It was obvious to their advisers that the Saudis' hearts were not at all in the coming ground war.

With the Kuwaitis rolling eagerly onto their own soil, the rest of JFC-North soon fell into long lines behind their Arab brothers. The Egyptians, overjoyed as their first few tanks and troops crossed successfully into Kuwait, stopped their advance and began celebrating. As the weather clouded over, bringing with it a clinging ground fog, Colonel Kraus turned to his command sergeant major. Both men had just noticed what appeared to be hundreds of ghostlike human beings moving toward their position, the eerie army was coming from the Iraqi positions still ahead of Coalition forces. "Who the hell are they?" asked Kraus. Sims, a huge African-American who ruled the 5th with an iron hand, offered little reassurance. "We'd better hope they're friendly, sir. Because if they're not, our asses are hanging way out there."

The wraiths turned out to be Iraqi soldiers, drawn to the berm by the sounds of the gingerly advancing armies. Approaching Kraus one of the Iraqi soldiers, his hands devoid of any weaponry, stopped. "Americans?" he asked. When the army officer nodded, the man smiled a smile of relief. "Where the hell have you been? We've been waiting for months for you to come and rescue us from Kuwait!" Kraus and Sims could only accept the man's surrender and point him toward the openings leading into Saudi Arabia.

By the evening of the twenty-fifth, elements of the 5th Group's 1st Battalion had made contact with the Kuwaiti resistance, which, trained and directed by U.S. intelligence agencies, had become active since the first day of the invasion. With initial guidance from U.S. Army major John F. Feeley, a member of Gen. Norman Schwarzkopf's Central Command, headquartered outside of Tampa, Florida, the resistance had monitored and reported on Iraqi troop movements and activities inside Kuwait City. Feeley, who'd arrived in Kuwait on July 28 to brief Ambassador Howell on the growing Iraqi military buildup just over the border, spent nearly a month operating on the streets of Kuwait as a resistance figure. His experience as part of Schwarzkopf's staff would serve him well as the situation grew more tense; reports from the embassy, sent out to Central Command, gave precise information as to what might be expected once hostilities commenced. Major Feeley would receive the Legion of Merit for his coolness under fire and superb help in creating the basis for a Kuwaiti resistance movement.

The resistance would prove to be a critical intelligence asset throughout DESERT SHIELD and DESERT STORM. Made up primarily of lower-class Kuwaitis and those having no formal affiliation with the ruling Al Sabah family, the movement also sheltered a number of Shiites whose loyalty was with Iran. In early September 1990, U.S. intelligence personnel had identified a cadre of Kuwaiti nationals, which they felt had the potential to develop the active resistance inside Kuwait City. The United States would not allow SOF assets to participate directly with such an unconventional force for purely political reasons. Instead, this cadre was recruited and trained by outside government intelligence operatives, with necessary communications equipment and weaponry provided by these same agencies.

Once their training was completed, SOF assets assisted the infiltration of the resistance cadre into Kuwait using crews and aircraft from special operations air assets and, via the sea, using SEAL surface craft and security personnel. Once the newly trained fighters were in the city, resistance cells began collecting and transmitting information into Saudi Arabia. Although the Iraqis could monitor such transmissions, especially those sent over mobile car phones, they could not locate their source. As a result, Central Command and Special Operations Command-Central (SOCCENT) were well aware of what was going on inside the capital throughout the campaign.

Sadly, the resistance was doomed from the moment it was established. "They were the victim of a back-room deal," a senior SOF officer explained. He went on to explain that because of its makeup, the royal family would not tolerate continued support of the resistance after the organization's usefulness as a covert intelligence mechanism was exhausted. The arming and training of such a movement was seen by the Al Sabahs as potentially dangerous because the resistance owed nothing to the royal family and some of its membership was openly faithful to Iran. Because of the great potential of a resistance, the Allies were able to convince the emir to allow such an organization to be raised. But it was agreed that the resistance would be cut loose once Kuwait City was declared secure and the emir's loyalist forces again held the reins of power. "We used them for six months, then left them," one veteran admits.

Contrary to popular belief, many Kuwaitis traveled from Saudi Arabia back into Kuwait to visit their families during OP-ERATION DESERT SHIELD. On seldom used roads, they freely moved along the coast, reporting on Iraqi-held positions via cellular phones in their automobiles. Specific resistance figures were infiltrated back into Kuwait City upon completion of their training by civil intelligence agencies or special forces units like the SEALs. By the start of the ground offensive, the resistance was active, following its orders to link up with Co-alition units as soon as possible. They were to provide up-to-date intelligence and act as ground guides when Coalition forces drove toward their objectives.

"Our guys made contact with the resistance and were asked if they'd like to go to our [the U.S.] embassy," recalls Lieuten-ant Colonel Brownlee, the 5th's senior operations officer. "They were told it wasn't permitted, and it wasn't one of our objectives. The resistance then asked if our guys would like to 'just go look at it' because there weren't any Iraqis left in the city." Accordingly, Brownlee's military intelligence detachment joined the Kuwaitis and headed for the capital, over a hundred miles away. At Central Command, Schwarzkopf's staff was stunned to learn that the resistance was operating so far for-ward of the city. When asked how they'd gotten through the Iraqi lines, they responded that there were no Iraqi lines. In fact, there were no Iraqis except for those offering to make a deal for a meal.

Upon their arrival at the city on the afternoon of the twenty-sixth, the SOF operators found the embassy secured as had been reported by the resistance. There were no Iraqis to be seen and the streets were deserted. Curious, the men entered the compound and made a preliminary search. They found no evidence of mines or booby traps nor of any damage to the grounds. When they radioed their observations to Special Op-erations Command-Central (SOCCENT), Lieutenant Colonel Brownlee was one of several to monitor their message. Even he was shocked to hear that special operations teams were al-ready inside Kuwait City. According to Lieutenant Colonel Brownlee, Col. Jesse Johnson, the SOCCENT commander, overheard the same radio transmission. "Colonel Johnson came barreling down the hallway to where I was, demanding to know why our people were anywhere near the American embassy," recalls the veteran Special Forces officer. After explaining that his men were only following their orders to assist the Kuwaiti resistance, Brownlee ordered the detachment to safeguard the embassy but to stay away from it until further notice. "One thing you might want to know," offered the somewhat irritated radio operator on the ground, "the American flag is flying over the compound." At SOCCENT, Brownlee shuddered inwardly. "Tell me," he pleaded, "tell me that you guys didn't put the flag up." To his relief, the Green Berets responded they hadn't. Locking the embassy's gates one more time, the MI detachment pulled back from the embassy until its official "retaking" could be acted out under the supervision of Colonel Johnson.

According to the war plan, none of the embassies in Kuwait City would be secured or reoccupied until the capital had been cleared of enemy troops. In December, Colonel Johnson had approached the 5th Group's commander, Colonel Kraus, with a request. Johnson, the SOCCENT commander, wanted one of Kraus's battalions in order to retake and secure the embassy once the city was in friendly hands. Kraus refused the request. The American embassy was not a tactical objective, and Kraus's teams were heavily committed to Coalition warfare taskings and other missions. Although SOCCENT had operational control over SOF units, it did not possess command control. That critical area belonged to Army Central Command (ARCENT). Special Operations Command-Central was responsible for organizing, tasking, directing, and planning SOF actions in the Gulf, but it could not order Kraus to relinquish troops. "SOCCENT had no tactical mission," confirmed one SOF insider. "In fact, they had long before abrogated any involvement in foreign internal defense [FID] missions. The 5th was under the command of the Army Central Command, or ARCENT. SOCCENT assumed a tactical stance by stating it would be responsible for retaking the embassy. No one else in SOF cared, or wanted the job."

Johnson was forced to ask for additional forces to get the manpower he felt necessary to secure the embassy. He couldn't turn to Delta, perhaps the premier unit responsible for such seizures, because it was under the command of Joint Special Operations Command. In addition, Delta didn't rescue buildings, it rescued people. After convincing the proper channels of his concerns, Johnson was able to get a battalion from the 3d Special Forces Group at Fort Bragg. After arriving in Saudi

Arabia, the battalion was dismayed to learn that there were no real missions for its teams. One suggestion made by command elements of the 5th was that the battalion "could help us out-load to go home." The 3d's operators didn't think the suggestion humorous.

To many, Jesse Johnson's credentials in special operations were fairly impressive; those who had served with the colonel while he was with Detachment Delta, saw him in a more balanced light. Johnson's intense interest in the embassy may have been prompted by his involvement during the early 1980s as the deputy director for Delta. One of the newly formed counterterrorist unit's priority missions was the retaking of occupied American embassies, which Johnson had earlier hoped to get a taste of while serving as the OIC of a Ranger blocking force during the failed 1980 attempt to free American hostages in Iran. In 1981, on the heels of Gen. James Lee Dozier's kidnapping by the Red Brigades, Johnson was ordered by the Joint Special Operations Command (JSOC) to deploy with a Delta team to Italy. But the colonel's I-report-only-to-JSOC attitude caused serious problems between European Command's Gen. W. Y. Smith, the American ambassador to Italy, and JSOC. Only after intense conversation between Washington and Ambassador Rabb was Johnson permitted to operate—as long as he understood he reported directly to the American ambassador. In the end, Italian counterterrorist forces rescued Dozier. Their success was a tribute to American technical counterintelligence agents as well as to an army CID agent with Mafia connections.

Because the ground war in Kuwait ended so quickly, the plan for the securing of the British, French, and American embassy compounds had to be revised. The operation would take place at 1200 hours on February 28. Each country's armed forces would be responsible for the securing of their respective embassies. SOCCENT was busy pulling an impressive array of special operations capabilities together, to include rotary aircraft from the 160th Special Operations Aviation Regiment (SOAR), SEAL fast-attack vehicles, selected Marine personnel, and an assault team from the 3d SFG(A). Consequently, the news that the embassy was in the hands of 5th Group operators on February 26, was less than well received by Colonel Johnson, who was determined to see his command garner recognition for securing the compound two days later.

By February 27, the liberation of Kuwait was well along.

The Marines had captured all their objectives, including the international airport outside Kuwait City. The Marines could easily have moved into the city but were held in place due to Central Command's orders that only special operations forces would assist their Kuwaiti counterparts in the clearing and securing of the capital, a politically important consideration. The Kuwaitis owed their limited battlefield capability to Kraus's 5th Group teams, which had literally rebuilt the shattered force from the ground up. Due to the lack of armed resistance on the part of the Iraqi army inside the city, it was felt the Kuwaitis could liberate the city with only the additional tactical support provided by their SOF advisers.

Around the embassy, a massive block party was taking place. Thousands of the city's residents were in the streets, welcoming their liberators with tears, gunshots, and makeshift American flags. The embassy was surrounded by the happy throng, making vehicle traffic nearly impossible. By this time, a number of 5th Group advisers were scattered throughout the neighborhood where the embassy was located. At one point, a Kuwaiti national approached a wary Green Beret to inform him of thirty-five Iraqi soldiers who had been caught attempting to disguise themselves as civilians. Unless the SOF soldiers could rescue the Iraqis, they would soon be hung by their angry captors, the informer offered.

Following the Kuwaiti, the Special Forces troopers soon hustled the terrified prisoners out of immediate danger. But the crowd followed them, becoming more hostile and threatening with every step. With nowhere safe to go, the Green Berets herded their POWs into the American embassy compound. Six hours passed before trucks could be sent to collect the frightened Iraqi prisoners. By that time, Colonel Kraus had visited the compound personally with Lieutenant Colonel Brownlee. Heading for the airport—launch site for the Special Operations Command operation—both men advised Colonel Johnson that the embassy was secure, undamaged, and in the hands of the 5th Group. Despite this firsthand intelligence from senior SOF officers, preparations for an all-out assault continued. Kraus was told to get his people out of the embassy so they wouldn't "be in the way" when the helicopters arrived on the twenty-eighth. Locking the gate behind him, the last 5th Group soldier left the embassy at midnight on the twenty-seventh.

At 1200 hours the following day, the American embassy was "retaken" and "secured" by combined SOF elements. As a Blackhawk from the 160th Special Operations Aviation Regiment hovered above the embassy's roof, 3d Group operators fast-roped into the compound, armed with light weapons, explosives, and claymore antipersonnel mines. The men moved rapidly to their objectives, followed closely by a Marine security element landed by an air force chopper, which nearly crashed when one of the embassy's patio umbrellas was sucked up through the whirling blades. The compound's interior began resonating with the sound of grenades going off as locked rooms were blown open and cleared. Rifle fire punctuated the smoke-filled air as soldiers dashed from building to building. SEAL fast-attack vehicles patrolled the streets, keeping the curious crowd and a scattering of media at bay. The scene being played out recalled the taking by British SAS troops of the Iranian embassy in London in 1980. The widely televised antiterrorist drama had confirmed the British ability to deal with embassy seizures. SOCCENT's version was easily as impressive. The difference was the Iranian embassy in London had been occupied by bona fide "bad guys" and *was* booby trapped with explosives.

Elsewhere in the city, British and French troops were quietly reclaiming their embassy grounds without fanfare. Down the street, "Johnson's Raiders" were blowing theirs up, much to the delight of the assembled crowd on the street. "We went back on the twenty-ninth for a meeting," Lieutenant Colonel Brownlee recalls. "The embassy was a mess, walls shot up, doors kicked in. All the damage was done when they stormed it." A State Department source at the embassy in Kuwait confirmed that no mines or booby traps were ever found on the premises by SOCCENT's demolition experts. Damage to the compound was estimated by those on the scene at roughly eight million dollars.

By the afternoon of the twenty-eighth, the American embassy in Kuwait City was officially secure. Colonel Jesse Johnson was photographed escorting the new American ambassador to the compound. On March 1, Edward Gnehm proudly raised the original flag that Ambassador Howell had carefully lowered that past December. It was also the same flag with which Gnehm was sworn in as ambassador earlier in Washington.

But what of the small American flag reported on the twenty-sixth to be flying by Brownlee's military intelligence (MI) detachment? If Ambassador Howell indeed lowered the original embassy flag, and the Iraqis took its replacement down, where did the third flag come from? Did the resistance raise it on the eve of the ground war to welcome their American liberators? Or did the Iraqis put one up to suck unsuspecting American troops into a heavily mined killing ground?

According to a number of sources, including SOF operators, senior special operations officers, senior Marine officers, and a senior State Department source at the embassy in Kuwait, the flag was raised sometime during the early hours of February 25 by a squad of Marines.

Encountering little resistance from Iraqi forces, the 1st Marine Expeditionary Force was sweeping rapidly toward Kuwait City. Ordered by Central Command to hold behind the Sixth Ring Road, the Corps stopped short of the city and began digging in. A squad of recon Marines, accompanied by their lieutenant, pushed forward, conducting their own version of special reconnaissance. They ended up outside the American embassy. Despite orders, the lieutenant entered the deserted compound with his men and proceeded to search the premises. Finding no Iraqi defenders, and encountering no booby traps or mines, the Marines prepared to leave. Before doing so, their officer removed a small flag he'd been carrying, ordering it raised. Perhaps recalling the Corps's humiliation in Iran, as well as their having to abandon the Kuwaiti embassy to the Iraqis without firing a shot, the squad quickly ran up the flag and prepared to return to their lines.

It was that flag which was found by army Special Forces operators on the afternoon of the twenty-sixth. For his transgression, the Marine officer was reportedly court-martialed for failing to obey orders. "The Marines were highly embarrassed over the incident," an SF officer recalls. "They were already smarting from beginning their attack earlier than General Schwarzkopf had ordered, and Special Operations Command raised hell about the embassy being entered against orders." Ambassador Gnehm would request troops from the 3d Special Forces Group to act as the embassy's guards upon its liberation, an assignment historically the Marines'. "It [the embassy] was never *officially* secured until the 1st of the 3d accomplished their mission," stated one SOF officer who escorted the new ambassador onto the compound. Maj. Craig Barta, public affairs officer for U.S. Special Operations Command, would call the incident "one of the most embarrassing moments for special operations during the entire Gulf War."

Many of his peers would later agree once the story became known throughout the SOF community.

In retrospect, the unfortunate destruction caused to the embassy cannot be attributed to a failure on the part of special operations personnel tasked to accomplish the mission given them. Operators from the 5th Group had followed their orders to exploit the battlefield situation, joining the Kuwaiti resistance at the earliest possible moment and undertaking a highly dangerous trek into the unknown confines of Kuwait City in order to provide up-to-date intelligence to those needing it. Other special operations troops would have to use the embassy compound as a sanctuary to protect the lives of their prisoners from the anger of hundreds of outraged Kuwaiti citizens eager for revenge. Even the unnecessary assault on the embassy was carried out professionally, with the economy of force assumed necessary to confront the dangers which the 3d's operators had every reason to expect. Ordered to clear and secure the grounds, the 3d's handpicked team made short work of the task, then ensured the physical safety of the diplomatic corps once the embassy was reopened.

The interesting question is why Colonel Johnson insisted on carrying out such a mission once informed it was no longer necessary. Poor decisions on the use of special operations forces have often been made by conventional commanders possessing little understanding of such forces, but Johnson's stubbornness in seeing Special Operations Command-Central as a *tactical* participant in DESERT STORM mirrors past SOF blunders. In his defense, Johnson's instincts as a "goer and doer" may have overridden his judgment as a staff officer.

In any event, the reoccupation of the American embassy demonstrates both the strengths and the weaknesses of special operations forces. Because of their daring, mobility, and ability to cooperate with indigenous forces, they are clearly capable of accomplishing extraordinary missions. Had the possession of the embassy been a tactical consideration, it is quite evident the 5th Group's teams could have occupied and held the diplomatic mission until relieved by a triumphant Kuwaiti army or other more conventional forces (such as the standby Ranger company stationed in Riyadh).

On the downside, the marriage between special operations and the conventional commander calls for the latter's needs to be met by those special operations forces at his disposal. Central Command's war plan did not designate any one embassy a tactical objective. Hussein's allowing foreign diplomats to leave in mid-December eliminated the potential hostage situations. It can be assumed that classified materials and equipment were brought out during the evacuation or destroyed prior to its being carried out. Therefore, the retaking of an empty diplomatic compound was correctly deduced at Central Command to be of little value to the liberation and securing of Kuwait's capital.

The creation of the embassy mission by Special Operations Command ran counter to Central Command's projected plans and ignored Colonel Kraus's indirect admonition that critical special operations assets should not be wasted on purely political objectives. Colonel Johnson's refusal to heed the Group commander's advice and Colonel Johnson's continued inability to take advantage of Lieutenant Colonel Brownlee's special reconnaissance teams, which had reached the embassy forty-eight hours before anyone could have imagined, is curious. For example, SOCCENT could have developed the situation in any number of ways without compromising the reoccupation of the French and British embassies once the capital was declared secure. Instead, Colonel Johnson elected to carry out a dubious mission despite hard intelligence that such an undertaking could no longer be justified.

Fortunately, this incident would be the single blemish on an otherwise spotless performance record set by combined U.S. special operations units during the Gulf War.

CHAPTER
TWO

Outside the orthodox warfare system is a great area of schemes, weapons and plans which no one who knows America really expects us to originate because they are so un-American, but once it's done, an American will vicariously glory in it.

GEN. WILLIAM DONOVAN
Office of Strategic Services (OSS)

Generally, special reconnaissance inside Iraq reflected Gen. Wild Bill Donovan's pragmatic understanding of both clandestine and covert warfare. In 1942, the OSS was preparing to leave operational teams behind as the German advance on the Suez Canal gained momentum. Relying upon Donovan's vast and highly effective unconventional warfare organization, the teams were to engage in intelligence gathering as well as sabotage. Inside Iraq, four OSS special intelligence (SI) operators were working alongside their British counterparts, collecting vital information on Kurdish tribes and Iraq's terrain. As the country was historically a route used by seven previous invading armies, Iraq's importance to the Allies could not be underscored. By all accounts, the OSS reports were of exceptional quality and importance to those receiving them. Special Forces reconnaissance teams tasked to infiltrate Iraq during the Gulf War followed in the footsteps of their special operations forefathers. Their terrain analyses would prove critical to General Schwarzkopf's successful "Hail Mary" armored thrust into Iraq at a time when the Kurds were again viewed as a possible insurgent force congruent to the Coalition's wartime goals. History, as it is said, does indeed repeat itself.

America's special operations capability began with Donovan's Office of Strategic Services, the OSS. Prior to World War II, the United States had relied upon a number of intelligence gathering agencies. President Roosevelt, possessing a better-than-average grasp of the importance of intelligence during peace and wartime, was committed to seeing a central intelligence office established within the government. But agencies already funded and awarded areas of responsibility were highly critical of the efficacy of creating an organization whose far-reaching powers would dominate their own. Particularly adamant were the army and the navy.

Donovan's appointment by Roosevelt brought about a proactive intelligence agency, featuring a cadre of above-average operatives, officers drawn from military and civilian circles and subjected to imaginative as well as demanding selection courses before entering the OSS training program. Donovan, himself a highly decorated veteran of World War I, was heavily influenced by the British approach to unconventional warfare (UW). In turn, the British supported the general's efforts, knowing that American participation in such activities was necessary, given the global scope of the war.

Despite the efforts of those opposed to a central intelligence service, Roosevelt appointed Donovan Coordinator of Information (COI) on June 18, 1942, giving Donovan direct access to the president and a classified budget for COI operations. He began by seeking out the best minds with which to create an intelligence gathering arm unlike any before in the United States. From its onset, the COI was considered outside of the normal military establishment; worse yet, its demand for only the best personnel and equipment emphasized its elite nature as a war-fighting unit. This perception would follow the COI/OSS throughout the war, ultimately contributing to its being disbanded as soon as victory had been proclaimed against the Germans and the Japanese.

Donovan, who'd become a successful lawyer after World War I, realized America was idealistic in her youth, generally respectful of international law, and given to disdain of "dirty tricks." But his travels revealed the ruthlessness of Germany and Japan, and he became a proponent of fighting the enemy by his own rules and on his own ground. It was this philosophy which guided the emergence of the COI during the early days of the war.

The first combat unit deployed by the COI was Detachment 101, commanded by Capt. Carl F. Eifler. Detachment 101's destination was Burma, its mission to support Gen. Joseph "Vinegar Joe" Stilwell's effort to keep the Japanese from swallowing up all of Asia. The detachment's goals included the gathering of information/intelligence, special reconnaissance, the training of guerrilla forces, sabotage, propaganda, and the execution of unconventional warfare in its darkest forms. Although Stilwell was unimpressed with Eifler's mission, to the general's credit he allowed the COI officer the opportunity to prove his unit's worth. For the rest of the campaign, Detachment 101 would make important contributions to the conventional war-fighting effort, using native guerrilla units to secure large areas of previously enemy-held territory and obtaining accurate and timely information regarding the enemy's intentions.

To carry out its wide variety of missions, the detachment relied upon a growing inventory of specialized weaponry and communications equipment. Special operations were bound by few rules; silenced weapons were employed for surprise attacks and assassinations. American agents set up jungle training camps where native tribesmen were taught clandestine radio operations, spying techniques, photography, agent recruitment, and guerrilla warfare. They carried out ambushes and raids against Japanese positions, conducting sabotage against railway lines and other targets of tactical importance. The war in the jungle was brutal, carried out quietly by the detachment's members, and little information concerning its conduct was passed back to the "brass hats." By the time the army began pushing the Japanese back, units such as Merrill's Marauders found themselves greeted by OSS field operators, whose unexpected appearances in the middle of nowhere was often startling. Detachment agents and their guerrillas became guides to the struggling infantrymen, protecting their flanks and mopping up bypassed enemy units as the conventional forces gained ground. The Burma campaign would become a classic study in unconventional warfare, Detachment 101 serving as a cornerstone for the development of the army's future Special Forces.

By June 1942, the COI found itself renamed as the Office of Strategic Services, or OSS. Donovan's organization thrived in an environment which was essentially free of military convention or civilian oversight. Volunteers continued to be encouraged from the ranks of the toughest and brightest candidates, with selection and training conducted at hidden camps under the strictest secrecy. The demands of OSS missions fueled research and development efforts, which produced hundreds of items, everything from tiny hideout knives to compact radio communications gear funneled to agents operating worldwide. OSS operatives were urged to experiment with new methods of intelligence gathering and warfare and often adopted the attitude that the ends justified the means in fighting Japanese and Nazis. As expected, this approach resulted in impressive successes, successes which Roosevelt acknowledged as being instrumental in the overall conduct of the war.

In Europe, the OSS adapted to the demands of the battlefield facing it. Unlike Burma, Japan, and China, occupied Europe possessed a number of organized partisan groups, which were waging war against the German invader. The task of the British Special Operations Executive (SOE) and the OSS was to recruit and develop these underground organizations so that their efforts contributed directly to the Allied effort. In 1943, Donovan's organization began supplying American recruits to the SOE in preparation for the deployment of three-man teams into occupied France. These teams would become known as Jedburghs, or "Jeds."

The Jeds consisted of one American and one foreign officer, with an enlisted radio operator. They were normally infiltrated by parachute, linking up with partisan units once on the ground. Elaborate efforts were made to prepare the teams for their missions, with clothing, identification papers, and cover stories only a part of the agent's overall covert arsenal. Capture by the Germans meant torture and, most often, death. Hitler's infamous "Commando Order" demanded the execution of Allied infiltrators, agents, and commandos, and indeed it was carried out with enthusiasm by German forces. One of the largest such executions took place in Italy when fifteen OSS raiders were trapped at their exfiltration point by the Germans. From the 2677 Special Reconnaissance Battalion, the men had successfully destroyed an important railway tunnel which ran between La Spezia and Genoa. Their PT boat exfiltration craft driven off by enemy fire, the men were captured and executed, their bound bodies thrown into a narrow trench and buried.

In both Burma and Europe, the OSS demonstrated the value of unconventional operations to the conventional battlefield commander. Thousands of enemy troops and materials had to be diverted to deal with the activities of Detachment 101 and the Jedburghs, whose guerrilla and partisan forces proved formidable against even the most aggressive measures thrown against them. In addition, individual OSS agents provided critical information for use by Allied planners, often plying their trade deep within the heartland of the enemy. Despite these accomplishments, the organization was distrusted by many of those in authority, especially those who felt Donovan's OSS enjoyed far too much leeway where command and control was concerned.

In truth, General Donovan was quite aware that his approach would be met with a high degree of hostility by military and civilian authorities. The OSS took secrecy to heart, with operational security an inviolate demand of the organization. Agents often conducted their business on the strength of verbal orders alone, leaving no trail of embarrassing written orders behind.

In its own way, the conventional military attempted to limit the efforts of the OSS by giving its missions low priority for supply and support. This was fairly easy to accomplish, given the organization disdained excessive paperwork and had no official Table of Organization and Equipment (TO&E). In addition, the use of secret agents, informers, turncoats, partisans, and guerrillas in conjunction with conventional forces was an alien concept to the U.S. military of the day. To many observers, Donovan's organization had yet to prove its worth; often its successes were classified, knowledge of them being restricted to a very small circle. To such people, the OSS appeared to be more an irritant than a weapon. To others, having more intimate knowledge of its function and viability, it was a threat to be dealt with at the soonest possible moment.

In their defense, the formal services were justified in their concern about special forces and special operations. They followed a fairly strict soldier's code which governed the profession of arms; the practice of warfare fostered by OSS was frequently in direct opposition to the views held by the Joint Chiefs of Staff (JCS). During OSS military operations, it was not unusual for agents to execute or assassinate traitors and enemy agents, often on the spot. Due process and the Geneva Convention were replaced by the grim realities of partisan warfare, with many OSS operations conducted with the understanding that they and their participants would be officially denied if compromised. For instance, at one point General Stilwell advanced the possibility that Chinese general Chiang Kai-shek might be assassinated due to his inability to conduct the war as Stilwell felt necessary. To prepare such a plan, the general turned to Detachment 101's commander, who accepted the challenge despite knowing his actions would never be supported by Stilwell if the plot were uncovered. In the end, due to the fortunes of war and international politics, the Nationalist leader was spared an unexpected visitor. It should be remembered that Donovan reported directly to the president whose interest in OSS operations and capabilities was great. It cannot be overlooked that the country's highest office no doubt supported, and possibly even suggested some of the more "black" efforts of the war as carried out by his Office of Strategic Services.

From the conventional military point of view, such operations and intrigues were outside the boundaries of the professional/career soldier. The battlefield was a place of honor, its awards and decorations governed by stringent requirements that paid homage to the lofty ideals promoted by the combined military establishment. Careers were based upon an intricate matrix of social and professional accomplishments in which adherence to a rigid military tradition played a major role. Assassins and guerrillas had no place within that carefully maintained caste system, and even the OSS's existence was deeply offensive to many in the professional military. There were more tangible reasons for this dislike, as well.

Physical and mental requirements for the OSS were high, with individual specialized skills keenly considered by OSS recruiters. To meet his personnel requirements, Donovan needed the best officers and enlisted personnel the military could offer. As a result, many army units often found themselves forced to give up their most promising and effective soldiers. In addition, OSS operations and their support demanded huge funding, which meant that less money was available to the other services for their needs. In effect, the nontraditional role of the OSS assaulted the very core of the professional military, while material support of such an organization detracted from the war-fighting arsenals, as well.

To add insult to injury, to the conventional military the OSS was an "elite" organization. Due precisely to the higher quality of manpower, training, and equipment allotted for such units, elite formations have long been recognized as effective during wartime by their uniformed sponsors. In a system which demands regimentation and across-the-board average performance levels, the elite unit is perceived as threatening to the status quo: it siphons off the best soldiers, uses a disproportionate share of the budget, and its soldiers are often difficult to deal with in the traditional manner because their loyalty is given first to the unit and only then to the unit's service. The elite soldier's heightened self-awareness and confidence in his abilities conflicts with the daily regimen of chickenshit activities forced upon the average soldier. Indeed, active duty soldiers are referred to as "regulars" whereas their elite-unit peers are most often called by their unit's specialty, e.g. "Rangers," "paratroopers," and most recently, "Special Forces," "SEALs," and "LRRPs." In the OSS's case, it was difficult to find a category in which to fit its operators and agents. They generally functioned beyond the touch of the conventional military system, often flaunting its authority, almost always creating new ways to accomplish missions that the regulars said couldn't be done.

In the end, that freewheeling attitude and disdain for accepted practices would be the death of the organization once the war was over. Like President John F. Kennedy, who would serve as the Green Berets most influential supporter in the early 1960s, Roosevelt's strong belief in the OSS essentially protected the unit from those favoring its disbanding during the war years. When Roosevelt died in 1945, the OSS's days grew swiftly fewer, and behind-the-scenes politics moved rapidly to ensure the organization's dismantling after the war's end.

Of the many contributions Donovan's men made to the embryonic special operations capability needed by the United States, the "routine" carrying out of special reconnaissance missions was one of the more impressive successes. Detachment 101's teams, operating in the classic unconventional warfare environment, gathered otherwise unobtainable information through clandestine patrols and static observation posts. In addition, the teams successfully targeted vital military installations for future attacks by Allied air power and eliminated key military/political figures so as to weaken the command and control structure of the Japanese in the occupied territories.

In Europe, the OSS carried out special reconnaissance under far more restrictive conditions than those that existed in Burma, its partisan bands and operational groups likewise gathered critical information about the enemy and pinpointed priority targets for bombing or attacked such targets themselves. Again, the selective assassination of military personalities as well as civilians deemed important to the German war effort was given the green light by those higher authorities to whom Donovan was responsible. One particular device so used was an explosive candle developed by OSS researchers. Provided to female agents, the candles would be lit after a night's lovemaking with German officers who'd been charmed by the OSS agent's attentions. Slipping out the door, the agent's final gift often ensured the officer's evening ending with a bang as the candle's internal explosive was ignited by its flickering wick.

Despite the contributions of the OSS to a final Allied victory, the OSS disappeared soon after the war's end. After a brief interval, it was resurrected within the Central Intelligence Agency (CIA), whose ranks boasted a large number of former OSS agents, including William Colby and Bill Casey, future CIA directors. Another former OSS agent was Lucien Conein, destined to become one of the Agency's most important agents in the Vietnam War. But not all veterans of OSS drifted to the CIA; other agents returned to the army. One of these was Aaron Bank, a young officer whose wartime experiences had been hard won in Europe, where he'd served with the Jedburgh teams. Bank possessed firsthand knowledge of partisan warfare, and he understood the kind of organization and personnel required to implement it. In 1951, Bank would have his shot at creating an official army unit tasked with the conduct of unconventional warfare. He and Lt. Col. Russel Volckmann, a veteran guerrilla fighter who'd fought behind the lines in the Philippines until MacArthur's return, would become responsible for the army's Special Forces, which was activated on June 19, 1952.

Along with Special Forces came special reconnaissance, a concept which would become a trademark of the Green Berets, beginning with their deployments to Laos and South Vietnam during the mid-1950s.

CHAPTER
THREE

By whatever name, this militant challenge to freedom calls for an improvement and enlargement of our own development of techniques and tactics, communications and logistics to meet this threat. The mission of our armed forces—and especially the army today—is to master these skills and techniques and to be able to help those who have the will to help themselves.

PRESIDENT JOHN F. KENNEDY
April 14, 1962

By 1947, the Central Intelligence Agency was a functioning organization, which absorbed its heritage from the OSS's special intelligence (SI) branch. With the void left by the loss of the special operations branch as a result of the dismantling of the OSS, the CIA assumed covert responsibility for both resistance movements and guerrilla warfare. This was a natural evolution because many CIA operators had been wartime OSS field agents with experience in Asia and Europe. Despite the Agency's interest and apparent headstart, the army was concerned enough about the impact of partisan warfare to evaluate its role as an army mission.

Unconventional Warfare (UW) is defined as those interrelated fields of guerrilla warfare, evasion and escape, and subversion against hostile states (resistance). Such operations are conducted behind the lines, normally deep within enemy-held territory or in the enemy's own backyard. UW is carried out by primarily indigenous personnel and supported/advised by an external power. During World War II, the British and Americans had been the primary sources of support and advice for resistance efforts. Through the OSS, the United States had supported guerrillas in Burma, Vietnam, China, France, Italy, and even Germany itself. Many lessons had been learned by its agents, all of these carefully documented for future use.

The United States Army saw unconventional warfare as a tool with which to foster political discontent within a country America might be at war with or one which was targeted as being within the scope of the United States' national interests. In any event, the first priority of UW was the support of U.S. conventional operations during a declared war under the direction of a theater commander. Such support would include intelligence gathering, including the use of reconnaissance teams within enemy-dominated territory. At the same time, it was understood that the emergence of resistance movements required a uniform response that could influence such movements and their leaders toward the United States. Ignoring the potential of internal uprisings could lead to conventional forces fighting both a resistance effort as well as the forces which the resistance was opposed to. Such a "war on two fronts" was not practical, given the experiences of World War II.

Special reconnaissance was seen as critical to a successful campaign as early as 1946, when Secretary of War Robert Patterson began advocating the creation of an airborne reconnaissance option by the War Department. Patterson's belief in such a capability was derived from the after-action reports gathering dust in OSS files. It is important to note that shallow reconnaissance—reconnaissance carried out just forward of friendly lines and within fire support of air and artillery means—was a standard tactic employed at division level and below. The secretary of war's emphasis was on a deep reconnaissance capability, such as that carried out by OSS Jedburgh and operational group teams and Detachment 101's extensive efforts. Such reconnaissance offered a wide variety of submissions to the theater commander, including the targeting of industrial areas, bomb-damage assessments, communications disruption, and the pinpoint destruction of command-and-control centers. At the war's end in 1945, all units capable of deep reconnaissance were disbanded and their personnel either discharged or transferred to other, more conventional, duties. Units affected included not only the OSS, but the Marine Corps's Raider and army's Ranger battalions, all of which had fought brilliantly throughout the course of the war.

Reacting to Patterson's interest in such a project, an Army Ground Forces (AGF) study concluded that such a unit had potential. Despite the proven value of deep reconnaissance and the volumes of information generated during the training and deployment of the OSS, the Raiders, and the Rangers, the AGF study called for the establishment of a forty-one-man cadre as an experimental unit. It is possible the AGF study's recommendation was meant to satisfy the secretary of war by appearing to take his concern to heart, when AGF would be just as pleased to drop the entire matter because of a perceived "elite" nature of an airborne reconnaissance unit. At any rate, once the intelligence division of the general staff (G-2) became involved, the idea of establishing an experimental cadre was dropped. Far more aware of the value of long-range reconnaissance because of its mission, the G-2 pushed Army Ground Forces to develop an overall concept for the training and formation of such units within the army. To do this, the AGF turned to a veteran OSS commander, Col. Ray Peers.

By the end of 1948, a hybrid solution for an airborne reconnaissance capability was being developed. With Peers's input, Army Field Forces (AFF)—as AGF was by then known— recommended the formation of a "Ranger Group," which would conduct a combination of Ranger and unconventional warfare missions. AFF was comfortable with the Ranger label, as there was precedent within the army for such units dating back to colonial times. In addition, the AFF was comfortable in dealing with Ranger missions because they were based upon small unit tactics and objectives. Colonel Peers's UW background (the colonel had commanded Detachment 101 for the OSS during the war) was lumped in with the AFF proposal, although it was obvious no one unit could be proficient in such a dual role. In any respect, the Ranger Group would never become anything more than a paper drill.

Still, unconventional warfare continued to be a topic of interest to the Joint Chiefs of Staff, which felt that responsibility for the conduct of unconventional warfare should be split between the CIA, for peacetime operations, and the army, for wartime operations. Further, that the army needed to provide some kind of training in UW to selected personnel so as to be prepared should such a capability be required. The CIA, blessed by a decision made by the National Security Council, assumed full responsibility for the support and execution of both unconventional warfare and the development and extended support of guerrilla movements deemed favorable to U.S. interests. Again, an obviously active OSS influence had been working overtime against a slow-moving and reluctant army. Now the Agency could rely upon the army to provide training for its agents and paramilitary cadres, knowing that only an act of declared war could drag the service into a UW role. With the Cold War slowly heating up and a host of smaller conflicts simmering around the world, the CIA was assured a broad operational arena under its new mandate.

Accordingly, the Agency moved faster to consolidate its hold on the unconventional warfare role. If the army was going to pussyfoot around regarding a force with which to fight such a war, the CIA determined it would raise its own army through the training facilities and instructors possessed by the army. By doing so, the Agency's peacetime responsibility for UW would be realized and could be proven as a viable mission for the intelligence service. Parallel to this was the CIA's hidden agenda regarding a wartime role. As long as the army declined to become firmly involved with UW, it could not hope to field an operational force to carry out UW missions during a declared war. If the Agency was already in possession of such a force, and that force had proven itself effective on the covert battlefield, assuming a wartime role from the unprepared and unblooded army would be assured.

As it turned out, an aroused secretary of defense successfully challenged an edict from the secretary of the army meant to disassociate the army from *any* recognition of or participation in unconventional warfare. Had this not occurred, the army would have stepped aside, leaving the CIA in full control of all future special operations forces and missions.

By 1951, both Aaron Bank and Russ Volckmann were hard at work devising a concept which would meet the needs of the latest JCS study regarding the army's position on unconventional warfare. In effect, the army was tasked to be the principal force of an effective UW doctrine. Additionally, it was to explore the formation of a unit tasked to conduct unconventional warfare and implement its findings as soon as possible. Falling back to old rivalries as seen in World War II, the army's G-2 was loathe to relinquish ground to the CIA where intelligence was concerned. The Agency was seen as simply an evolution of the old OSS, whose control over intelligence had been a source of contention to all of the agencies involved in its collection and analysis. Because of the army's concern over losing a wartime mission, unconventional warfare, and possibly becoming a weak sister in the intelligence game, the creation of Special Forces became a belated necessity.

A more capable team to draft the plans for such an organization could not have been found. Aaron Bank and Russ Volckmann were products of the conventional army whose experience with UW had been brought about by the circumstances of war. Bank possessed the devil-may-care philosophy of the OSS and had worked extensively with foreign nationals in Europe during his service with the Jeds. Volckmann was a stay-behind when Douglas MacArthur was forced from Luzon by the Japanese. Charged with carrying out guerrilla warfare until MacArthur's return, the young captain joined with the guerrillas and began a three-year campaign against the occupation of the Philippines. Working alongside a small group of Americans, Captain Volckmann watched the small partisan bands grow until over twelve thousand guerrillas were operating as an effective combat force.

Perhaps because his background leaned more toward the conventional, Volckmann appeared to understand the army's wish to soften its acceptance of a special operations unit by associating such a unit with the politically correct Ranger concept. Such units had been part of the army's heritage since Roger's Rangers had been formed in 1756. During World War II, six Ranger battalions had been formed, all seeing combat. In addition, the army likened the 5307th Composite Unit (Provisional) to being essentially a Ranger-type unit, its operations in Burma earning the 5307th the nickname Merrill's Marauders. In October 1951, the chief of staff of the United States Army had directed formal Ranger training to take place so as to "raise the level of infantry training, army-wide." With the 1948 "Ranger Group" concept still on the books, appealing to the army's open admiration of Ranger operations and employment may have appeared a wise compromise to the former guerrilla leader.

Bank was not as convinced. Although Ranger operations included such activities as raids, ambushes, and reconnaissance patrols, they did not include unconventional warfare, encompassing special reconnaissance, assassination, forgery, safecracking, photography, agent handling, intelligence networks, a knowledge of foreign languages and customs, an ability to instruct in a wide variety of military skills, and enormous patience. Ranger operations were geared toward direct-action missions, such as ambushes and raids against specific targets.

Although the Rangers were assigned an antiguerrilla role, neither training nor becoming guerrillas had been part of their mission.

Added to this was the difference in mind-set between the army Ranger and what Bank believed the Special Forces soldier should possess. Rangers, then and today, follow a highly regimented system of command checks and balances. Rangers are not taught to operate as individuals, but as a coordinated team. In this manner, they have become some of the finest light infantry soldiers in the world. Bank knew that the unconventional warrior would have to function as both a team member and individual, capable of making instant decisions, often without the immediate supervision of a higher headquarters or superior. In Bank's opinion, the Special Forces recruit needed to reflect those characteristics which General Donovan had sought for the OSS. In short, the Ranger concept could not be imprinted over what would be required in Special Forces.

Volckmann and Bank had studied recommendations offered by numerous parties since 1946 on an unconventional capability. Both men understood the implications of the CIA's position regarding UW and knew an army organization tasked to conduct such a mission had to reflect a strategic impact upon general-war doctrine. Should they allow the Ranger mission to be attached to UW, there was little doubt the unit would soon find itself supporting tactical commanders in the field, conducting shallow reconnaissance, raids, and ambushes instead of deep-penetration missions and other UW taskings. If that were the case, the CIA would be able to point out that the army was ignoring UW and would offer to step in to exploit and develop resistance and guerrilla movements in enemy territory.

The challenge, then, was to deliver to the JCS an organization that reflected the personnel requirements and missions first established by the OSS but which was acceptable to the U.S. Army. Emphasis would have to be on the specific UW missions envisioned by Bank and Volckmann and required under the JCS mandate, with little mention of small-unit tactical capabilities, which could be identified with Ranger operations. In a conversation with Volckmann on where to put their emphasis, Bank offered the following: ". . . in my opinion, we should, where possible, stress and emphasize employing the OSS heritage."

The Special Forces concept was primarily concerned with Eastern Europe, which had been gobbled up by Russia during and after the Second World War. An ideal UW theater, Eastern Europe had numerous pools of potential resistance movements and guerrilla forces available for development. At the same time, the Soviets were quickly tightening their grip on every facet of social activity within the conquered territories, and intelligence sources were drying up. Bank realized an army Special Forces intelligence-gathering capability operating behind the Iron Curtain could reap benefits.

Special reconnaissance would play a part in SF's warfighting role, although it would not be termed as such until much later. Under the unconventional warfare umbrella of capabilities, the army required its unconventional forces to support combat operations of both the theater and the tactical commander. For the theater commander, SF/UW forces could expect to be assigned intelligence missions "such as target acquisition and damage assessment," which are critical missions because the existence, makeup, and exact location of military targets must be confirmed by ground assets before being struck and, generally, such confirmation had to be done by U.S. "eyes and ears" as these sources were the only ones an American commander would trust without reservation when preparing to launch aircraft or missiles.

The tactical commander would need unconventional warfare forces to capture key installations or to prevent their destruction, to carry out diversionary attacks in support of deception plans, and to use as reconnaissance elements in support of local operations. It is of interest that all of the proposed early missions (developed and published in FM 31-21 in September 1961) were undertaken to one degree or another during OPERATIONS DESERT SHIELD/STORM nearly thirty years later.

Special reconnaissance, as we have discussed, includes a far broader array of submissions than reconnaissance in the conventional sense. The latter concerns itself with both short- and long-range patrols meant to collect information within a defined area. Normally, such recon or recce patrols are no larger than an infantry squad and operate within the range of effective fire support such as artillery and air. Missions include target acquisition, reconnaissance, and surveillance. Generally, such missions do not last more than seventy-two hours because of the high levels of stress involved and the team's limited ability to protect itself during chance enemy contacts.

The developers of Special Forces knew that the conventional commander would most likely not be concerned with UW as the conduct of such warfare would be outside his immediate battlefield goals. Therefore, Special Forces could not be seen as an excellent source of recon teams if they were available to such a commander. Both Bank and Volckmann saw SF as a strategic option, meant to serve the theater commander's needs within the big picture. The theater commander would require intelligence collection and other efforts beyond the capabilities of his tactical commanders' forces. This meant special reconnaissance, and SR demanded Special Forces.

Since the inception of Special Forces in 1952, the definition of "special reconnaissance" (SR) has evolved as Special Forces operators have conducted missions in support of a number of wars and conflicts. Today, SR activities are unilateral, meaning they are directed by a U.S. Special Operations Command rather than being coordinated through a foreign power. Missions are not much different than first defined in 1961, with many having to do with forms of reconnaissance, target acquisition, and surveillance. Teams directed to conduct SR may become involved in long-term information collection efforts, which normally support additional collection systems such as high-altitude imagery (spy satellites) and intelligence-agency agent networks. As already mentioned, SR puts trained personnel "on the ground" to acquire, verify, or deny intelligence data, which will influence tactical decisions. Signal intelligence (SIGINT) is vulnerable to equipment malfunctions, weather, and countermeasures, while remote intelligence sources may provide unreliable or dated information. Conventional reconnaissance provides information regarding the immediate front; special reconnaissance offers a far larger picture from well behind enemy lines, and it permits "active" options once the information is received and analyzed. Unlike the conventional recon mission, SR can be of long duration and carried out well beyond friendly fire support. In fact, the range of SR teams is confined only by the method of infiltration (delivery) and the manner of secure communications with the rear.

During their conduct of special operations, OSS operators often wore no distinctive uniform or emblem which would have identified them as U.S. forces. As a result, many were shot as spies or commandos once they were discovered. Today's SR operations may also involve the use of equipment, clothing, or weapons which are nonissue, and normally untraceable to the sponsoring power.

The Cold War threat faced by Bank and Volckmann in the

early 1950s demanded a strategic capability which would allow the army to gather timely intelligence utilizing possible resistance movements within the Soviet Union as well as U.S. ground personnel who would carry out unilateral taskings. Though many confuse unconventional warfare to mean guerrilla warfare, the term "unconventional warfare" was intended to apply to a series of actions which could be taken by a theater commander in support of declared or undeclared conflicts. Special Forces teams would be expected to train and advise insurgent organizations to act as guerrillas during peace/wartime, but the trainers/advisers themselves would also be available to carry out, via special reconnaissance activities, such missions as locating Soviet nuclear installations for future attention by U.S. military planners.

When approached by army operations and asked if his Special Forces could conduct Ranger missions as well as UW, Bank replied SF teams could indeed execute raids and reconnaissance, but not as frontline troops. "However," he said, "to use Special Forces' highly trained and specialized personnel for that type of activity would be a terrible waste." Colonel Bank's opinion would be validated during the Vietnam War's overuse of Special Forces to conduct conventional reconnaissance and hunter-killer missions throughout the embattled country.

By summer's end, 1951, the birth of Special Forces was a done deal. Despite a Third Army effort to have the unit's training center and first group headquarters situated elsewhere, Fort Bragg, North Carolina, was selected and approved. Aaron Bank was chosen to serve as the Special Warfare Center's first commandant, and his future command of the 10th Special Forces Group (Airborne) assured once a suitable replacement was transferred from the Infantry Center. Colonel Bank's selection to head up Special Forces was based upon his understanding of unconventional warfare and his "ground time" as an operator with the OSS in Europe. The necessary personnel slots had been made available several months earlier through the deactivation of the army's Ranger companies in Korea. At the same time, the European Command voiced its feelings that formal Ranger units were no longer necessary in that theater. Both commands believed that Rangers could not conduct UW because of a lack of skilled linguists or an inadequate supply of soldiers of the proper race. Almost as an afterthought, the Army Field Forces offered that any formal association between

Rangers and Special Forces should be declined as SF would be engaged in sub-rosa activities. The army didn't want to stain its pristine Ranger mission with black warfare.

On June 19, 1952, the tiny cadre of 10th Special Forces Group (Airborne) was activated.

CHAPTER
FOUR

> But the Special Forces were also animals, which offended
> all the prancers, and they considered themselves an elite
> force, which offended almost everybody else. General
> Abrams *hated* them. Yet, if these Green Berets had been al-
> lowed to run the show, there's little doubt in my mind that
> the outcome of the war would have been quite different.
> COL. DAVID H. HACKWORTH
> *About Face*

Animals. Certainly that was how the conventional army pre-
ferred to view Special Forces during the Vietnam conflict, a
"counterinsurgency" which President Lyndon Johnson and his
staff were convinced could be won by tanks, aircraft, and spit-
shined boots. But as history would later show, it was President
Kennedy's approach to Southeast Asia's multiple limited conflicts which possessed the greater opportunity for a politico-
military victory with the least amount of investment. Sadly,
after Kennedy's assassination the presidential emphasis on special operations evaporated, and the mission statements of
special-operations units were corrupted by the hierarchy of the
conventional military and by intelligence services such as the
CIA.

Kennedy's support of special operations and the units designed to carry them out had grown from his own experiences
as a PT boat commander during World War II. Such units operated on the basis of speed and stealth, attacking enemy ship-
ping when it was least expected and undertaking clandestine
infiltrations of U.S. and Allied commando teams far behind
Japanese lines. It was his own wartime experiences with special operations which influenced the president's healthy interest

in creating organizations and tactics which could better deal with the numerous Third World conflicts facing his administration in early 1961.

Kennedy's first challenge was in Laos, a tiny country considered by military thinkers to be critical to the stability of Indochina. The pro-Communist Pathet Lao forces supported by the Soviets were gradually gaining control over the countryside, forcing the United States to consider various means of defending the legitimate government, including one plan which called for the use of nuclear weapons. A Communist victory in Laos would make possible further expansion, into Thailand, South Vietnam, and Cambodia, via the Ho Chi Minh trail. In a sense, the use of Laos as a staging and logistical platform by Communist forces could be likened to the *tache d'huile*, or spreading-oil-stain method of securing an ever-expanding area of control by either guerrilla or counterguerrilla forces. Kennedy's challenge was to prevent the fall of Laos into Communist hands, while keeping the United States from establishing an overt presence in the country, which might be challenged by Communist China, a far more dangerous adversary.

In the end, the president would agree with his Laos task force that the United States could only realize its political objectives by encouraging the defeat of the Pathet Lao on the battlefield, thereby allowing the kingdom to declare itself neutral toward all parties concerned. OPERATION MILLPOND, as it became known, would begin with the introduction of Special Forces advisers who were charged with a number of tasks, the primary one being the reconstitution of the *Forces Armees de Laos*.

This "introduction" would prove to be no more than an expansion of the deployment of Special Forces operators in Laos which had been begun in 1959. At that time, Laos was under the administration of France, which supported Laotian king Savang. Because of the Pathet Lao and their support by North Vietnam's Communist government, France and the United States agreed to cooperate on an upgrade of the Royal Lao Army headed by Gen. Phoumi Nosavan. U.S. Special Forces teams would enter the country secretly because the Geneva Accords made their military involvement illegal. At first the Special Forces teams taught classes on basic military skills such as weapons proficiency and radio communications, and French advisers were responsible for combat training. This relationship survived until an attempted coup in August 1960 saw the U.S. advisers assigned directly to the pro-Western forces of General Nosavan. This decision prompted the withdrawal of France's military presence from Laos. Once the general's army was reconstituted and deemed capable of retaking the capital of Vientiane, Special Forces personnel were permitted to join the *Forces Armees de Laos* in a combat role. By the end of December 1960, Vientiane had been recaptured, and the neutralist government, which had been installed by Capt. Kong Le, was replaced by King Savang.

With a degree of political stability once again established, the role of Special Forces was quickly expanded, and additional teams were deployed from the 1st and 7th Special Forces Groups. The Laotian army was enlarged until it could field twenty-one battalions. To ensure continued training as well as tactical expertise, U.S. advisers were assigned to each battalion. On March 9, 1961, President Kennedy accepted the advice of his Lao task force and authorized preparations for a large-scale military buildup to include what were to become known as White Star Mobile Training Teams. In fact, Special Forces operators were already advising the Royal Lao Army, but had initiated the basis for a counterinsurgency program involving Kha tribesmen in the I, II, III, and southern IV Military Regions. By the end of April 1961, Special Forces personnel were actively prosecuting the war against the Pathet Lao in what was becoming a classic counterinsurgency.

Still, the Pathet Lao remained a formidable force, with growing support coming from the North Vietnamese. Since control of the Ho Chi Minh trail was considered vital to the strengthening of Viet Cong forces in South Vietnam, the North Vietnamese increased their assistance to the Pathet Lao. To counter the growing battlefield threat against the Royal Lao Army, White Star teams enlarged their training program of the tribal groups to include the Meo. Such paramilitary forces could conduct counterinsurgency as well as proinsurgency activities behind enemy lines and across defined borders. The regular army was tasked with protecting the Lao government and defending the country's most strategic areas, but the paramilitary forces developed at Phou Bia (Meo) and in the Plateau des Bolovens (Kha) were recommended to U.S. conventional military authorities as a force that would support Royal Lao Army objectives, undermine the Pathet Lao in his own backyard, and set the stage for exporting an insurgency to the North Vietnamese.

This foresight would be largely ignored as the Joint Chiefs of Staff in Washington had long held to either a full-scale *conventional* intervention in Laos or no involvement at all. By that time, South Vietnam was being seen as the place to take a stand against Communist aggression because its insurgency was seen as less well developed than that taking place across the border in Laos. At this critical juncture, due to the conventional military's severe lack of understanding and acceptance of Kennedy's belief that guerrilla-style conflicts were the future challenges to democracy worldwide, Special Forces would realize its first politico-military defeat. Where Special Forces commanders were applying the mutually supporting concepts of protracted struggle and foreign internal defense, the conventional (and politically much more powerful) military wanted to emulate France's conventional military approach to eradicating North Vietnam's "insurgency" without committing the errors which led to France's defeat in Vietnam. As the United States had never fought an organized insurgency in its short history, the Special Forces cowboys-and-Indians approach to the war in Laos was perceived to be more of a holding action than a method of actually bringing the conflict to a favorable conclusion.

At the same time, the JCS feared that a successful counter-insurgency program, given the necessary financial and logistical support required to see it through, would undermine the agenda proposed by the JCS, which argued that a full-scale military presence was the only way to maintain Laos under U.S. influence and control. But even as Kennedy was being urged to follow through with the seventeen-step OPERATION MILLPOND—a plan which ultimately called for the deployment of a massive military force in support of King Savang—it was becoming apparent that the conventional military forces of the United States were incapable of inserting the manpower and equipment into Laos that would allow a conventional war to be mounted immediately against vastly better prepared Communist forces. This in itself made a mockery of the Laos task force solution promoting a battlefield defeat of the Pathet Lao, to be followed by an announcement of neutrality by King Savang. General Nosavan's army had failed to defeat the Pathet Lao in 1959, had been thrown out of Vientiane by Kong Le's paratroops in 1960, had lost the battle for the Plain of Jars, and had been further humiliated by being slaughtered in a Pathet Lao counteroffensive in 1961. It would see final defeat in 1962 as the Communists overran huge portions of the country prior to the Declaration of Neutrality, being signed on July 23.

In short, the only means of saving Laos from the Communists was the introduction of U.S. special operations forces with the missions of nation-building and aggressive counterinsurgency. The lack of a coherent political policy toward Laos by the Kennedy administration was aggravated by the JCS's lack of concerted military support for Special Forces operations. These two factors successfully hamstrung the Special Forces' efforts against an enemy which knew very well where its beans and bullets were coming from and what its final objective was.

By the summer of 1962, it was painfully clear the United States could not hope to maintain control over the situation in Laos, and U.S. policymakers were rapidly turning their sights on South Vietnam, the Pentagon offering that the dismal results of the war in Laos justified sending selected forces to Vietnam for "training purposes." Four hundred of these troops were to come from the 1st Special Forces Group based on Okinawa. Within seventy-two hours of their arrival, the term "training" would be dropped, replaced by "combat."

Back in Laos, the Special Forces teams under White Star were preparing to depart. Of the nearly fifty teams operating in country, eighteen had concentrated on counterinsurgency. This effort utilized the Meo and Kha tribes as paramilitary forces for long-range reconnaissance, strike operations, raids, ambushes, and harassing operations. The war-savvy mountain people were superb combat soldiers whose loyalty was aligned with their Special Forces advisers and opposed to the Laotian government, which held them in general distaste. Using equipment, weaponry, and funds provided by the CIA under its charter to support the conduct of unconventional warfare during peacetime, the program was seeing positive results against Pathet Lao forces and was creeping toward the conduct of combat operations against the Ho Chi Minh trail. But intense pressure from the Laotian government cut the legs out from under the Meo/Kha irregulars because the Laotians feared a well-armed and trained coalition of tribes might become yet another independent political element once the Americans left the country.

The employment of Special Forces in Laos resulted in a number of lessons which would prove useful in Vietnam. Unfortunately, the bulk of those "lessons learned" was responded to by the SF organization itself rather than by the conventional senior military commanders who would be responsible for directing special operations assets throughout the Vietnam War. As well, Special Forces operations in Laos gave rise to a number of negative attitudes concerning the employment of Special Forces. These attitudes serving the purpose of those who felt such forces were unnecessary or unreliable within the conventional military. To some, the loss of Laos supported the opinion that a massive infusion of U.S. combat troops earlier on would have saved the day. The practice of counterinsurgency was in its infancy, and despite its remarkable accomplishments in the field, the ultimate withdrawal of the United States did little to win support for such warfare in Washington.

The CIA's underwriting of the Special Forces' war in Laos was gladly accepted by the advisers, primarily because such support was not forthcoming from its parent organization—the U.S. Army. But the CIA had its own agenda for the war in Southeast Asia and was far more perceptive in appreciating the impact that Special Forces and special operations were having in furthering that agenda. The relationship between CIA and Special Forces would grow as emphasis was placed upon winning the war in Vietnam, but it would greatly sour the professional relationship between Special Forces and the remainder of the U.S. Army.

Finally, the ability of the Special Forces to father aggressive irregular defense forces such as those represented by the Kha and Meo tribesmen proved to be a facet of special operations the conventional military never quite grasped. Disparaging such forces as "secret armies" detracted from the tactical value such forces provided, and later, in Vietnam, every such organization of irregulars was, ultimately, abandoned by its U.S. sponsors. The lesson that was learned by those at the Pentagon was that Special Forces could dramatically influence foreign policy through its proven talents in organizing, training, and leading diverse political factions, but that by doing so, SF became a challenge to the traditional approach of implementing U.S. policy.

Though no more than 433 Green Berets and 317 Military Advisory Assistance Group (MAAG) personnel ever operated inside Laos at any one time, the JCS awarded the 7th Special Forces/White Star project an Armed Forces Expeditionary Medal. This campaign medal only applied to those who'd served in Laos between April 19, 1961, and October 7, 1962. It is the only such award given to date for a counterinsurgency mission.

Special reconnaissance was an integral part of the Special Forces effort in Laos. Recon teams led or advised by SF personnel were successful in locating Pathet Lao supply routes, base camps, staging areas, and command-and-control sites. The Kha and Meo irregulars were hugely successful in securing large areas of the countryside under their control and in fielding reconnaissance efforts ever closer to North Vietnam. Special Forces camps and mission support sites (MSS) were remotely situated, often supplied by rugged light aircraft landing on hard-packed dirt strips.

The success of these early reconnaissance gathering efforts would serve as the foundation for the multitude of special reconnaissance projects soon to be birthed by the war in Vietnam.

CHAPTER
FIVE

We didn't fit the mold. We just didn't fit in. We were renegades used to operating independently, with few people pulling our strings. We disregarded the established rules and created our own. We did whatever the situation demanded, developed our own courses of action, never questioning the morality of what we did to survive and complete the mission.

FRANKLIN D. MILLER (MOH)
Reflections of a Warrior

Reconnaissance—(DOD, NATO, IADB) A mission undertaken to obtain, by visual observation or other detection methods, information about the activities and resources of an enemy or potential enemy; or to secure data concerning the meteorological, hydrographic, or geographic characteristics of a particular area.

U.S. Department of Defense

In Vietnam, Special Forces and reconnaissance became almost synonymous, the war birthing a host of conventional and special projects for the collection of intelligence throughout Southeast Asia. Supported by Gen. William C. Westmoreland, Special Forces would undertake the bulk of the training mission where tactics, techniques, and specialized equipment was concerned.

Vietnam was no stranger to U.S. special operations. Occupied by the Japanese in 1940, Vietnam had been a French colony since 1887. With France itself conquered by the Germans, there was little resistance to the Japanese invasion by French settlers, many of whom collaborated with the Japanese to maintain control over the Vietnamese population. A guerrilla army was formed by Ho Chi Minh, who would later become the leader of North Vietnam's Communist government. Visited by an OSS team, Ho would receive advice, training, and equipment from it in his struggle against the Japanese. By the war's end, the United States elected to recognize French interests in Vietnam over Ho's vision for a unified nation. Accordingly, the French attempted to regain control of the country in a war which was won by Ho's forces in 1954 with the fall of the French garrison at Dien Bien Phu.

Vietnam became two separate countries divided at the 17th Parallel. Ho Chi Minh's long-range goals for his homeland did not include such a division, and he began a protracted struggle to throw out "foreign aggressors," i.e., the United States. Although Ho had carried on cordial relations with his OSS visitors during World War II, the support of the French by the United States had left him with few illusions once the war was over. By mid-1954, the U.S. Military Assistance Advisory Group, Vietnam (MAAG-V) was fielding over 340 advisers. The next year, China and Russia publicly sided with Ho. Their support promised new pipelines of funds, advisers, and equipment with which he could conduct warfare in South Vietnam.

Ho also provided sanctuary for Laotian prince Souphanouvong, who had formed the Pathet Lao in 1951 to throw the French out of Laos. Two years later, his forces, assisted by Hanoi's Viet Minh, reentered Laos and began a civil war against King Savang's government. The political and strategic importance of that war has already been made quite clear. Souphanouvong's forces would split the country by 1954, the Geneva Accords giving him the two most northern provinces with King Savang retaining the remainder. But the Pathet Lao continued guerrilla operations until the "Declaration on the Neutrality of Laos" was signed in July 1962.

Unfortunately, Laos would be anything but neutral as the war in Vietnam began to escalate.

His logistics into South Vietnam secured with the help of the Pathet Lao in 1954, Ho could conduct guerrilla warfare inside South Vietnam with greater intensity. By 1959, the insurgency was running rampant throughout the South's countryside, the United States–backed government of President Diem content to hold the urban areas of the country while the Viet Cong gained control of its rural power base. Special Forces became active in South Vietnam in 1957, when a training team instructed the South Vietnamese 1st Observation Group in Ranger tactics. That unit would become the South Vietnamese Special Forces, the counterpart organization of U.S. Special Forces.

Teams from the 1st Special Forces Group (Airborne) and 7th SFG(A) began training in earnest as the CIA exercised its mandate to conduct covert warfare in defense of U.S. national interests. With the understanding between the JCS and the CIA that Special Forces would be the instrument in such activities, the Agency began developing ties with the Montagnard tribes who, it hoped, would become the first line of defense against the encroaching Viet Cong. The successful operations carried out by SF in Laos with the Meo and Kha served as examples that such a project was worth pursuing, especially in light of the fact that Special Forces advisers had little difficulty adapting to the primitive life-styles of those they were training. But the SF advisers appear to have overlooked the animosity of the Vietnamese toward the Montagnard races, which was very much like that of the Laos for the Meo and Kha. As the 'Yards became more organized and effective on the battlefield, the Vietnamese grew more hostile and afraid of a Montagnard uprising within the country. One did occur in 1964, but Special Forces advisers were instrumental in resolving the rebellion before too much damage could be done by either side. According to those who led them into combat, the "hill people" would become known as perhaps the most effective counterguerrilla operators of the war.

In October of 1964, the entire 5th Special Forces Group (Airborne), with an authorized strength of 1,297 personnel, was deployed to Vietnam. The 5th's command was charged with conducting a vivid counterinsurgency program which included

The destruction of the Viet Cong
The establishment of firm South Vietnamese governmental control
The enlistment of the population to support the government

Additionally, the 5th would conduct border surveillance missions, aggressive operations against infiltration/supply routes, and combat operations against Viet Cong–held territory and installations. All of these missions required a strong reconnaissance capability, something which at the time did not exist within either the South Vietnamese army (ARVN) or the U.S. military command soon to become known as MACV. To compensate for that fault, the 5th began tentative planning to establish a recon school for its U.S. and indigenous personnel. Concurrently, General Westmoreland had his own thoughts regarding the importance of reconnaissance, based upon his experience with the 101st Airborne's RECONDO School in 1958.

While the 5th SFG(A) was gearing up to carry out its MACV-directed commitments, another organization which would be charged with *strategic reconnaissance* had already gone operational in January of 1964. The Studies and Observation Group (SOG) represented all the services' unconventional warfare interests via a task force hidden beneath the umbrella of Military Assistance Command Vietnam. Although never a Special Forces project, MACV-SOG drew the bulk of its operators from Special Forces, Marine Force Reconnaissance, navy's SEAL platoons, and air force Air Commando squadrons. In the army's case, the 5th Group was tasked with creating the special operations augmentation section to process SF volunteers for SOG in secret.

By early 1964, Special Forces had already laid the groundwork for special reconnaissance with PROJECT LEAPING LENA, a combined U.S. and Vietnamese long-range recon effort meant to conduct intelligence gathering missions about the enemy inside South Vietnam and Laos. LENA was an SOG operation, entrusted to the classified unit because MACV was not authorized to conduct military operations in Laos. Six- to eight-man teams of South Vietnamese were parachuted into Laos to attack VC transportation routes and to collect intelligence. Sadly, few of these efforts bore fruit, many of the teams being compromised, then killed or captured by the Pathet Lao or Viet Cong. Nevertheless, LENA served as a basis for a more sophisticated project to be administered by the 5th Special Forces. Five months after LENA's initiation, PROJECT DELTA replaced it as the primary means of conducting special reconnaissance by Special Forces, although DELTA's missions were run only in South Vietnam. By mid-June 1965, DELTA's growth saw the creation of a specific headquarters charged with the planning and conduct of the project's missions. This headquarters was called Detachment B-52, and one of its first priorities was the development of a reconnaissance training program designed to meet the specifics of DELTA team missions.

PROJECT DELTA became the core structure for all other special/strategic reconnaissance projects deployed during the Vietnam War. DELTA teams specialized in raids against Viet Cong bases and lines of communication, as well as conducting hunter-killer missions against selected VC/NVA targets. In addition, DELTA developed the first deception operations meant to mislead the enemy about the intentions of friendly forces, and it conducted numerous photographic reconnaissance missions for tactical and strategic commanders. B-52's responsibilities also included Allied POW recovery operations and targeting missions for the terminal guidance of airborne munitions. The groundwork laid by DELTA/B-52 would influence special operations for the duration of the war, and affect future special reconnaissance projects such as those which would be mounted in El Salvador twenty years later.

Serving field force commanders were PROJECTS OMEGA (B-50) and SIGMA (B-56), both providing special reconnaissance teams to corps tactical zones. In 1967, these projects would be turned over to MACV-SOG, but they were replaced by Detachment B-36 (RAPID FIRE) and Detachment B-20. The rapid replacement of such projects serves as a testament to their worth on the battlefield where both intelligence and small-unit combat are concerned. Of particular note is the development of reaction forces to complement the reconnaissance teams within each project. These forces served two purposes: a large, heavily armed, rapidly deployed rescue effort for teams in danger; a way to exploit information obtained by project recon teams. Relying on the recon team (RT) to guide them in, the reaction forces conducted raids and ambushes against newly identified targets with great success. More importantly, such combat actions were the result of U.S. and Vietnamese cooperation, the majority of the military personnel involved being from South Vietnam's armed forces.

In 1967, strategic reconnaissance (SR) became the priority of MACV-SOG, whose charter allowed it to conduct a variety of missions *throughout* Southeast Asia. SOG had assumed many of the clandestine and covert projects begun by the Central Intelligence Agency prior to the United States' official entry into the war, thus enforcing the linkage between the CIA's responsibility for peacetime unconventional warfare and the army's assumption of that responsibility during wartime. In 1948, only a year after the Agency's creation, the CIA's role in political, economic, and paramilitary warfare was expanded.

Further evolutions within the intelligence organization saw former OSS station chief (Rumania) Frank Wisner head up the Office of Policy Coordination (OPC), which became responsible for the CIA's covert-action capability, a capability first exercised during the Korean War. Carried out in parallel to the overt war in Korea was the National Security Council's (NSC) mandate of April 14, 1950, which called for a "nonmilitary" offensive against the Soviet Union to include various forms of clandestine, unconventional warfare. Under direction from the NSC, the CIA sought to develop its covert warfare forces while carrying out a "nonmilitary" offensive against Soviet satellite nations. As a result of the support of China and Russia for North Vietnam, it was inevitable that the Agency's attentions would become focused on Indochina.

Under MACV, SOG sought to collect both tactical and strategic intelligence throughout Southeast Asia. Such information assisted U.S. policymakers in their decisions regarding South Vietnam, Cambodia, Laos, Burma, China, and North Vietnam. Additionally, SOG was charged with carrying out a host of unconventional warfare missions outside the acknowledged political restraints of the United States. Many such missions became the basis for future SpecWar operations long after the conflict in Vietnam had ended. Despite being included in the MACV wiring diagram, SOG actually worked directly for the Joint Chiefs with only MACV's planning officer (J5) having knowledge of the unit's activities; with the exception of South Vietnam, MACV was not permitted to conduct military operations in the countries which were assigned as SOG's areas of interest. SOG's overseer was the special assistant for counterinsurgency and special activities (SACSA) at the Pentagon. SACSA approved all SOG operations, which were passed from MACV through the commander in chief Pacific (CinCPAC) to the JCS in Washington, D.C.

Often overlooked is the relationship between the South Vietnamese special operations community and that of the United States. Although SOG was activated in April 1964, Special Forces had been working alongside the Vietnamese since the inception of the 1st Observation Group in 1957. This unit was made up of roughly three hundred Vietnamese, most of them coming from North Vietnam. The 1st OG's mission was to conduct special warfare inside South Vietnam, targeting the growing Viet Cong infrastructure. Under the sole command of the South Vietnamese president, the 1st Observation Group would later be designated as a Special Forces command. By 1964, with the transfer of responsibility for U.S. covert warfare from the Central Intelligence Agency to the army (OPERATION SWITCHBACK), the Vietnamese activated the Special Exploitation Service (SES) which worked parallel to and in conjunction with the newly created MACV-SOG. The 1st Observation Group conducted a number of highly classified missions against the North, including agent infiltrations and raids. U.S. military advisers from Special Forces and the navy's SEAL teams assisted in training as well as ground combat, although the bulk of such operations were run by all-Vietnamese teams. Nevertheless, though well intentioned and fully supported, far too many 1st OG missions were compromised and resulted in heavy casualties to their agents.

The first successful Studies and Observation Group project was SHINING BRASS, whose commander was former White Star project officer, Col. Bull Simons. The first SHINING BRASS teams were launched in September 1965. A combined U.S.–Vietnamese effort, special reconnaissance teams infiltrated Laos to conduct combat operations against the Pathet Lao and NVA. Additional missions included bomb damage assessments (BDA), strategic reconnaissance, interdiction of VC/NVA supply lines, downed-pilot searches, and POW recovery efforts. Granted permission to operate a depth of fifty miles into Laos, SHINING BRASS would become one of the most controversial and consistent SOG programs of the war. Renamed PRAIRIE FIRE in 1968, the project continued through 1971, when it was turned over to the Vietnamese.

SOG's expanding role in "strat recon" soon undertook the form of PROJECT DANIEL BOONE, authorized by the Joint Chiefs of Staff via Gen. William Westmoreland. This time Cambodia was the target, given the country's use by the Viet Cong as a safe sanctuary for major supply and personnel bases. DANIEL BOONE marked the first time Special Forces was assigned a specific border surveillance mission, utilizing a series of outposts built along the border between Vietnam and Cambodia. DANIEL BOONE recon elements served in much the same capacity as their SHINING BRASS counterparts. Because Cambodia was a far greater threat to South Vietnam's security than Laos, the project's outposts were a trip-wire warning system for major VC/NVA troops concentrations and movements; despite accurate and timely reports from teams operating inside Cambodia, no serious interdiction efforts were launched against massive troop buildups, which became main-force enemy units during the 1968 Tet Offensive. In that case, the value of strategic reconnaissance was ignored despite the fact that pinpointing such buildups was a primary reason for initiating the project.

By 1966, SOG was rapidly becoming its own special operations command. Its organization included air assets (90th Special Operations Wing) consisting of four squadrons of mixed fixed-wing and rotary aircraft, as well as a maritime force of fast boats. SOG conducted its own special reconnaissance training school at Long Thanh, and mounted psychological warfare efforts against the enemy from a headquarters in Saigon. Roughly seventy-five recon teams were available through the Ground Studies Group, with additional forces, up to company-size, provided as both security and exploitation elements.

SOG's best-known configuration would be its three field commands, Command and Control South (CCS), Command and Control Central (CCC), and Command and Control North (CCN). The distinct separation of area responsibilities took place in 1967 and continued until 1972. The three commands were charged with the conduct of unconventional warfare in North and South Vietnam as well as inside Laos and Cambodia. It is known that CCN recon teams made incursions into Communist China to gather intelligence and conduct other classified operations of strategic impact. Of the three, Command and Control North was always the largest project. CCN teams often used Chinese Nung mercenaries or CIA-supported Meo tribesmen to conduct operations against the North. Of all three projects, only CCN could field both high-altitude, low-opening parachute teams (HALO—RT Idaho, RT Michigan, RT Ohio) and a HALO/SCUBA RT (Python). SOG recon teams were normally made up of three Americans and six to nine indigenous personnel.

SOG's primary interests lay in cross-border operations, the tracking and attempted rescue of U.S. and Allied POWs, the formation of agent networks inside North Vietnam, and psychological operations directed against the North. Additional missions included special operations such as POW snatches and the salting of enemy equipment caches with faulty ammunition as well as assassination and the recovery of sensitive equipment from downed aircraft. These operations were so successful that the North Vietnamese began targeting SOG recon teams, specifically those assigned to CCN. Beginning in late 1968, CCN casualties began to mount due to compromised missions and new NVA counterinsurgency tactics. Intelligence pointed to newly formed NVA "headhunter" battalions which were to locate, isolate, and overrun SOG ground teams. Training these battalions was a large cadre of Chinese advisers. By late 1970, this cadre's location was pinpointed at being a small installation just outside the city of Son Tay.

The *Real* Son Tay Raid

In the spring of 1969, intelligence analyst Norval Clinebell finally began to fit together the pieces of a six-month puzzle. Assigned to the air force's 1127th Field Activities Group at Fort Belvoir, Virginia, Clinebell was part of the unit's escape-and-evasion branch. His duties centered on intelligence about American POWs, which was passed on to both the Central Intelligence Agency and Defense Intelligence Agency (DIA) for further action. Some of these actions included SOG-CCN missions to effect the release of U.S. and Allied POWs held in Laos or North Vietnam.

A year after encountering the first hints of a POW compound being possibly located near Son Tay City, Clinebell was finally confident he had a case to make. His report was forwarded to the office of Col. Rudolph C. Koller, who in turn took it before Maj. Gen. Rocky Triantafellu, an air force rescue and recovery expert. General Triantafellu agreed with Clinebell's analysis and approached Brig. Gen. James R. Allen, deputy director for plans and policy. General Allen turned the report, with comments, over to his best covert operations planners, with instructions to come up with a rescue scenario within a week. He then made plans to meet with the army SACSA chief, Brig. Gen. Donald Blackburn, who he felt would be inclined to take action once made aware of Clinebell's discovery.

As a colonel, Blackburn had commanded MACV-SOG from 1965 to 1966. His experience with special operations and unconventional warfare began during World War II when he elected to remain behind Japanese lines in the Philippines, organizing and leading a Filipino guerrilla army of twenty thousand fighters by 1945. Blackburn himself commanded a unit of Igorot headhunters, which were some of the most feared guerrillas faced by the occupying Japanese forces.

In 1957, Blackburn was sent to Vietnam as a senior adviser to the Vietnamese. Returning to the United States, he took command of the 77th Special Forces Group, leaving in 1960 to organize and command the White Star Project in Laos. The colonel's assignment as "Chief, SOG" in 1965 was seen as a natural extension of his expertise, and in 1970, he became the special assistant for counterinsurgency and special activities at the Pentagon. As we have seen, the SACSA was SOG's true supervisor, and Blackburn's firsthand understanding of this unit's capabilities made him indispensable as an ally at JCS.

By June, the Joint Chiefs had approved continued planning for a POW raid to be conducted by a specially picked team of Green Berets. Blackburn turned to Col. Arthur "Bull" Simons, who had served under him during the White Star project and again while Colonel Blackburn commanded SOG. Simons was to pull the mission together and then execute it. In his usual gruff manner, the Bull began recruiting his team from a flood of volunteers at Fort Bragg while intelligence continued to arrive regarding the prisoners at Son Tay. Air force assets were likewise coordinated, with an isolated portion of Eglin Air Force Base in Florida selected as the project's training area. Now known as IVORY COAST, the Son Tay raid was well on its way with a projected launch date of late October.

To this day, it is not known why the mission was not assigned to SOG's assets at CCN. With its experience at mounting operations against the North, CCN offered not only recon teams capable of infiltrating the Son Tay area, but Hatchet Forces and SLAM companies which could be used as both assault and security elements for such a raid. As the SACSA, Blackburn should have been able to assign such a mission to SOG. After all, one of the unit's primary responsibilities was the recovery of POWs in North Vietnam. A CCN task force could have been quickly assembled, briefed, and then launched from the same bases in Thailand later used by Bull Simons. A fact about POW recovery missions was that intelligence regarding a suspected POW site needed to be acted upon in the shortest amount of time possible because Viet Cong or NVA captors would move their charges as soon as discovery became a possibility. It would take six months to mount IVORY COAST, even though the first intelligence of the POWs' being moved from Son Tay was analyzed two months after Clinebell's original report went to General Triantafellu.

There are any number of reasons which could be considered as to why SOG wasn't used to conduct the raid at Son Tay. Two of the most persuasive have to do with interservice politics and the circumstances surrounding SOG's operations in North Vietnam. According to one source, the fact that IVORY COAST was generated from within the Pentagon immediately dispelled any possibility of the sure-and-simple route offered by SOG's in-country assets. The political windfall which could be accrued through a joint-service rescue operation made it necessary to share participation among the army, air force, navy, and Marines. As the JCS exercised enormous power of approval over how far such an operation might go, Blackburn needed to successfully walk a political tightrope if he wanted to see the mission undertaken at all. Second, SOG's cross-border operations into Cambodia, Laos, and North Vietnam were outside parameters established for U.S. ground operations. A successful raid against a POW compound less than twenty-three miles from Hanoi, conducted by CCN operators and mixed indigenous forces, would have ripped away the veil of secrecy surrounding the SOG war effort. Worse yet, a failed mission, which left dead or wounded rescue forces on the ground in North Vietnam, would become a massive national embarrassment if it could be proved that those forces were part of a covert army which routinely crossed borders into countries where the U.S. said its ground forces were not fighting. If SOG was to play a role at Son Tay, it would necessarily be a limited one.

A firm believer that the United States should conduct special operations inside North Vietnam, General Blackburn believed that an impressive success—as was possible with IVORY COAST—might open the door to further such operations against targets vital to the North Vietnamese. According to Blackburn, "It [IVORY COAST] was bigger than getting the POWs out. There were too many people who didn't have the perception to understand what this was really about, or could accomplish." Due to their firsthand knowledge of nearly seven years of SOG's highly successful operations in Southeast Asia, Blackburn and Simons were two of the few covert warriors who understood the capability possessed by SOG-CCN to carry out such missions. If using a composite force to wedge open the door for further operations inside the North was required, Blackburn would go along in his role as SACSA. It was the best possible solution because SOG's cover would not be compromised by the mission's success or failure. And should Simons succeed, that would still clear the way for future SOG missions of the variety Blackburn had in mind.

Meanwhile at CCN, the chances of an operator's surviving the next mission were getting progressively worse. By mid-1969, the NVA was assigning specially trained battalions to areas known to attract CCN recon teams. Working with trail and landing-zone (LZ) watchers, a battalion monitored its assigned area until a watcher reported an insertion. After a CCN recon team realized it had been detected, standard operating procedure called for it to maneuver toward a preplanned extraction point, avoiding confrontation. But the enemy's trackers would use various methods to alert the NVA headhunters and to channel the team toward them, hoping to crush the small patrol between themselves and a much larger force before an extraction could be made.

Because of their small numbers and light weaponry, a recon team facing heavy contact often sought to occupy the highest ground it could find from which to fight. Knowing that, the headhunter battalion, with the help of its trail watchers and trackers, would force the RT to assume such a defensive position because given the firepower a battalion could muster against incoming aircraft, a helicopter extraction would be near suicide. Once a recon team was brought to bay, the battalion would launch continuous assaults against its perimeter until the team's members were dead, wounded, or out of ammunition. Enemy losses were not important because the destruction of a SOG recon team was considered a major victory by the NVA. At SOG headquarters, the list of decimated recon teams was getting longer. The question was: where had such effective tactics been devised and who had devised them?

By October 1970, Simons was ready to launch his POW raid, but political considerations—among other problems—intervened. Intelligence about the camp and its surrounding facilities was so accurate that an exact model and mock-up of the Son Tay compound had been built to aid in the unit's planning and rehearsal phases. In addition, over 170 dry runs would be conducted to ensure the highest degree of accuracy where the air and ground portions of the operation were concerned. Simons had divided his fifty-six-man raiding party into three groups. Capt. Dick Meadows would lead Blueboy, the fourteen-man rescue team charged with crash-landing inside the Son Tay compound and freeing the sixty-one POWs reported being held there. Capt. Daniel Turner's twenty-man force, code-named Redwine, would provide command and control just outside the compound, with Lt. Col. Elliott Sydnor overseeing this portion of the operation. Capt. Udo Walther would command the twenty-two-man support group of which Simons was part. Titled Greenleaf, Walther's team would land outside the compound along with Redwine to help to secure the area as well as to prevent an enemy reaction force from interrupting the planned twenty-six-minute occupation of North Vietnamese territory.

As a precaution against the loss of one team through accident or combat, each of the three elements cross-trained in each other's tasks. It was determined that two teams could carry out the actual raid against Son Tay in this fashion. As events later revealed, Simons's planning would pay off.

Despite careful planning, extraordinary intelligence, and one of the most effective security nets ever erected around such an operation, the nagging concern over the prisoners' status at Son Tay continued to grow as premission preparations continued. In July, overhead photography collected by SR-71 spy planes and Buffalo Hunter drones offered definite indicators that Son Tay was abandoned. Weeds were growing in the courtyard, and no POW laundry was arranged in international code patterns as was first discovered by Clinebell's analysis. These overflights continued well into October, with one of the last SR-71 flights bringing back perfect pictures of the compound. To everyone's concern, not one photograph indicated the presence of POWs at Son Tay. They did reveal that the camp was apparently occupied once more, but by whom and for what reason remained unknown.

Delayed for another month, it would be November 18, 1970, before OPERATION KINGPIN, as IVORY COAST was then known, would receive its "Red Rocket" message from the National Military Command Center to execute the raid. By that time, Simons and his force were already in Thailand, prepared to launch, but poor weather was hampering a final decision on which day to send the raiders into North Vietnam. Then further proof that the POWs had been moved was received by Blackburn. Provided by a reliable North Vietnamese source with access to POW information, the message listed both active POW camps and the number of prisoners being held at each one. Son Tay was not on the list, although a new camp, Dong Hoi, was.

This latest information supported the photographic evidence gathered by the spy planes/drones, to include photographs of the vastly improved camp at Dong Hoi. Despite anguish on some of the planners' part that the raid should be at least postponed, with perhaps Dong Hoi targeted rather than Son Tay, other reports of POWs dying at an increased rate pushed KINGPIN's planners toward a launch decision. It was decided that even if Son Tay was a dry hole, the mission could be explained to the media and North Vietnamese using one of the five cover stories which had been devised for just such an event. General Blackburn's strong personal opinion was that a raid into an empty camp was better "than no raid at all." At this point, the raid on Son Tay had taken on a life of its own. The services had successfully gathered, trained, and fielded a capable strike force without its being compromised despite the extensive six-month train-up period. The POW issue was gathering importance in the negotiations at the Paris peace talks. The reports of prisoners dying—gathered through a number of intelligence sources of which one was exceptionally illegal— urged that action in some form be taken. If there were POWs at Son Tay, their revelations regarding inhumane treatment at the hands of the North Vietnamese could prove invaluable. At the White House, President Nixon needed a trump card, and with Thanksgiving fast approaching, *any* rescued U.S. prisoners would provide just that.

In the end, KINGPIN was given the green light, and the mission was launched near midnight on November 20. Only hours before, Bull Simons had revealed to his assembled force that they would be assaulting a POW camp deep inside North Vietnam, and there was a fifty-fifty chance of mission success. Further, the Special Forces officer offered there were "seventy" POWs at Son Tay, and "maybe more." After a brief silence, the raiders had begun applauding their commander's announcement. To a man, they were undaunted by the target's location and the possibilities of things going wrong once they were on the ground. Simons, normally not an emotional man, would later recall being nearly overcome by their response and obvious dedication to the mission. Despite being fully informed that there were probably no prisoners at the camp, the Bull elected to keep his force's morale high as they prepared to leave Thailand.

As it turned out, the ground operators were among the last to know their objective. Simons's immediate team leaders had been fully briefed during the early stages of planning, and the air force helicopter-pararescue personnel assigned to fly the mission had been informed during their training at the Eglin training site. Secure communication between the raiders and General Blackburn was available despite the distances separating them, so intelligence updates were easily conveyed to Thailand as the launch window grew wider. Early on, air force brigadier general Leroy J. Manor had been selected by the Joint Chiefs to be the designated field commander for IVORY COAST/KINGPIN. His job as the air force's special operations commander made him acutely aware of the needs and challenges of such an operation. Particularly since it was his job to instruct the air crews that were supporting Blackburn's SOG operations in Southeast Asia. Manor was on the ground with Simons at the Thai airbase at Takhli, awaiting the final message for mission launch.

Operational security for the raid was not only tight, it was organized in such a way as to ensure that each element involved knew only what it needed to in order to accomplish its portion of the mission. For Simons, it was the only way to run such an operation, especially if changes needed to be made at the last moment. The fewer people you had to explain things to, the fewer questions needed to be answered.

On Friday the twentieth, General Manor advised Simons the mission was a "Go." The threat of poor weather in the Hanoi–Son Tay area urged Manor to move up the launch date by twenty-four hours, a decision which eliminated an SR-71 overflight that was meant to provide last-minute intelligence to Simons about who was, or was not, at the compound. At 1800 hours, Colonel Simons briefed his ground operators. Final preparations were made, with lift-off from Udorn scheduled for just before midnight. It would be a three-hour flight to the objective, with in-flight refueling planned over Laos. Heavily armed, and prepared to rescue prisoners or to fight a last-ditch battle on the banks of the Con River, each team boarded its helicopter.

The flight was uneventful, although it required some of the most difficult precision flying its pilots had ever conducted. In order to keep up with the far faster C-130 Combat Talon, the H-3 carrying Meadows's assault team had literally drafted directly behind the airplane's wing tip in a maneuver developed specifically for the operation. The H-3s were faster than their smaller cousin, and were able to maintain the Talon's pace without problem. Col. Warner Britton was flying Apple 1, one of six helicopters involved in the raid. He recalls the aircraft formation from Thailand through Laos being "very tight" with the helicopters flying within rotor lengths of each other and the two C-130s involved. A second Combat Talon would link up with the airborne raiders over Laos, bringing with it a flight of A-1 attack aircraft. This C-130 would lead the helicopters on their final approach into Son Tay.

CHAPTER
SIX

Anybody who gets in our way is going to be dead.
COL. ARTHUR "BULL" SIMONS
The Raid

Although the raid has been carefully researched and presented in a number of respected publications, certain events have continued to elude full explanation. The centerpiece of controversy surrounds the so-called secondary school which was colocated with the prison. During the assault, Simons's support force of twenty-two Green Berets was landed by mistake at this compound, where they became engaged in a furious firefight, which killed between 200 to 250 enemy soldiers. Long afterward, events revealed Simons and his men had effectively destroyed a company-size unit of Chinese advisers billeted at the secondary school. Although no POWs were recovered by the Son Tay raiders, the attack led by Simons was seen by many to have made up for the disappointing conclusion to the greatest single raid conducted into enemy territory by a special operations unit.

Did Simons and his command group know beforehand that the POWs had been moved? Were they aware of the Chinese, and if so, was it really pilot error which put Simons at their front gate? Finally, if Simons did know the prisoners had been moved, and the raid was launched with the secondary school's inhabitants as the primary target rather than Son Tay itself, what would be the reason for undertaking such an effort with so much at stake?

The answer lies in what may be one of the most daring special reconnaissance missions undertaken by Special Forces, a mission which until now, never existed.

By mid-November 1970, Simons's Son Tay raiders had arrived at the Takhli military airbase in Thailand. Intelligence reports were flowing in regarding the status of the POW compound, with overhead photography giving strong indications of activity at both the prison and a smaller compound located four hundred yards to the south of the raiders' primary target. Both the CIA and DIA had provided exceptional information regarding the NVA military threat, identifying nearby units and estimating their ability to respond once the fireworks began over Son Tay. It was agreed an enemy reaction force could arrive at the prison within four minutes, traveling by road at night. Simons allowed he'd need to accomplish the operation in less than twenty-six minutes to avoid becoming involved in a major ground confrontation. Although a massive deception operation was to be carried out by carrier-based attack aircraft over Hanoi during the assault, the raiders could expect a strong response from elements of the North Vietnamese air-defense system.

The smaller compound was called a secondary school by intelligence analysts, but Simons was concerned by its location and about its true purpose. Why would the Vietnamese have a school in the midst of what was primarily a military zone? Were military personnel using the compound? The SR-71 and drone overflights strongly supported that conclusion, and in Simons's mind, the school became a major threat. Located only four hundred yards from Son Tay, the school's occupants could be at its gates within minutes of the first shots being fired at Son Tay. As to how many guards were actually on the prison's premises, Simons didn't know. His intelligence updates were only confirming *someone* was on the grounds, but not whom and how many. For all the Special Forces officer knew, his airborne force might hit a dry hole where POWs were concerned, while racing directly into the jaws of the NVA. The outcome of such an encounter was too horrifying to consider.

According to one of the pilots assigned to fly into Son Tay, the secondary school was briefed as being a threat at the onset of the mission's training. It was brought up again while final preparations were being made in Thailand. "We were told there were enemy troops at the secondary school," recalls Apple 1's copilot, Alfred C. Montrem. "It concerned us because the school was so close to the prison." Montrem later remembered seeing "strange radio or television antennae" atop the two-story, pagodalike structure inside the secondary school's walls during his multiple flights over Son Tay during the raid. In Washington, concern was growing about the raids even being launched. More and more, intelligence indicated that the camp was devoid of POWs. Weather concerns were affecting the final decision, as well. With the most likely weather window open from between 21 and 25 of November, it was anyone's guess how much time might pass before Mother Nature would again cooperate with the raiders.

And there was another reason for the raid's being conducted. For nearly eighteen months SOG's CCN recon teams had been suffering extensive losses on the ground. According to Maj. Gen. (Ret.) John K. Singlaub, who served as chief SOG from 1966–1968, a high-level intelligence leak was responsible for their compromise. "We suspected they [the North Vietnamese] had been successful in placing an agent inside the prime minister's office," says Singlaub. It was at this level that Singlaub and others assigned to SOG believed information was being collected by the North Vietnamese intelligence agent. "After the war I heard the man responsible was decorated in Hanoi for his services," the former SOG commander remembers.

At CCN, the effects of the agent's penetration were threatening the entire project. By mid-1969, the North Vietnamese had recognized CCN's areas of interest and methods of inserting its RTs into both Laos and North Vietnam. Soon afterward, a coordinated system for watching trails and potential landing zones was established, along with specialized tactics tailored to deal with the Americans and their indigenous mercenaries. A former CCN one-zero (team leader) whom I'll call "Frank Capper" remembers the effectiveness of these tactics. Capper did five tours with CCN and today is a successful businessman in California. "They [the NVA] saturated every trail and possible LZ with watchers. It was their job to alert what we were calling headhunter or hunter-killer teams when a team was inserted. The trail watchers had a primitive but effective communication system that relied on a number of audible signals, like gunshots, to communicate with the main body of troops. What they wanted to do was channel us toward the hunter-killer teams, which consisted of four hundred to five hundred troops.

"Once we were compromised on the ground, you just wanted to get the hell out. My team discovered the best way to break contact was to rush right at the trail watcher's position when he fired. Too many other teams didn't do this, and they ended getting waxed. Because we were so small in numbers, but carried such incredible firepower, the idea was to get to the highest point of ground in the area and set up a perimeter. An SOG RT could hold off an awful lot of people until an extraction ship could get in . . . provided it had the time. With the new enemy tactics, time was what you didn't have. Once they had our position pinpointed, they'd begin throwing human-wave attacks against it. We're talking fifty to sixty men at a time until they simply overran the perimeter and everyone inside it. They didn't give a damn about their own casualties, they just wanted that recon team dead.

"The NVA were well trained and expertly led," continues Capper. "Their information was so good about our missions that we knew they were getting our actual eight-digit grid coordinates prior to the missions even being launched. They'd have these hunter-killer units sitting on the primary and secondary insertion points, just waiting for us to arrive. We had teams get hit as soon as they jumped off the bird—just waxed—totally destroyed."

As it turned out, Chinese advisers were responsible for the creation of the tactics and units being deployed against CCN. All indicators pointed to the cadres being located near Hanoi, where they could operate and communicate in relative safety from U.S. reprisals. Capt. Udo Walther, Simons's executive officer for Greenleaf, admitted in 1984 that "It wasn't a secret that there were Chinese there [at Son Tay], and it wasn't a secret that there were a bunch of them." Walther said he'd informed someone about this fact, and that he "took some photographs" although he doesn't know what happened to the pictures after they were developed. What the captain did possess was the Chinese officer's belt he'd removed from a body on the grounds of the secondary school during Greenleaf's surprise attack, a belt presented "on loan" to Texas billionaire H. Ross Perot.

Meanwhile back in Thailand, Bull Simons was growing impatient. As it turns out, Son Tay was a familiar subject to the man who'd commanded SOG's Ground Studies Group (OP-35) under then-colonels Blackburn and Singlaub. "Bull had been brought over by Don Blackburn to be his deputy commander," recalls General Singlaub. "When Don left to become the SASCA and I took over SOG in 1966, Simons was in charge of OP-35. That project was responsible for all cross-border operations into Laos, Cambodia, and, later, North Vietnam." It was during his time with SOG that Simons worked alongside two of the officers he later handpicked to lead teams Blueboy and Redwine into Son Tay. They were Dick Meadows and Elliot Sydnor, both of whom became legendary personalities in the special operations community. Meadows, considered by his peers to be one of the best SF operators in the business, also possessed firsthand experience with deep penetration missions into North Vietnam. Between General Blackburn as SACSA, Simons, Sydnor, and Meadows, the SOG fraternity and its interests were well represented within the command structure of the Son Tay task force.

According to General Singlaub, a raid against Son Tay had been examined by SOG in late 1968. Under OP-35, over two hundred POW Bright Light rescue operations had been mounted against suspected sites in Laos and North Vietnam. *All* had been dry holes. SOG's OP-34 was responsible for escape-and-evasion networks in North Vietnam, and was administered by the Joint Personnel Recovery Center (JPRC). "Our intelligence gathering teams entered North Vietnam whenever we wanted to," explains a former one-zero involved with Bright Light missions. "It was common for us to evade their radar using helicopters flying in from several hilltop launch sites along the northern Laotian border. We pretty much came and went as we pleased." It was during one of these early missions that word about a POW compound outside of Son Tay City began surfacing.

"We began work on a study regarding a raid on Son Tay, but as best I can recall, I'd left SOG before it was completed," says Singlaub. In fact, according to the retired officer, the study was finished under SOG's new commander, Col. Steve Cavanaugh. It was then presented for operational consideration, but was turned down. "In retrospect, it was probably a wise decision not to let SOG undertake the raid," says Singlaub today. "The serious intelligence leak at the prime minister's level likely would have compromised the mission either before it got under way, or once it was on the ground inside North Vietnam." Could SOG's assets have pulled off such a raid if approval had been given? Singlaub believes SOG had the equipment and personnel capable of doing so, although keeping the training secret would have been the planners' greatest challenge. "Son Tay was not a secret to us. We knew about its status as a POW camp well over a year before the raid was launched."

* * *

According to Cmd. Sgt. Maj. Mark Gentry, a veteran Green Beret who was in Vietnam during the Son Tay raid, his project was going to infiltrate an "Earth Angel" team into the Son Tay area seventy-two hours before Simons's scheduled launch date. Earth Angels were Vietnamese who dressed in enemy uniforms and conducted intelligence gathering missions well behind the lines. Most often they were infiltrated by free-fall parachute or HALO. On this occasion the mission was canceled the very night the Earth Angel team was to jump into North Vietnam. Gentry says no reason was given, but he was told later that the rescue attempt overrode the Earth Angel tasking.

According to Frank Capper, fromer One-Zero for RT PYTHON, the Vietnamese Earth Angel mission was scrapped in favor of an American-led special reconnaissance mission into Son Tay during the same period. Relying on three volunteer CCN One-Zeros, two North Vietnamese Kit Carson Scouts from the Son Tay area employed by CCN, and at least one CIA operative, the hastily recruited team launched from SOG's Heavy Hook mission site located in Thailand.

As Heavy Hook's rotary aircraft were so heavily armored that their range of operations was limited, the team was "loaned" one of Simons's reserve helicopters then positioned at his project's launch site, located deeper inland than Heavy Hook, which was on the border of its host country and Vietnam. Refueling at a CIA mission support site inside northern Laos (Longcheng), the chopper successfully infiltrated into North Vietnam using one of the oft traveled air lanes relied upon by CCN's RTs for several years. Landing several kilometers away from Son Tay, the team moved by foot to a position where it could conduct a careful reconnaissance of the entire area, to include the supposed prison site and the secondary school.

According to Capper—one of the three One-Zeros on this mission—it was Sergeant Dale Dehnke who led the recon team into Son Tay. The men, guided by their North Vietnamese scouts, were able to confirm specific bits of information about the immediate area and, to a certain degree, who was present. For example, it was during this mission that the Chinese cadre was verified as occupying the secondary school, and that they stacked their weapons in the school's inner yard at night. Knowing the defenders were essentially unarmed proved invaluable to Bull Simons when he elected to order his misplaced team to assault the compound.

As it was impossible to see through the Son Tay prison's walls, the recon element was unable to state whether or not American POWs were still being held there. But, they were able to confirm the presence of North Vietnamese troops (guards?) inside the compound, lending credence to the possibility that such prisoners might have still been under watch. Exfiltrating at night, the CCN team "abducted" a baby water buffalo from the nearby rice paddy where its borrowed helicopter was waiting. The animal was taken off the aircraft at Heavy Hook, back in Thailand, and made the project's mascot thereafter. It was this water buffalo which invoked the wrath of Henry Kissinger when it was "rumored" such an event had occured during the actual conduct of the Son Tay raid, and buffalo dung was discovered inside one of the helicopters assigned to Simons's air fleet. As no one outside a small core of the raid's command and control group ever knew of the unauthorized CCN reconnaissance of Son Tay on behalf of Simons, the investigating body charged with discovering the missing water buffalo never visited Heavy Hook, where, Capper says, the animal grew "fat and sassy" with time.

In light of this mission, the raid was launched with an American "eyes on the ground" update which provided precise intelligence as to the deployment of Chinese and North Vietnamese forces at Son Tay, but gave no reason to doubt that American POWs were present. Blackburn's observation was that even one such prisoner was worth the operation continuing. With this in mind, the raid was carried out.

Dale Dehnke was killed in action on May 18, 1971, while operating in the Da Krong Valley, inside Vietnam. The team he was with was, ironically, discovered and overrun by an NVA headhunter battalion trained by Chinese advisers. Frank Capper survived the war, and confirms that the third CCN One-Zero on the Son Tay mission did also. Sadly, the man—now living in Florida—is said to suffer severe personal problems due to his wartime experiences.

Colonel Eldon Bargewell, former deputy commander for the Army's DELTA Force, also served as a One-Zero with CCN. Says Bargewell, who knew both Dehnke and Capper during his tours in Vietnam, "If there was a recon mission run prior to Son Tay then people like Elliot Sydnor and Dick Meadows would know about it." Attempts on the author's part to speak with both men were met with silence, although former CCN One-Zero David Maurer—a personal friend of Dick Meadows—did recall several post-raid discussions with Meadows which strongly indicated far more was known about the events leading up the assault of Son Tay than was ever published before now.

Soon after the team's return to Heavy Hook, Bull Simons knew he was facing a major threat to his mission's success with what lay in wait at the secondary school. The question was then how to effectively deal with the information confirmed by CCN's reconnaissance effort. Simons, whose trademark was the safety and security of his men, knew it would be "hairy" to assault the school with even his largest team, flown in on Apple 1. But with an American-led SR team's precise information as to the disposition of its troops and weapons, the ground commander knew he'd face little organized resistance if he used surprise and initiated the contact. Further, Simons understood that every element of the raiding party needed to be in its assigned position during the ground operation. "Simons would never have deviated from the original plan," says his former commander, General Blackburn. "The Son Tay raiders were handpicked from the very best in Special Forces. When I talked with him [Simons] after he'd returned from Thailand, he told me he'd been landed by accident at the school. It was a mistake."

To deal with a reaction force coming from the Chinese barracks—as well as other designated targets—Simons was to rely on the A-1 attack aircraft, which would be circling the immediate area. Offers a veteran SOG team leader, "The A-1s could have slaughtered everybody in that compound with one pass. Simons didn't need a ground assault to deal with it [the secondary school]; he could have called in the fast-movers and it would have been all over within seconds." Assigned as a ground target for the A-1 sortie, the secondary school would be given special treatment once the raiders were safely off the ground and headed for the Lao border. Indeed, Simons would order the sortie to strike all assigned targets once he was airborne in Apple 1, the raid less than twenty-six minutes old.

By November 20, the verdict was in. At the Pentagon, no one could prove to General Blackburn's satisfaction that there were no longer POWs being held at Son Tay. "I felt we owed whoever *might* have been there the effort," Blackburn recalls. "I knew we could get in without being detected. I believed there would be no casualties on our side because of the level of training and the caliber of the men involved. Plus, there was the additional impact of letting the North Vietnamese know we could mount such an operation. Until then, it had been their pattern to do whatever they pleased inside South Vietnam while we just stood by." At 2318 hours, the Son Tay raid was under way.

Aboard Apple 1, Maj. Alfred C. Montrem settled himself in the HH-53's cockpit. He was somewhat surprised to find himself flying Simons's twenty-two-man Greenleaf team. Aircraft for the raid were assigned by rank, and in Montrem's case, Lt. Col. Warner A. Britton, who was the task force's senior air force commander, had elected to fly the mission despite having less than thirty hours flying time in an HH-53. Britton had personally selected the aircrews for the raid, and was one of the original IVORY COAST planners. According to Montrem, who had logged over one thousand hours as a Jolly Green pilot, Warner Britton was one of the inner circle when it came to knowing every facet of the mission they were about to fly. He'd asked specifically for Montrem as his copilot, knowing the major had participated in every practice run made during the Florida train-up phase. Montrem's experience would be invaluable as Colonel Britton's time had been spent primarily in the planning and logistics side of the operation. According to Montrem, he was "supposed to fly the aircraft when needed." That night would be the first time Warner Britton would fly an HH-53 into combat.

In Apple 2, Lt. Col. John V. Allison was carrying Elliot Sydnor's twenty-man command-security team. Code-named Redwine, Sydnor's men were responsible for securing the southern portion of Son Tay while Greenleaf took up positions to cover the northern sector. Inside the compound, Dick Meadows's Blueboy team was to free the POWs, blowing one of the prison's exterior walls at the same time. This would allow Meadows to move his team and the rescued prisoners to Apples 1 and 2, Blueboy's helicopter (code-named Banana) requiring destruction after crash-landing inside Son Tay to deliver its lethal cargo of Green Berets.

Apple 3 was commanded by Maj. Fredrick M. Donohue. His copilot was Capt. Thomas R. Waldron, a veteran rescue-and-recovery pilot. It was Donohue's job to lead the formation into Son Tay once released by the task force's Combat Talon, code-named Cherry 1. Apple 3, using its 7.62mm miniguns, would knock out two of the three guard towers. The third tower was to be left standing as a POW punishment cell was said to be situated below it. His mission completed, Donohue would head for a common holding area less than a mile and a half to the west of the compound. There he would await further orders.

Apples 4 and 5 would serve as backup rescue aircraft, with Apple 4 also ready to support Cherry 1 should it not accomplish its secondary mission upon releasing the task force just outside of Son Tay. These two HH-53s would land at Finger Lake, eight miles away from the compound. If they were needed, someone in the chain of command would order them in. In the meantime they were to maintain a low profile on one of the tiny islands dotting the lake.

Supporting the five Jolly Greens and one H-3 would be a sortie of A-1 attack aircraft circling one minute from the compound. Cherry 1 would drop napalm to mark their rally point on the ground, then head for home. Several miles away, a second Combat Talon was circling, ready to lead the task force back through Laos and into Thailand once the ground portion of the operation was over. The A-1s would provide a final saturation of cannon fire and bombs to cover the task force's escape. In most cases, they would be flying at treetop level.

At 0206 hours, Cherry 1's navigator broke radio silence for the first time after leaving Udorn. Noting a slight wind drift, which he believed could affect the helicopters during their final approach, he ordered a new heading of 072 degrees. This was five degrees left of the original flight plan and was meant to funnel the formation directly to its landing zone outside Son Tay's walls. Thirty seconds away from the objective, Cherry 1 released the helicopters and climbed rapidly to fifteen hundred feet, the altitude from which handheld illumination flares would be dropped. Maintaining his air speed at 105 knots, Montrem turned over command of Apple 1 to Colonel Britton for the final approach.

In Apple 3, Major Donohue increased his speed to 120 knots, pulling away from the rest of the formation where he'd been flying in the far right-wing position. As the first of Cherry 1's aerial flares ignited, Donohue adjusted his direction somewhat, although he could still not see their objective. By now the entire flight was less than fifty feet above the earth, racing toward what they believed was Son Tay. The weather was clear outside the tense cockpits, a half-moon adding to the flares' limited illumination. Slightly behind Apple 1 flew Maj. Kalen's smaller H-3, the majority of its navigational aids removed to adjust for the full load of men and equipment stuffed inside the cramped cargo bay. Meadows had ordered the aircraft's window glass taken out as a safety precaution. Kalen lowered the rear ramp as he prepared to follow Donohue's gun run over the prison compound.

Suddenly Donohue caught sight of a compound, roughly four hundred meters to his front but slightly to the right of his direction of travel. Making a quick adjustment, the pilot lined his aircraft up on the dim apparition, noting Banana 1 was directly behind him and coming on strong. As Apple 3 slowed, the giant HH-53 cleared the facility's southern wall, Apple 3's two pararescue men prepared to open fire on the guard towers, which were their assigned targets. Almost immediately, Donohue and his copilot noticed there was something wrong. Where was the Song Con, supposed to be just outside the prison's walls? A rapid inspection of the walls showed there were no guard towers present and that the interior structures didn't match up with the picture-perfect mock-up built in Florida for Donohue's much-rehearsed assault. Both men understood they'd somehow mistaken the secondary school for Son Tay, four hundred yards farther north. Donohue ordered his gunners not to fire, opening up the throttles and racing forward toward the distant prison.

Meanwhile, Banana 1 had lined up on Donohue's aircraft and was preparing to crash-land inside the compound. Kalen watched as Apple 3 failed to fire its weapons, then zoomed off over the far wall into the darkness. As Banana 1 slowly crossed the southern wall itself, its occupants watched as men began pouring out of a two-story building, which appeared to be a barracks area. Kalen identified the same problems as Donohue, noting the absence of the river, the guard towers, and the presence of a two-story structure. At Son Tay, there were no such buildings. Yelling into his intercom mike, the pilot ordered his M-60 machine gunners not to fire. Unfortunately, Meadows's assault team was not hooked in to the aircraft's internal communications system. As Banana 1 floated over the now active courtyard below, Blueboy opened up with everything they had from the glassless windows along the H-3's flanks and from its lowered rear ramp. They stopped only when Kalen poured on the power, now racing to catch up with Apple 3 as it made its gun run over the correct objective.

Onboard Apple 1, both Britton and Montrem had their hands full. They'd watched as Apple 3 adjusted his flight pattern; Britton followed suit, lining up behind Banana 1 now several hundred yards ahead of him. As Donohue crossed over the compound, Britton noted the absence of the expected minigun fire and observed to Montrem that "He must have had a malfunction." Both men then watched as Kalen's H-3 went over the wall, satisfied all was well as gunfire erupted from Banana 1's windows and rear ramp area. Montrem, assigned to monitor Apple 1's instruments while Britton focused on what was going on outside the cockpit, was now unable to assist in properly identifying the compound. Had he been flying the aircraft, he probably would have discovered what both Donohue and Kalen had, and reacted appropriately. As it was, he would not recognize Britton's error until Simons and his men were offloaded and Apple 1 was again airborne.

In April 1992, Warner Britton recalled his last impressions before setting Apple 1 down outside what turned out to be the secondary school. "We'd been warned while training at Eglin Air Force Base in Florida that such a mistake was possible," he said. "I wasn't paying attention to the final physical checkpoints as I made our approach. I wasn't looking for the road, or the river [Song Con], which was supposed to be right outside the prison. When I saw the outline of the structure, that's what I headed for."

Seconds before landing, Britton swung the HH-53's tail around so it almost faced the school's outer wall. His portside waist gunner, believing they were at the correct objective, opened fire into the interior courtyard now alive with angry and confused Chinese advisers. The deadly minigun wreaked havoc, killing the Communist soldiers even as they were desperately attempting to retrieve their unloaded weapons. Then Apple 1 was down.

"We touched down, and I switched our radio to the internal net," remembers Montrem. "I yelled 'Debark!' three times, wanting to get the soldiers off as soon as possible. The rear ramp jammed, for whatever reason, and it took several seconds to get things working. The crew chief advised me the Green Berets were all out and taking up positions in the rice paddy we'd landed in."

Lieutenant Colonel Britton remembers how surprising the assault was to the guards at the compound he still thought was Son Tay. "We'd just landed when I saw someone running to-

ward the helicopter. He was half-dressed, and appeared to be a
native, maybe he was a guard. He ran right across my front,
right underneath the cockpit. I never saw him again after that."
Bull Simons may have, as seconds after Apple 1 lifted off, he
emptied his .357 Magnum into a half-dressed North Vietnamese who popped up next to him.

Meanwhile, in Apple 2, Lt. Col. John Allison was trying to
correct Britton's mistake. Flying in trail, well behind the other
aircraft, Allison was able to view the entire proceeding, due in
part to the blue navigational lights positioned atop each airframe. Even as Apple 3 was heading for Son Tay after realizing the error in positioning, Apple 2 was realigning itself to
follow Banana 1, who was now also en route to the objective.
Breaking radio silence, Allison attempted to inform Britton
that he was preparing to land at the wrong compound. But by
now, Montrem had switched to the internal net, effectively
cutting off communications with the other aircraft involved
with the operation. Only momentarily frustrated, Allison ordered the task force to undertake Plan Green, which called
for Redwine to assume Greenleaf's mission responsibilities.
At Son Tay, Apple 3 was cutting the guard towers down with
accurate minigun fire, and Banana 1 was just seconds from
crash-landing Blueboy inside the tiny courtyard now alive with
NVA guards.

Strapped into the right seat of his HH-53, Apple 3 copilot
Tom Waldron chanced a look back even as Donohue was
clearing Son Tay's far wall upon successfully destroying its
guard towers. With alarm, Waldron watched as Britton's chopper began to flare for a landing, its portside minigun hammering away at the secondary school's courtyard. Activating his
radio the copilot yelled, "Apple-1 . . . get the hell out of there,"
to Britton and Montrem. His warning went unheeded due to
Apple 1's use of its internal communications system, necessary
in order to advise Simons he was free to exit the aircraft.
Donohue, hearing Allison's command to switch from their
original plan to the backup, gained altitude and headed for the
helicopter holding area west of Son Tay.

With Cherry 1's successful flare and napalm drop, Apples 4
and 5 were able to view the mix-up in objectives from their
position fifteen hundred feet above the action on the ground.
Seeing Allison's HH-53 make a successful landing outside the
prison, and hearing Blueboy's radio transmission that they

were safely inside the compound, the two support aircraft turned and headed for their holding area at Finger Lake.

"We knew we'd made a mistake as soon as we lifted off from the rice paddy," remembers Montrem. Britton made a sharp right turn to take the Jolly Green away from the secondary school, heading west toward their assigned holding area where Apples 2 and 3 were to meet them. Meanwhile, Bull Simons and his Greenleaf team knew immediately they'd been landed at the wrong objective. Ever the professional, Simons ordered the wall facing him breached with a satchel charge, and he and his men began killing whomever was in front of their weapons' muzzles. Quite a bit of damage had already been done by Meadows's team as well as by Apple 1's minigun. Thoroughly confused and essentially unarmed, the Chinese were easy targets for the CAR-15 assault rifles wielded by Greenleaf's practiced riflemen. Roughly two minutes passed as Simons and his men poured murderous fire into the secondary school's interior. Then the call went out for an extraction.

"We went west for maybe three-quarters of a mile, then just hovered about one hundred feet above the ground, watching both the firefight just north of the secondary school [at Son Tay] and where we'd just dropped Simons off at. I remember being briefed prior to leaving Udorn about a number of troops being at the school and that they had some vehicles. It would only have taken them thirty seconds to travel the distance between the school and the prison, had they gotten out the gate." Montrem also recalls seeing "strange antenna" atop the school's two-story building as Apple 1 was pulling away from its rice-paddy landing zone. Maintaining the hover, Montrem returned Apple 1 to its open radio net. By then, Greenleaf was calling for extraction.

"We heard Wildroot [Simons's call sign] request extraction," says Montrem. "We needed a flare to guide us in, and after asking for one, both Britton and I saw a strobe light activated almost exactly where we'd originally landed. We just flew in and picked them up, shuttling them over to Son Tay and dropping them off outside the wall." After doing so, Apple 1 headed for its holding area to await recall from Simons.

At the prison, Blueboy had accomplished its assigned tasks to perfection. Meadows's demolitions specialist had blown the wall through which the team would escape, hurrying back to place further charges inside the damaged H-3 in the courtyard.

Likewise, Redwine had secured Greenleaf's assigned sectors, which included the bridge across the Song Con. Sydnor's men assigned to destroy the bridge reported dropping it while a column of vehicles filled with NVA troops was attempting to cross, their apparent objective Son Tay. Meanwhile, at treetop level, the A-1s were hitting targets which included a footbridge connecting the secondary school to Son Tay. This target had been called in by Simons as Apple 1 was landing Greenleaf at the correct objective. NVA surface-to-air missiles were being launched; one of them, reported by Montrem, exploding high in the air over Finger Lake. With Simons at Son Tay, Plan Green was canceled and the original plan reactivated. Twenty-six minutes after the task force was released by Cherry 1, the raid was over.

Despite no POWs being recovered from Son Tay's cells, the raid was considered a success by many in the special operations community. In an interview conducted in April 1992, Gen. Donald Blackburn, recovering at his home from open-heart surgery, said this about the outcome of Son Tay. "At that particular time there was a lot of pressure in the United States about what we *were not* doing for our POWs. I saw the raid as a means of sending a message to the North Vietnamese as well as to our men being held. As it turned out, the news traveled fast, and later reports from released POWs proved me correct.

"There was another reason to launch the mission. The Russians were rebuilding the North's electrical grid system, which would greatly enhance their ability to continue the war effort. I, and a group of others who believed in special operations, believed we could disrupt this system using small groups of highly trained men operating inside North Vietnam. But first, we had to prove we could get people in and out again, with few casualties. Son Tay could demonstrate that capability if the raid was carried out." At the same time, Blackburn insists he would never have allowed the task force to leave Udorn had there been concrete proof there were no POWs at the prison. "No one could tell me there weren't prisoners at Son Tay," he recalls. "There are times when certain risks have to be taken to accomplish certain things."

At CCN, the intense pressure caused by the Chinese-trained NVA hunter-killer battalions dropped off dramatically after the raid's conclusion. "Without their Chinese advisers to coordinate and train them, the NVA couldn't move effectively against our teams," says a former reconnaissance team member. "Son Tay was a success where we were concerned."

Indeed, the raid on Son Tay was a success in every respect. As early as 1969, MACV-SOG knew the compound to be a prison which held U.S. POWs. What became of SOG's own plan to assault Son Tay after it was submitted for approval is uncertain, but we can deduce that many of the camp's early intimate details may have been gleaned from the plan's being reviewed by the IVORY COAST task force. For example, where did the information identifying a POW punishment cell being located underneath the third guard tower come from? There are other equally intriguing questions concerning Son Tay's physical layout and routine which have yet to be answered by those involved with the mission's planning.

It should be remembered that, back in Washington, General Blackburn demanded proof from his technical intelligence staff as to the presence or absence of POWs at Son Tay. The same question was asked in Thailand, where a ground reconnaissance capability was available to provide eyes-on intelligence impossible to gather by SR-71 or drone overflights. In the end, the only reasonable conclusion was that it was *possible* American POWs were being held inside the cells at Son Tay on November 21, 1970.

As a special operation, the Son Tay raid demonstrated that the United States military, using highly trained personnel with dedicated delivery systems, could penetrate far behind enemy lines and deliver the goods. As a result of the operation, American POWs were consolidated for the first time and afforded better treatment than what had been previously experienced. In addition, the morale-building nature of such an attempt was immeasurable in the minds and hearts of those held prisoner in North Vietnam. Chinese and Russian responses included putting shorter leashes on their in-country advisers, which inhibited the effectiveness of their presence. For the North Vietnamese, the raid was a lesson in the reality of being a selected target, regardless of location and distance.

In the end, Bull Simons brought all his people home in one piece.

CHAPTER
SEVEN

It is unfair to compare our little paddle through the swamp with that most difficult and complex operation [Son Tay], which was in fact a nice tactical piece of work. But ours was a success. I only wish we could have found a few GIs in those cages.

CAPT. RICHARD COUCH
"My First Firefight"

It was morning on the Cua Lon River, and United States Navy SEAL Dick Couch was preparing to meet with a local village chief about information provided only hours before. One of the SEAL officer's Kit Carson scouts had brought a local fisherman to his quarters, a man who claimed to know the location of a POW camp not far away. The scout believed their informant, but Couch wanted further confirmation. If he got it, he'd begin planning a rescue operation. Prisoners of war were priority items, and hard intelligence had to be acted on quickly if such a mission was to succeed. The SEALs were operating at a base called Solid Anchor, on the Ca Mau Peninsula in South Vietnam. They were deep in Indian country, surrounded by Viet Cong.

Wanting to speak with the village chief, who was openly anti-VC, Couch loaded up a boat with a security team and headed west along the Cua Lon. His objective was farther north, at Square Bay. The POW camp was said to be hidden along one of the many canals flowing into the southern portion of the bay. If the information was good, the SEALs would make the attempt.

The information was good.

Couch gathered his raiding party. He would take ten men

plus himself ashore. Six would be SEALs, three Kit Carson scouts, the fisherman as guide, and another Vietnamese as the SEAL officer's interpreter. They would use three sampans to negotiate the fifteen-foot-wide canal. The attackers would be heavily armed, carrying one Stoner light machine gun, one M-60 light machine gun, several 203 grenade launchers, M-16s, and AK-47s. Grenades, flares, and smoke would round off the raiders' arsenal. The plan was a simple one. Slip into the canal, paddle roughly two thousand meters upstream, locate the camp, and hit it. Couch coordinated with his air support, several Seawolf gunships from the HAL-3 detachment, the SEALs' special operations aviation unit. Waiting out in the bay would be one of Solid Anchor's patrol boats, ready to retrieve the SEALs and the former POWs once the assault was over. Back at the base, a second squad of SEALs was standing by with a helicopter. They would be the quick-reaction team should the firefight turn against Couch's ground party.

The operation commenced at 2200 hours. Slipping up the bay in the patrol boat, the SEALs transferred to the sampans when the guide indicated that they were near the right canal. Careful to make as little sound as possible, the raiders paddled up the suspected canal. Close to first light, it was discovered the team was on the wrong waterway! Fearful they wouldn't be able to get into position once the sun began coming up, Couch ordered their return to the bay. Reaching the mouth of the canal, the point men in the first sampan noticed a second canal just one hundred meters east of the one they had just left. Couch attempted to contact his support boat by radio, only to discover he'd lost communications. Deciding to drive on with the mission, the SEAL opted to use a handheld illumination flare if he needed the boat's immediate support.

After some hard paddling, the SEALs found themselves less than thirty minutes behind schedule, and a half hour before daylight, Couch reasoned they were near the camp. Suddenly, muted coughing could be heard just ahead of the sampans from somewhere along the canal's right bank. The raiders drifted to a stop, spending the next ten minutes listening intently. They were able to make out a small shack, supported above the water by stilts. It fell to the point men in the first sampan to investigate the source of the coughing, which Couch believed would turn out to be a not-so-alert sentry.

The brief glimmer from a red penlight confirmed the guard's capture. Couch moved in to question the frightened man, wanting precise information as to where the camp was and how it was laid out and guarded. He got nowhere until one of the scouts offered to "help." A phrase mumbled to the shackled guard by the former Viet Cong soldier was all it took. Information began flowing from the man's mouth. They learned the camp was less than one hundred meters away. It was a POW camp, lightly guarded and with few automatic weapons. More importantly, the prisoners were kept apart from the guards' quarters, making it easier to assault the compound with somewhat less concern for the POWs' safety. Dragging their prisoner along, the SEALs dumped him into the third sampan.

They ghosted into the camp, its cooking fires sending thin tendrils of smoke skyward. No one had spotted the armed flotilla as it gently beached itself on the muddy bank. Couch wanted his men to form a skirmish line, advancing until contact was made before firing their weapons. But that plan changed when the handheld flare the SEAL commander was relying on to alert their patrol boat slipped from Couch's grasp and clattered down into the empty sampan.

There was a challenge, shots, then the fight was on. The SEALs immediately began gaining fire superiority over the Viet Cong, laying down a heavy wall of tracer-led steel as they advanced into the camp. The POWs, awakened by the deafening noise, flattened themselves onto the floors of their bamboo cages. Totally surprised and devastated by the volume of firepower directed at their positions, the VC guard element ran for the safety of the jungle. Couch and his men set up a quick defensive perimeter, then began cutting the locks from the doors of the prisoners' cages. Couch remembers the feeling as he helped free those inside the rancid jungle cells as being "one of the highlights of my brief active naval career."

Whiskey Platoon, SEAL Team One, had just rescued nineteen South Vietnamese POWs from the innermost sanctum of the Viet Cong. Some of the men had been held in captivity for years under the most primitive conditions. Loading them into the sampans, the SEALs headed back down the canal. Overhead, alerted by the patrol boat crew which had seen Couch's signal flare high in the air above the camp, the Seawolves were on station. Radio communications were reestablished, and soon the raiders were married up with their patrol boat and headed back to Solid Anchor.

Shortly thereafter Dick Couch learned of the Son Tay raid, which had been mounted just hours before he was introduced to the helpful Vietnamese fisherman. Despite the success of Whiskey Platoon's rescue, it would be overshadowed by the events at Son Tay. Several newspapers reported the early morning raid on Square Bay, but national attention was drawn elsewhere. And, since the released POWs were all Vietnamese, the team's success might have seemed less important to some. Certainly Secretary of Defense Laird did not acknowledge the SEALs' successful Square Bay raid to the Committee on Foreign Relations, which held its hearing on the events at Son Tay just two days after Couch's platoon was back at Solid Anchor. If he had, it might have put a different light on the difficulty and uncertainty of rescuing American POWs, whether they were in North or South Vietnam.

"It was my first combat mission as a SEAL," Couch recalled twenty-two years later. "We had good intelligence, which was acted on quickly. POW rescues are perhaps the most challenging of any military mission. Plans change, and decisions have to be made immediately, with no hesitation. Few people understand the courage required to undertake such a mission; fewer yet understand the extraordinary courage it requires to abort a mission when you feel its objective cannot be accomplished."

Two POW rescue missions were mounted within hours of each other in November of 1970. One into North Vietnam, the other into Viet Cong–held territory in South Vietnam. In their own ways, both succeeded. In one way, both failed. Not one American prisoner of war was found and returned to safety.

CHAPTER EIGHT

Special Forces need not be ashamed of Vietnam, but the confidence of the Army in Special Forces was adversely affected by that conflict. In order to rebuild that confidence, Vietnam needs to be forgotten.

RICHARD W. STEWART, Ph.D.
Command Historian, USASOC

Where the second Indochina War demonstrated the unique talents and capabilities of a special operations force (Green Berets, Marine Force Recon, navy SEALs, Air Commandos/PJs), it was also a Pandora's box to the ultraconventional U.S. military. The political confusion and indecision experienced in Laos offered Special Forces its opportunity to conduct unconventional warfare as well as counterinsurgency, whereas the conventional military could do little more than observe events in that country as they unfolded.

By the time U.S. conventional forces were committed in support of South Vietnam against the North's increasing military pressure, Special Forces had been operating in there for eight years. Their early experiences with the South Vietnamese had led many of them to take note of the gross corruption within the South Vietnamese government and its effect on that government's ability to lead the country in time of war. In addition, SF advisers were critical of the limited capability of the Army of the Republic of Vietnam (ARVN) to wage war against both the Viet Cong and the North Vietnamese. Unable to affect the country's internal political structure, U.S. Special Forces advisers turned their attentions to the military question, which was within their ability to mold. SF's involvement in Laos showed that even the troops of a corrupt government could be formed into effective combat units if proper selection criteria were established and held to during the recruiting and training phases. SF also knew that units formed from the many mountain tribes were critical to long-term campaign successes and loyal to those who trained them and provided for their needs. In light of this knowledge, Special Forces actively cultivated and relied upon recruits and mercenaries drawn from ethnic groups that were despised by racist South Vietnamese. There were dedicated and successful ARVN combat units whose sacrifices and bravery cannot be questioned, but, the majority of ARVN special forces projects were flawed, and inspired little confidence in their American counterparts.

While U.S. Special Forces cadres were raising teams of indigenous troops, the army's conventional commanders were intent upon building, and seeing deployed, a South Vietnamese fighting force which was capable of conducting successful conventional operations in the field. To accomplish this, MACV assigned its own advisers to South Vietnamese units. For example, Norman Schwarzkopf spent his first tour in Vietnam assigned as a MACV adviser. His battlefield experiences in support of the ARVN resulted in strong beliefs about the ability and valor of the properly trained and led South Vietnamese soldier. At the same time, there was a fierce competition between conventional force advisers and Special Forces advisers, which often led to brutal back-room military politics. Abrams, who succeeded Westmoreland as MACV's commander in 1968, held in contempt Special Forces and its opinions about the South Vietnamese military. He was a powerful enemy of Special Forces for the remainder of the war in Vietnam, and he continued his efforts to dismantle the organization once promoted to chief of staff of the army. Schwarzkopf, who would command coalition forces in the Gulf during DESERT SHIELD/ DESERT STORM, inherited his professional feelings about both Special Forces and special operations from his schooling at West Point and through his personal and professional relationship with Abrams, whom Schwarzkopf looked upon as a mentor. This early contact with CENTCOM's future commander would come back to haunt Special Forces.

With America's withdrawal from Vietnam and President Nixon's "peace with honor" signed, sealed and delivered, the army began cleaning up after itself. The fragile truce which had been enjoyed by Special Forces during its early relationship with General Westmoreland had been shredded under the command of General Abrams. While Westmoreland was more politically astute than Abrams, seeing the emphasis placed upon unconventional warfare by the Kennedy administration beginning in 1962, but he still came from the rigid conventional upbringing which affected both Abrams and Schwarzkopf. Assuming conduct of the war in Vietnam in 1964, Westmoreland relied upon those forces he had in country, which included a heavy contingent of Special Forces and SEALs. Believing it would be better to take the war into Laos, Cambodia, and North Vietnam itself, Westmoreland saw the potential in special operations and utilized it. When Abrams assumed command of MACV in 1968, he had a massive conventional force available for operations, and special operations was losing its importance as it became apparent the war would have to be turned over to the South Vietnamese to prosecute. Ironically, as the war was concluded, General Abrams would find himself turning more to his Special Forces assets because conventional American military units and capabilities were being withdrawn as the Vietnamization policy gained momentum.

Abrams, a strongly conventional armor officer, was a graduate of both West Point and World War II. His perceptions about special operations resulted from his background, one which considered that such forces and operations were outside of the army's traditional role. Special Forces had been introduced to the army as an experiment in 1952, but had not been accepted by the institution as anything more than that. Forced to host special operations in Vietnam, Abrams—as well as the majority of his peers—was furious that such operations and those responsible for them were not under the full control of MACV. During Abrams's watch the infamous "Green Beret murder trial" took place after a small group of Special Forces officers was accused of killing an enemy intelligence agent found within their organization. The case was highly embarrassing to the U.S. war effort (read: conventional military), and was made even more so when the CIA refused to provide critical documents to the court, pleading that to do so would compromise operations and/or national security. The CIA's move, along with strong evidence that the men were innocent of murder to begin with, saw the case dismissed. General Abrams was not informed of the Son Tay raid until *after* it had been conducted. The results of the raid were mixed, and because of its singular failure to recover American POWs, fingers pointed at anyone having anything to do with the operation. General

Abrams, responsible for all U.S. military personnel and activities taking place in Indochina, could only comment in embarrassment as, once again, his command had been left out of the special operations information loop.

With Abrams's promotion to chief of staff of the army, an effort was made to dismantle Special Forces. At the same time, a similar effort was conducted by the navy, whose SEALs were viewed in the same light by their commands. "Everyone forgets Special Forces was essentially an experiment in 1952," recounts noted special-warfare historian Shelby L. Stanton. "After Vietnam, in my opinion, the army would have been pleased to simply do away with the entire unit. But this was not possible, for a number of reasons." The approach taken was to get rid of as many Vietnam-era Special Forces operators as possible, through a number of means. Says Stanton of this purging, "The army wanted to start with a new Special Forces, one whose ranks were untainted by everything Vietnam encompassed. In a sense, they wanted to take Special Forces back to the experimental stage, when the army exercised nearly total control over the unit's actions and makeup." To the credit of navy's SpecWar officers and enlisted men, SEAL mission emphasis was shifted toward the emerging submersible-dive-vehicle (SDV) program beginning to gather steam. "A select group of senior SEALs realized we needed to return as quickly as possible to the mainstream of fleet priorities after Vietnam," says one twenty-five-year SEAL veteran. "The Special Forces can exist and do their mission without the army, due to their other agency connections and missions. But SEALs need the navy and are intent on maintaining their place within its structure."

The army's reorganization of Special Forces left only three active duty Special Forces groups on the rolls, the 5th, 7th, and 10th Groups. Budgets were cut, and manpower reduced. Green Berets found themselves policing pine cones on Fort Bragg instead of attending language school, or acting as gate guards at Fort Devens rather than developing small-unit tactics. For many, the message was clear. "I saw it all changing back in 1973 when I got out," remembers David Maurer, who'd been a one-zero with CCN, MACV-SOG. "I knew they were going to screw it up. They were starting to send some of our best people to the then forming Ranger battalions ... historically the army has never tolerated elite units for very long. They use them when they need them, then water them down or get rid of them when they don't need them any longer."

But experienced special operations personnel were not the only branches being pruned from the unconventional warfare tree. Pre- and post-Vietnam records—including the organization's after-action reports, lesson plans, and even class graduation lists from the Special Warfare School—were thrown away by the boxful. "Records from the old days are limited," says Richard Stewart, the current command historian for the United States Army Special Operations Command (USASOC). "It's as if they wanted to get the bad taste of Vietnam out of their mouths." Fred Fuller, a longtime research assistant for the JFK Center's special warfare library, remembers discovering several file cabinets containing classified CCN after-action reports sitting in a garbage dumpster. "When I realized what someone was throwing away, I called our military intelligence folks immediately. Besides being classified, this was historical material that we could never hope to recover once lost."

What saved special operations/Special Forces was a combination of military institutionalism and the CIA. "The army could not abolish SF entirely, because its [Special Forces] mission and organization had been mandated to be an army responsibility," offers one longtime SpecWar expert. "Now the army could whittle away at the organization, cutting its budget, its manpower, curtailing its officers' promotions, and so on, but it could not wipe it out." At the same time, the army rewards those within its ranks which are most like itself. Special Forces was not a runner on the fast track to acceptance and promotion, in fact, it was the odd man out on those issues.

Externally, the Central Intelligence Agency demanded Special Forces be maintained in the inventory for its own purposes. Unable to field large numbers of qualified paramilitary advisers and instructors on its own, the CIA had enjoyed having the navy's UDT/SEAL platoons available (Korea/Vietnam) and the army's Green Berets. Unlike the conventional services, the intelligence community remembered the past successes—and understood the future opportunities—such forces represented. Vietnam was over, but the Cold War was not. In addition, the many brushfire wars springing up around the world demanded U.S. attention. Special operations during peacetime fell to the CIA to conduct, but the army and navy were responsible for providing support and manpower.

Within the conventional military, a realization was slowly

evolving about the nature of warfare in the future. Vietnam had taught a bitter lesson about politics and war in the bush. More than ever, the two were intertwined, and this mating required attention if future debacles were to be avoided. Due to the political nature of warfare and the intense political overtones represented by the deployment of Special Forces elements, special operations could become nightmares. The range of special operations missions—including special reconnaissance, direct action, unconventional warfare, and assassination—left the door wide open for serious, far-reaching political consequences. Special Forces, operating on a need-to-know basis for the military or the individual intelligence agencies, could have a profound effect on the battlefield, one which local commanders would want to be aware of before it took place.

Of even greater concern was the understanding that a single Special Forces effort could determine, or change, the foreign policy of a nation the way British support of Tito's guerrillas during World War II stamped events taking place in Yugoslavia today. One is also reminded of the OSS's early contact with and support of Ho Chi Minh during the Second World War. Had the United States followed up on that initial contact, the events of the Second Indochina War might have been significantly changed or avoided altogether. By choosing one guerrilla army over another, and supporting it with arms, ammunition, advisers, and political clout, a superpower can install a political platform favorable to its own interests inside a nation experiencing revolt or revolution. This was most certainly on the mind of Gen. Norman H. Schwarzkopf during DESERT SHIELD/DESERT STORM, who gave military-political concerns in postwar Iraq the highest priority.

During DESERT STORM, Schwarzkopf, who had witnessed the very real capabilities of Special Forces working with indigenous ethnic groups within South Vietnam, did not want his operational detachments, or A-teams, making contact with the various political factions attempting to establish their own agendas within Iraq. Despite the potential for a viable and effective guerrilla force operating in Saddam Hussein's backyard, using for instance the Kurds, the possibility that such a force might unbalance the political structure of Iraq through a successful campaign (with its subsequent creation of a Kurdish homeland) was in opposition to the goals of the United States and its major Coalition partners.

"You have to remember the history of Vietnam where Special Forces is concerned," advises USASOC's historian, Dr. Richard Stewart. "Many conventional commanders—which Norman Schwarzkopf was—formed the opinion that Special Forces became too involved personally with their projects in the field.

"Now imagine General Schwarzkopf ordering an A-team to infiltrate northern Iraq to train a Kurdish faction in guerrilla warfare. What if the team's commander becomes a little bit too involved with the people he's living with? Perhaps he elects to provide more support than he's allowed to because their cause has become his? He might obtain a few extra cases of ammunition from sources outside the norm, or offer training in subjects which will give the band an edge over not only the enemy, but the guerrilla chief's competing peers. Or he could simply make promises in order to ensure the support of the guerrillas, promises General Schwarzkopf could not honor due to the military-political constraints placed upon his command. You can see the far-reaching implications a single team can have unless its actions are carefully and strictly defined, as well as monitored."

Gulf War special operations reflected these constraints. No report can be found of any Special Forces teams making contact with Kurdish or any other rebel faction within Iraq, before or during the war. The Coalition did not want to see the dissolution of Iraq through a general uprising, nor its partitioning through the establishment of tribal/religious homelands. Such an event would create a power vacuum in the region, which would most likely be filled by Iran. In addition, the Turks have their own problems with the Kurds and would be against the support and establishment of a Kurdish state within Iraq as a Kurdish state's influence could easily spill over Turkey's border. Therefore, the employment of organized guerrillas trained and supported by Special Forces was neither of strategic nor tactical value to the Coalition.

According to sources close to Schwarzkopf during the war, these thoughts did indeed cross the general's mind when considering both *if* and *how* he would employ Special Forces in the Gulf. As we will soon see, based upon his experiences in Vietnam and Grenada, the CENTCOM commander didn't trust Special Forces to begin with. Schwarzkopf was also concerned about providing Hussein with additional POWs, some of which might be captured while conducting behind-the-lines special reconnaissance and direct-action missions. This was especially true during OPERATION DESERT SHIELD, when the Iraqis stopped their uncontested advance toward Saudi Arabia. The discovery and capture of U.S. commandos could have become Hussein's excuse to escalate hostilities at a time when CENTCOM was ill prepared to meet an advancing foe.

With the Special Forces unconventional warfare mission once again shelved, such mission planning reverted to civilian intelligence agencies on a case-by-case basis. An armed resistance movement inside Kuwait held priority where unconventional forces were concerned, and "black" special warfare personnel assisted in specific areas of training for individuals and resistance cells. Schwarzkopf initially elected to use his special operations assets as mobile training teams to conduct instruction in conventional force operations for Arab units and Coalition forces. Their efforts would support the CinC's views and needs as the buildup in Saudi Arabia continued. In this manner, CENTCOM could justify a special operations presence and utilization.

Schwarzkopf's views reflected the army's long-held philosophy about what it considered to be "nasty" warfare. Because of Vietnam's less than satisfactory conclusion, the army first began washing its hands of the taint brought about by a reluctant support of unconventional warfare in Indochina. Nevertheless, to supplement a quick-strike capability, two Airborne/Ranger battalions were activated within the continental United States (CONUS). Ranger units had been stood up during the Korean War and Vietnam. In both conflicts, individual Ranger companies conducted tactical reconnaissance missions in support of conventional commanders. They also carried out direct-action missions (raids, POW snatches) and ambushes. Although the army does not favor elite units of any kind, it could live with the "Ranger" imprint because such formations were essentially light infantry, which paid attention to appearance and discipline.

According to former Special Forces officer Shelby Stanton, the army had already been successful in combining Special Forces with the Ranger concept. Deployed in 1967, Special Forces Operational Detachment A-41 was tasked to develop a Ranger training program for the Thai army. Because the course had to meet specific requirements under the military assistance program offered the Thais, it was decided that the Ranger Department at Fort Benning, Georgia, would have to sign off on the program's overall concept and lesson plans. The department did so, but only after being assured A-41's enlisted cadre would all be Ranger qualified, its officers either graduates of the demanding course, or their records and experience deemed acceptable to the school. Because of this, A-41 became the first and only Special Forces (Airborne/Ranger) detachment in army history. Its members trained Thai rangers for the next eight years, while also conducting combat patrols with their graduates in both Laos and Vietnam.

In short, the army's traditional role was not threatened by Ranger battalions, which appeared to be capable of carrying out the kinds of missions most often assumed by Special Forces during Vietnam. The one exception to this was the unconventional warfare role, a role for which the army saw little future use after its withdrawal from Southeast Asia. Rangers, not Special Forces, would be the elite conventional unit of choice for the army's real go-getters. As for those who were determined to wear the green beret, the already tough times were going to get tougher.

Four separate events would breathe life back into the special forces/operations concept. In 1979, with the successful revolution in Nicaragua as a backdrop, the United States began deploying Special Forces advisers to El Salvador, a tiny Central American country undergoing its own Marxist-inspired revolution. This event marked the beginning of a twelve-year counterinsurgency that would see thousands of U.S. advisers rotated through El Salvador until peace could be negotiated in early 1992. In April 1980, the United States military would suffer a stunning disaster in the barren deserts of Iran as a hostage rescue effort caved in under its own weight. The nightmare of Desert One demonstrated the U.S. military's lack of an organized task force readily prepared to mount such operations. Seen as a national embarrassment, Desert One would mark the rebirth of a coherent special operations capability within the U.S. arsenal. In October 1983, the tranquil island of Grenada would host the first joint military operation mounted since Vietnam. Despite its ultimate success, OPERATION URGENT FURY revealed continuing flaws in the military's effort to rebuild itself. Downplayed, special reconnaissance nevertheless had a major role in the invasion's success, although the role of special operations was underplayed, and some charge intentionally distorted by elements in the conventional military leadership. Finally, the 1989 invasion of Panama (OPERATION JUST CAUSE) provided the first coherent employment of special operations forces in conjunction with the conventional army. Still, despite impressive contributions to the operation's stunning success, Special Forces personnel were subjected to poor mission assignments and minimal support. The combination of these two factors would prove disastrous for the navy's SEALs, who would see an entire platoon decimated during a single engagement.

In order to fully understand the extraordinary missions undertaken by our special operations forces during the Gulf War, a brief but intense study must be made of each of the four operations mentioned. It was through each that further refinement and acceptance was accorded to a fledgling special operations command, charged with ensuring the United States would never again suffer the anguish brought about by failed missions in hostile lands.

CHAPTER
NINE

". . . we would not want to underestimate the magnitude of
the American achievement during phase one of U.S. involvement in El Salvador, running from 1980 through 1984.
Credit for the achievement goes above all to the Salvadoran
soldiers who did the fighting. Clearly, however, the Salvadorans could never have succeeded without American arms,
advice, and training."

> Lt. Col. James D. Hallums
> *The Case of El Salvador*

The moment you deploy Special Operations Forces, you
have declared war.

> Lt. Comdr. Michael J. Walsh
> *The American Warrior*

The deserts of Kuwait and Iraq are quiet now, the majority
of the Coalition's forces back in their barracks, the tools of war
again relegated to training exercises and endless inspection for
cleanliness. If there was ever a war to have gone to, Saddam
Hussein's ill-fated invasion of his neighbor was the one. One
hundred hours of high-tension combat and then . . . liberation.
In a single charge across the desert, the stigma of Vietnam was
forever laid to rest, the mistakes of past U.S. military operations left for historians to address.

In 1981, fifteen Green Berets were sent to El Salvador to
augment the advisory group already in place. According to the
Pentagon, the Special Forces soldiers were chosen for their
"linguistic ability and training expertise." Deployed from the
3d Battalion, 7th Special Forces Group ("3/7"), then located at
Fort Gulick, Panama, the group was split up and sent to three

separate training areas said by State Department officials to be secure. Their mission was to train the struggling Salvadoran army in communications, logistics, and intelligence. The timing of this move was critical. Beginning in January, the Communist-led FMLN guerrillas had launched a major offensive against government forces. This offensive signaled the guerrillas' capability to conduct formal military operations against the army. The Reagan administration, having inherited the Sandinista victory in Nicaragua from President Jimmy Carter, announced its intention not to remain passive where El Salvador was concerned.

But El Salvador would also serve as a proving ground for the United States military's new foreign internal defense (FID) policy, developed to bring about an end to the losing streak being experienced in Third-World wars. Prevented from employing large numbers of conventional troops in the brewing civil war, the Joint Chiefs ordered a series of mobile training teams (MTTs) be sent to bolster El Salvador's essentially frontier police/military. American advisers began working alongside Salvadoran military units in 1962 when an MTT was deployed to conduct a counterinsurgency/civic-action/psychological-operations survey. On June 30, 1972, Panama's 8th SFG(A) was deactivated and replaced by a single battalion from the 7th SFG(A) as part of the army's downgrade of Special Forces. It would be this battalion which would carry out the bulk of those MTTs developed to support the war effort in El Salvador over a twelve-year period.

The announced presence of Special Forces advisers in El Salvador in 1981 brought about a wave of liberal protest and conservative concern in the United States. Hadn't U.S. involvement in both Laos and Vietnam begun in much the same manner? Was Reagan going to repeat history, sending in the Green Berets first, following with the Marines as the war gradually escalated? Political stakes were high, with a strong and convincing propaganda war mounted by the political arm of the primary guerrilla organization, the FMLN, from its headquarters in Mexico City.

Forced to appease public opinion at home, the Pentagon devised a plan to establish a limit on Special Forces advisers in country. In 1979, total U.S. military aid to El Salvador was $12 million. Fifty-five or so advisers were already stationed in El Salvador conducting training and assistance to its military forces. When the decision was made to increase aid to the Salvadoran government, the question asked by the administration and Congress was how many more advisers it would take to get the job done. Not wanting to jeopardize the greater funding and fearful that any increase would result in a general pullout of all U.S. advisers, the then-current number of military specialists was said to be satisfactory by the Pentagon. After that announcement, the adviser manpower ceiling was "etched in stone" according to one former MilGrp commander. In 1982 (fiscal year 1983), U.S. military aid to El Salvador jumped to $80 million. This dramatic increase brought about an equally dramatic increase in mission requirements. It was obvious more advisers were required to carry out the additional taskings, yet the limit of fifty-five would not be challenged. "No one in El Salvador wanted to take a chance of seeing the increased aid canceled in Washington," says another former MilGrp veteran. "It was felt that asking for the ceiling to be lifted on trainers would invite disaster." At the same time, the Pentagon knew that several policy loopholes allowed for additional SF-qualified personnel to be assigned in country; positions allotted to the embassy-based U.S. MilGrp could be stocked with Special Forces operators who would not be counted under the formal fifty-five limitations. In this fashion, the number of uniformed military advisers actually assisting the Salvadoran war effort stood at between eighty-five and one hundred at any given time. Those advisers were supplemented by an additional fifty to seventy-five CIA contract personnel, many of whom were either former SOF operators or had been recruited from Special Forces reserve units.

Arriving in country, the "trainers," as they were now titled by the Pentagon, were reassigned from the 3/7th to the U.S. Military Group (MilGrp). Located at the American embassy in San Salvador, the MilGrp staff oversaw all operations and taskings undertaken by U.S. military advisers in the field. One of the first requirements was to arm the advisers. Although advisers were formally not to participate in Salvadoran combat operations, officials at the Pentagon concluded they would be "allowed to use their weapons only if attacked." The only weapon an adviser could carry was the issue .45 automatic pistol, a policy meant to demonstrate (to whom is still not clear) the official noncombat role of American forces in El Salvador. Confusion about this policy was evident once in country. A number of permanent MilGrp operators were authorized locally to carry either Uzi or MP-5 submachine guns, much more formidable weapons than the issue .45, but trainers arriving from Panama would not be issued such weapons until 1984.

According to former army captain David Morris, whose A-team deployed to El Salvador in March 1981, the rules of engagement were a sure way to get one killed on the ground. "I made sure my team was appropriately armed at all times due to the high threat," he remembers. "That meant M-16s, M-60s [light machine guns], M-79 grenade launchers, grenades, etc." Morris went on to describe how his team was listed by name on a guerrilla "hit list." The far right was looking to murder them, as well. "My team received combat pay, and each of us has affidavits signed by the U.S. MilGrp commander that state we were exposed to hostile fire," Morris concluded. The author has personally reviewed such documents.

Indeed, the threat level was so intense that many SF advisers made use of the embassy's unique purchasing plan for civilian small arms. Using their own funds, operators ordered large-caliber revolvers such as the Smith & Wesson .44 magnum or high-capacity 9mm automatics like the Sig Sauer P-226 for personal carry. Discounts offered by weapons manufacturers were impressive, allowing advisers to more appropriately arm themselves at reasonable cost. "The issue weapons were so shabby, most of us didn't want to trust our lives to them," one adviser recounts. "Plus, we were so badly outgunned by the guerrillas that buying your own self-protection just seemed to make sense." Issue .45s ended up in secured footlockers as bigger and better personal side arms were delivered to the embassy, courtesy of the free-enterprise system.

In the meantime, the guerrillas were increasing their operations, concentrating their attentions on American trainers because their vulnerability and high political profile made them handsome targets. Meanwhile, the army was doing all it could to underscore the fact its personnel were operating in what was an undeclared combat zone. As an insurgency, the war would only be brought to a successful conclusion by combining military methods with a broad array of economic, political, and diplomatic means. The similarity to the war in Laos cannot be overlooked, as that country's insurgency had been handled using the same tools in equal application.

The war in El Salvador was just that. It has rarely been referred to as anything other than a war by politicians or the media, especially in light of the over seventy-five thousand Salvadoran nationals who have been its victims. Yet in Washington, labels were being explored which would prevent the bitter reality of the guerrilla war from being presented as an armed and deadly conflict where American military lives were at stake. The assessment made by the JCS was that the Salvadoran army could defeat the insurgency if properly trained, led, and equipped. This solution would preclude American ground-combat troops being needed, of which there was little chance of any such authorization being granted. In 1979–1980, it was impossible for either the Pentagon or Congress to gauge the demands which would ultimately be made on U.S. trainers. The already expanded artificial ceiling imposed by the U.S. military upon itself soon required that individual Salvadoran units be sent to the United States, Honduras, and Panama for badly needed military instruction. But according to one former Southern Command commander in chief, "We *were* at war. We'd been at war—at least since 1981." It was no coincidence that Captain Morris made the same assessment when his team locked and loaded their "illegal" M-16 assault rifles in March of that same year.

The massive and violent escalation of the war by the FMLN in 1982 sent government forces reeling. Determined to split the country in half, guerrilla forces began assaults on army *cuartels* at San Vicente, San Francisco Gotera, San Miguel, Usulutan, and La Union. The two bridges across the Rio Limpa became primary targets, with FMLN raids successfully dropping spans which had to be quickly rebuilt by government forces. On the ground, Special Forces advisers were working eighteen-hour days to improve the military capability of their assigned units, often accompanying patrols and company-size operations on limited forays outside the safety of the barracks. "You cannot present yourself as a combat expert and then stay behind while your students take all the chances," a former adviser said. "It was no secret in country that we were in the field; they knew full well at the ambassador's level what we needed to do to get the job done." Sgt. Joseph Vigueras, who served as an adviser during the war in 1988, echoed the same thoughts when he said, "The only way an SF trooper can effectively evaluate soldiers is by actually participating in the training. Improvise. Adapt. Overcome. That was the only way to accomplish the mission."

By then, American trainers were operating throughout the country. From Fort Bragg, North Carolina, came one of the first immediate reaction battalions (BIRI), the now infamous

Atlacatl. Thrown into battle, this aggressive combat unit utilized SF combat skills to successfully engage and defeat the surprised FMLN. Atlacatl's impressive demonstration soon birthed additional BIRIs, such as the Arce, Atonal, and Ramon Belloso immediate reaction battalions. In March of 1983, a Special Forces A-team graduated the first Salvadoran paratroop battalion, a unit trained entirely in El Salvador. Following the paras came the first long-range reconnaissance company, known as the PRAL. That unit trained in Panama, then returned to El Salvador where they came under the direct advisement of U.S. counterinsurgency specialists. The PRAL conducted special reconnaissance, often directing the paratroopers onto guerrilla base camps hidden high in the mountains. From forward staging areas, U.S. advisers assisted in launching six-man teams, using assigned UH-1H helicopters which were part of the PRAL "air force." PRAL missions included not only battlefield intelligence gathering but surgical strike missions against targeted FMLN military commanders and strategic sites controlled or occupied by the guerrillas. The PRAL would be expanded to battalion size and retitled GOE—or Special Operations Group—with close command-and-control ties to the CIA.

In 1993, the UN released its human rights report, detailing a number of atrocities carried out against Salvadoran civilians by members and units of the country's military. The Atlacatl was singled out as being particularly brutal. Indeed, in 1984, while visiting the battalion's modern base, this author witnessed the final transformation of a human skull into a desk lamp, at the orders of a Salvadoran officer. The skull was reputed to have belonged to an FMLN guerrilla who was killed during a recent Atlacatl operation. An ESAF soldier had been assigned to clean the "trophy" up and then wire it as a lamp. Questioning showed that no U.S. advisers were then assigned to the battalion, and indeed no Americans had been allowed or invited to accompany Atlacatl troops to the field during combat operations for some time. "Had Special Forces advisers been more free to participate in the combat theater," points out one of the early Atlacatl trainers, "there can be no doubt that far fewer atrocities would have taken place by ESAF forces." Until now, it has been unknown that U.S. advisers were formally assigned by the MilGrp to monitor their units both in garrison and the field, with specific instructions to gather and report information about those ESAF military personnel either suspected or rumored of war crimes or to be involved with right-wing death squads like the White Hand. When this tasking became known within Salvadoran military circles, some officers mounted a virulent program to have the advisers kept behind the walls of their assigned *cuartels*. Unfortunately for hundreds of Salvadoran civilians, U.S. policy made possible this sleight-of-hand effort by the worst of the offenders.

By mid-1982, the Green Berets had carried out forty-six separate mobile-training-team missions (MTTs) with Salvadoran forces. These included counterguerrilla operations, planning and assistance, small-unit tactics, field medical MTTs, patrolling, harbor security, airfield security, communications training, dam security, SCUBA training, border-patrol training and security, arms-interdiction surveys, advanced photography, airborne training, and heavy-weapons employment. The work load increased in 1983, the war shifting to the government's favor by 1984. Before that shift, though, a major event would change the face of the war in El Salvador for the advisers serving there.

In early June 1983, Lt. Comdr. Albert Schaufelberger was attacked by FMLN urban guerrillas in downtown San Salvador. Shot several times in the head at close range, Schaufelberger became the first armed American adviser to die at the hands of the FMLN. The assault was carried out by guerrillas of the Popular Liberation Forces (PLF), one of the five guerrilla organizations then under the command structure of the FMLN. Schaufelberger's death was called "a legitimate action of national self-defense" by rebel radio stations, which broadcast the news throughout Central America. This announcement supported the FMLN's policy which considered U.S. military personnel as willing participants in the civil war. Therefore, their engagement by FMLN units across the urban or rural battlefields was, in the guerrillas' own terms, legitimate.

The lieutenant commander was a carefully selected target, but he was not the only target. The MilGrp commander himself had recently shaken off two guerrilla surveillance units. After Schaufelberger's death, the MilGrp began using chase vehicles, which would deal with suspected urban terrorists as they were spotted, meaning they were intercepted and either killed or captured. According to former MilGrp commander John Waghelstein, this tactic soon "solved the problem."

"Up until that afternoon, things were pretty tranquil," recounts a former adviser in San Salvador the day of the killing. "I was at the Sheraton [hotel] when we got the news about Al. The embassy ordered everyone to stay put, they were calling all over the country trying to locate our people. Weapons were coming out of everywhere. I saw one captain pull a MP-5 out of his tote bag. On the other hand, at least two Special Forces senior types on a staff visit were totally unarmed. They were asking for anything extra we had available in terms of firepower. The Gs [guerrillas] missed a major opportunity to take more of us down that night. We were totally confused and centrally located; it would have been an easy hit."

Schaufelberger's tragic death stunned the MilGrp community. The following day, a careful migration of armed and wary trainers arrived at the heavily beefed-up U.S. embassy compound. With as many advisers present as he could safely bring into San Salvador, MilGrp commander Col. John Waghelstein stated, "The guerrillas have changed the rules of the game." What he was saying was that the party was over as far as a noncombat role was concerned.

In light of Al Schaufelberger's death, Congresswoman Pat Schroeder (D., Colorado) introduced an amendment to the House which recognized El Salvador as being a foreign area "where they [U.S. military personnel] were subject to the threat of physical harm or imminent danger on the basis of civil war, terrorism, or wartime conditions." Until then, hostile-fire/imminent-danger pay had been granted on a case-by-case basis, normally awarded to those assigned to a full tour with the MilGrp. Schroeder's amendment established the reality of military service in El Salvador for the record. It was a courageous act on the part of the Democrat from Colorado, but one which did not sit well with the Pentagon. The authorization of hostile-fire pay recognized that El Salvador was indeed a combat zone despite the Pentagon's public stance that it was somehow something less than such. The increased number of advisers actually working in country, along with combat operations of a far greater depth than Congress was aware, was a constant source of concern at the Pentagon. Combat pay made it more difficult to maintain the charade being carried out. In February 1991, a formal memo circulated within the U.S. MilGrp confirmed the granting of a military tax exemption for those serving in El Salvador. Under Section 112 of the U.S. Tax Code, compensation is to be received "for any month during any part of which such member served in a combat zone."

Further, the Commerce Clearing House—Standard Federal Tax Report Reg. 1.112.1 (k) (3), paragraph 1142.011 stipulates "a member of the Armed Forces who performs service in an area not designated as a combat zone, which service is in direct support of military operations in a combat zone and is performed under conditions that qualify the member for Hostile Fire Pay, is deemed to have served in such combat zone." Finally, the memo, signed by then MilGrp commander Col. Mark R. Hamilton, offers that the Department of Defense Pay & Entitlements Manual designated El Salvador as "an area of hostile fire or imminent danger."

By 1984, the war was heating up for American advisers in El Salvador. Their Leave Earning Statements (LES) reflected the additional sixty-five dollars per month hostile-fire/imminent-danger pay invoked by Pat Schroeder, the Pentagon term a semantic evolution of what was formerly known as combat pay. Trainers/advisers were no longer restricted to the worn-out .45 automatics; MP-5s, Uzis, and even CAR-15 assault rifles were being issued by the embassy's arms room. "You weren't supposed to carry the automatic weapons in the open if it could be helped," one adviser recalls. Another said, "The word games were incredible. Submachine guns and the carbine version of the M-16 [CAR-15] were now considered *defensive* weapons because of barrel length. Full-size rifles were *offensive* weapons, and since we weren't actively conducting such operations with the Salvadorans, defensive weapons were authorized for carry. It was all for the politicians and press—our main concern was being able to fight back with more than just our dicks in our hands."

The adviser's concern was real, as during the course of the war, the following combat actions took place.

In March 1984, two-man Special Forces communication teams assigned to critical Salvadoran election points came under harassing fire from FMLN guerrillas. One base had been earlier overrun by the guerrillas and was considered a prime target for a repeat performance during the elections. In Honduras, a U.S. Army Ranger platoon was standing by with assigned aircraft support. The Rangers were to act as an extraction/body-recovery element, should the Green Berets come under attack and be unable to exfiltrate the area on their own. "We were to get them, or their bodies," remembers a former Ranger who was there.

In late May 1984, a contingent of Special Forces personnel

monitoring the elections at the *cuartel* in El Paraiso came under fire by guerrillas. The same *cuartel* had also been over-run, with heavy losses suffered by the army (its wounded were bayoneted in their beds by FMLN forces). An AC-130 gun-ship, code-named Bield Kirk, was scrambled from its base in Honduras. Using sensitive night-vision equipment, Bield Kirk advised the encircled Green Berets of hot spots considered to be possible guerrilla positions. Most of the *cuartel*'s troops were on liberty when the attack occurred. "We evacuated the radio bunker and manned whatever weapons were available. The guards were new recruits, with maybe two magazines per man of ammunition for their rifles. The embassy was preparing to order U.S.-piloted helicopters from the capital (San Salvador) to extract us. That didn't happen, but we stayed low until the sun came up," recounted M. Sgt. (Ret.) Mike Campanelli.

Outside the *cuartel* in San Vicente, SFC Steve Antonelli took command of a small army element which had come into contact with guerrilla forces during a training maneuver. "The Salvo officer was young, and he just froze. I knew we were going to catch it if something wasn't done," the Special Forces NCO reported. The Green Beret noncom successfully engaged the enemy in combat and was later awarded a Joint Service Commendation Medal for his efforts at San Vicente.

At the *cuartel* in San Miguel in 1984, an A-team from Bravo Company, 3/7th SFG(A), was awakened as the base came under intense ground attack by a major guerrilla force. Again, the attack was launched when many of the *cuartel*'s forces were on leave. Manning .30-caliber Browning machine guns the team's weapons sergeants had rebuilt in the *cuartel*'s armory, the Green Berets fought a night-long battle from atop their barracks. "The barrels began overheating, but we had pre-pared number-10 cans filled with motor oil to pour over them," one of the defenders remembers. "When those ran out, we lay on our sides and pissed into the cans, pouring urine over the barrels to keep them up. It stunk like hell, but it worked!"

The next morning Col. "Smokin' Joe" Stringham flew into San Miguel to view the carnage. Recommending the entire team for Combat Infantry Badges, Stringham would be over-ruled by SOUTHCOM commander Gen. Paul Gorman. Special Forces advisers would not be acknowledged to have partici-pated in combat regardless of the circumstances, and Gorman was intent on maintaining this charade at all costs. SFC Leroy

Sena, S.Sgt. Peter Moosey, and the smoke-soiled veterans of the all-night battle would be denied their due combat credit.

In 1985, Green Beret Robert Kotin secured an M-60 light machine gun while under heavy FMLN attack at San Miguel. As ESAF forces abandoned the base's perimeter, falling back to the *cuartel*'s helicopter launch site, where both Kotin and a Marine Corps captain were dug in, Kotin began firing. "Kotin asked for cover fire from the Marine officer," recalls M.Sgt. (Ret.) Bruce Hazelwood, who served as an adviser in El Salvador for seven years. "He [Kotin] then moved forward under fire and secured a position from which he could cover the retreating Salvadorans while slowing the guerrilla advance. The Gs had penetrated the base, and were close to overrunning it until this took place." With the SF trooper pouring fire into the guerrilla ranks, his Marine counterpart assembled a force capable of mounting a counterattack. Using Kotin's outgoing fire as cover, the Marine led his ESAF stragglers in an assault that threw the guerrillas out of San Miguel. Both Americans would be recommended for Bronze Stars with valor (V) devices, but only the Marine's chain of command would actually grant their combat award. "The Marines maintained a separate service administration even at the MilGrp," points out Hazelwood. "The army downgraded Kotin's award for purely political reasons, but the Marine Corps acknowledged the participation of their officer in combat without any negative feedback." As we shall see, the army's awards-and-decorations policy in El Salvador was deceptive at best.

A fifteen-man adviser element in La Union discovered itself tasked to establish a regional training base (CEMFA) for the Salvadoran military. Deep in Indian country, the trainers were dismayed at the lack of perimeter defenses and a competent security force for the badly needed project. Within one week, they were on alert, a sizable force of guerrillas reported to be preparing to storm the ragged *cuartel*. "We each had an MP-5, a .45, and about one hundred rounds of ammunition," one adviser recalls. "We were in a ditch all night long, just waiting for the Gs to hit. One hundred rounds would go through a submachine gun pretty damn fast."

Just days later, Colonel Stringham declared a zone twenty-five kilometers in circumference around the base to be "training area." This recommendation had originally been made during early planning stages by Special Forces Major Charles Zimmerman, responsible for the construction and security of the new training base. The concern was that his advisers be allowed to patrol the area for signs of guerrilla activity that could endanger the early phases of the base's construction. The MilGrp commander only supported the major's observations after an argument with the embassy's defense attaché, whose report on the defensive situation at CEMFA contained those tactical considerations originally submitted by the young SF officer. "The attaché and MilGrp commander were rivals," says one close observer at the time. "They did not work hand in hand as might have been expected."

After being embarrassed by the attaché's report, Stringham ordered the composite team to arm themselves with "whatever you can get ahold of, just stay alive." The advisers did so, drawing brand new M-16s, M-79 grenade launchers, claymore antipersonnel mines, and several M-60 light machine guns from Salvadoran stocks at CEMFA. The SEAL platoon located several miles away at La Union provided small arms munitions and intelligence updates. "Our primary concern was to be able to fight from inside the *cuartel* if attacked," one of the original team said. "But we had our people out in the bush conducting training both day and night. We went on patrols, during one of which a suspected guerrilla was captured spying on the base from a tree.

"During one battalion-size training operation [Biat Bracamonte] the Salvadorans changed their minds after leaving the *cuartel*, deciding to turn it into a combat op, during which the town of Conchagua—a confirmed guerrilla R & R center—was encircled and searched. We had armed advisers in the field for over twenty-four hours. All we could do was tell them to go with the flow."

In 1985, CEMFA was attacked by combined FMLN units whose number totaled nearly one thousand guerrillas. The *cuartel* was partially overrun, with at least five Green Berets caught on the premises and taken under fire. Contrary to embassy reports, the Americans fought back against the advancing guerrillas, rallying ESAF security forces deep within the confines of the base and leading a valiant counterattack. A senior SF medic is credited for much of the team's success, and Capt. Danny Egan was recommended for the Bronze Star with V device along with those other advisers who survived the assault. Shamefully, forces within the embassy ordered both men out of the country within hours of the relief force's occupation of the shattered training center. Again, State Department influences were working overtime to ensure the Reagan/Bush administration's noncombat campaign would remain intact.

How extensive has the combat been for U.S. military advisers? At least five Purple Hearts are known to have been awarded to Special Forces personnel for wounds obtained in El Salvador. The first went to S.Sgt. Jay Stanley, who was wounded while returning fire from a low-flying helicopter during a battle with FMLN guerrillas manning a roadblock. On a somewhat more humorous note, S.Sgt. George Reyes received his Heart after being accidentally shot by his own officer while training NCO cadre for the Arce Immediate Reaction Battalion.

Awarded the Purple Heart posthumously in 1987, SFC Gregory Fronius was struck down by small-arms fire when three FMLN guerrillas confronted him during a well-coordinated attack on the headquarters of the 4th Infantry Brigade at El Paraiso. According to the message sent the 3/7th after the young NCO's death, Ambassador Edwin Corr stated in part that ". . . those who were critics of the policy before will find in SFC Fronius's death fresh grist . . . or [will] misconstrue his training role as involvement in combat." Sixty-five Salvadoran troops were also killed in the attack, as well as seven of the FMLN sappers. Corr's position was a political one, which sought to maintain the facade of non-U.S. combat involvement in the war. First Sgt. Ray O. Emerson, an SF administrative NCO assigned to the 3/7th, recalls the fight that went on to see the dead sergeant justly acknowledged for his sacrifice. "He [Fronius] was submitted for the Bronze Star with valor device along with the Purple Heart. There was a huge fuss put up by SOUTHCOM over this, particularly after the award was approved at 7th Group headquarters, the Special Operations Command, and the Joint Task Force. In the end, Fronius's Bronze Star—a combat award—would be transformed into a Meritorious Service Medal, the peacetime equivalent of the original award. According to sources then in Panama, the Purple Heart was authorized only after much debate."

As a final insult, Fronius was depicted as being killed while huddling in a defensive position while his attackers swarmed over the compound. According to former SF adviser Joseph Vigueras, who visited the base and interrogated the surviving ESAF soldiers shortly after it was secured by government forces, the following actually took place. As FMLN sappers assaulted the perimeter, the Salvadoran officers left their troops in a panic, electing to flee the compound. Fronius, the sole armed American adviser on site that day, left his defensive position and began rallying those soldiers he could immediately lay hands on. According to Vigueras, it appears Fronius was attempting to do what so many other Special Forces personnel had done before him—mount an effective counterattack in the face of the enemy. It was at this point that Sergeant Fronius was confronted by the three guerrillas who shot him. His body was later struck by mortar fragments where it lay. "I observed the spot where Greg's body was found," confirmed Vigueras, "and saw where bullets had struck the wall behind him." Joe Vigueras would be awarded the Joint Service Achievement Medal for his "meritorious achievement" as the Special Forces radio operator responsible for the daily operations of both the tactical and nontactical communications system used by the MilGrp. His citation in part reads, "He greatly assisted these efforts, as well as the overall Salvadoran war effort through his devotion to duty and professionalism."

According to Emerson, a document packet pertaining to the entire incident was prepared, and included several hundred photos of the battle area as well as eyewitness accounts and formal recommendations for Greg Fronius to receive the Bronze Star in light of his actions that day. The report, said to still be locked away in the S-2's safe at the 7th Special Forces Group's headquarters, has been mentioned to retired Gen. Carl W. Stiner, commander in chief, United States Special Operations Command, in the hope of seeing it used to upgrade the peacetime decoration to the combat award earned by Sergeant Fronius.

Today, in light of growing support both inside the military and through the Veterans of Special Operations, the Bronze Star Greg Fronius should have received is being fought for by his former comrades-in-arms. It is hoped the army will do the right thing by Greg's wife and two children.

A number of carefully worded "sanitary" award citations have been issued, many of these beginning "While under great terrorist threat . . ."

For instance, in 1986, it was discovered one such officer responsible with approving awards for both enlisted and commissioned advisers in El Salvador was routinely downgrading the enlisted awards. Rather than approve Joint Service Medals for enlisted men, one of the most coveted and respected available for service in El Salvador, the officer downgraded such recommendations to Army Achievement Medals, the lowest possible acknowledgment for peacetime actions above the norm. His explanation, according to one Special Forces officer, was that "only officers merited joint service awards, with Army Commendation Medals and Army Achievement Medals appropriate for enlisted personnel, regardless of their activities or the recommendations of their immediate superiors."

In fact, it now appears the Pentagon and JCS actively supported use of peacetime and noncampaign awards and decorations to acknowledge U.S. adviser actions in El Salvador. According to one senior SF officer with intimate knowledge of the embassy's internal directives, other MilGrp commanders after Joe Stringham have attempted to have the Combat Infantryman's Badges (CIB) authorized for those who served in El Salvador. Cols. Milton Menjivar, Mark Hamilton, and James Steel submitted formal documentation and arguments for CIBs, but their recommendations were denied. In addition, by 1989 all advisers were taken off jump status and denied hazardous duty pay. Joint awards became a thing of the past, to include the mundane but much respected awarding of Salvadoran jump wings to advisers who conducted a parachute operation with Salvadoran armed forces. "Officer evaluation reports and enlisted reviews were sanitized to reflect not a hint of combat action," says one senior officer. "This was done for the sake of political sensitivity." These questionable actions seem to have resulted in career-damaging, less-than-favorable reviews during the current drawdown of the armed services. And promotion boards have apparently received no instructions to alert them to the true status of service in El Salvador. "[Such service] is treated as dead time by the boards." In fact, advisers who served in El Salvador have reported being threatened with the destruction of their military careers if detected in battle or vocal about the unfair treatment handed out to them upon completion of their assignments. Yet for a twelve-year period they were expected to produce combat results while subject to being shot at or mortared at any time.

"We were in a combat zone where over seventy-five thousand lives have been lost," an SF veteran of Central America comments. "We drew combat pay, we carried weapons, we were in the field, and we were caught up in 'shit happening' where, in at least two cases, our people died. We've lost more advisers since Fronius. For instance, Lieutenant Colonel Pickett and Specialist Dawson were executed by the guerrillas when their bird was shot down." Additional Special Forces casualties include S.Sgt. Lynn Keen, killed in a July 1987 helicopter crash while providing medical aid to wounded Green Beret Timothy Hodge. SFC Tom Grace, also aboard the chopper, was severely injured in the accident. Pickett, commander of the 4/228th Aviation Battalion, was returning from an inspection of his forward assault helicopter detachment, which was stationed at the Illopongo military base outside of San Salvador. Unknown to the American public, U.S. Army aviation crews were flying combat missions in support of MilGrp operations, and, in fact, several Air Medals had been approved for their pilots. CW03 Ken Shirley, now assigned to Ford Hood, Texas, was one of those combat aviators. Infantry-qualified door gunners from the 193d Infantry Brigade in Panama provided armed security for the specially equipped Huey helicopters, but were denied aircrew wings by the Southern Command. Pickett, whose body was struck over twenty times by FMLN bullets before he died, was forced to witness the single-bullet execution of his crew chief before attempting to evade his captors.

Some of those who are part of the "Double Nickle" fraternity are disdainful of official recognition for their actions while serving in El Salvador. "If you're in SF, it's part of the package," one senior retired noncom offers. "We're supposed to be quiet professionals. Sometimes you get credit for shit, sometimes you don't. I don't think getting a CIB or combat patch out of that situation should be too high on one's priority list."

But many others disagree. Both active-duty and former Salvadoran veterans believe such a philosophy is easily espoused by those who earned their combat decorations in earlier or later conflicts and can therefore afford to disregard what took place in El Salvador. They point out the broad interpretation of the army regulation covering the award of the Combat Infantryman's Badge during Vietnam. OPERATIONS JUST CAUSE and URGENT FURY raised similar observations. "I'd just come in off a patrol and was having a beer when news of the invasion of Grenada got to us. Three days later, we heard the Rangers were all getting their CIBs. Now, the Rangers earned it, and I've got no bitch about that. But they gave over *eight thousand* awards and decorations away for URGENT FURY. By the time Grenada went down, many of us had been humping El Salvador for months." Indeed, in a February 1993 interview with the chief of Army Awards and Decorations in Alexandria, Virginia, the subject of CIBs was touched upon. According to Major Wawrzyniak, the Combat Infantryman's Badge has been awarded to many DESERT STORM veterans "who never crossed the line of departure, saw the enemy, or were fired upon." Further, the major was clear to point out that far too many CIBs are today being worn by soldiers who didn't earn them, while those who have are denied the award. In a 1987 memo reply to a question by then Secretary of the Army John O. Marsh, the former chief of staff of the army, General Wickham offered, "I don't have a problem with the CIB for Special Forces members ... clearly Special Forces troopers serving in El Salvador–type duty, for example, clearly warrant [the] CIB."

Many of the advisers who served with the U.S. MilGrp see the problem as one of recognition. In 1986, the Joint Meritorious Unit Award (JMUA) was awarded for the first time to those personnel who served over sixty days with the U.S. MilGrp in El Salvador from January 1, 1981, to June 7, 1985. According to Maj. Jose Rodriguez, the J-5 politico-military officer for SOUTHCOM in 1986, "The unit ... participated directly in furthering vital national security interests and foreign policy objectives of the U.S. government in Latin America." According to the army's Awards and Decorations Office at the Department of the Army, this was the only such award given to MilGrp personnel during the course of the war.

What Major Rodriguez failed to add about the JMUA was this. Authorized by the secretary of defense in June of 1981, the award is "given to joint activities (all services) for meritorious achievement or service, superior to that which is normally expected, for actions in the following situations; combat with an armed enemy of the United States, or during a declared national emergency, or under extraordinary circumstances that involve the national interests." In light of its definition, and considering the fact that U.S. military personnel were formally entitled to imminent-danger pay as of October of 1983, the JMUA appears to be a unit combat award. Award narratives provided to the author by those assigned to the MilGrp refute the army's claim that there had been only one award of the JMUA to MilGrp personnel. The narratives for all *four* awards of the JMUA have been obtained from military sources. They tell quite a story about U.S. adviser involvement in Central America's longest civil war.

In a memorandum to the director of the Joint Staff, channeled through the commander in chief of the U.S. Southern

Command, former embassy chargé d'affaires, Mr. David Passage, wrote:

> Operating under the potential and real dangers of both political and physical fire, U.S. Armed Forces personnel designed and carried out a program to help build the Salvadoran Armed Forces from a small, ill-equipped and poorly led force, to the point where it is now well on the road to becoming one of the finest fighting forces in Latin America.

Passage, whose duty station was the embassy in San Salvador, goes on to point out that military group personnel "have been shot at" and "that they are high priority targets for enemy attacks." According to the memo, then-ambassador Thomas Pickering "specifically requested to be associated" with the recommendation that the Joint Meritorious Unit Award be given to those members of the MilGrp assigned and attached and who served for over sixty days in any capacity between January 1, 1981, and June 7, 1985. "The Military Group has been paid the ultimate compliment," wrote Passage. "The Communist-backed guerrillas have publicly ascribed to them the fact that the guerrillas are losing their war. No commendation can be written that is so credible a testament to their effectiveness."

This discreet manner of acknowledging exposure to, and the conduct of, actual combat in a counterinsurgency environment mirrors the award of the Army Meritorious Unit Commendation (AMUC) to those who served with MACV-SOG from 1965–1970. In this case, the AMUC replaced the Combat Infantryman's Badge as a unit award, although CIBs and Combat Medical Badges (CMB) *were* authorized for SOG recon team members. In the case of Laos, Col. Bull Simons's White Star Project earned combat badges and patches, as well as an Armed Forces Expeditionary Medal (AFEM) for service between April 19, 1961, and October 7, 1962. Sadly, the awarding of the JMUA in 1986 appears to have been promoted not to protect the identification of a covert war or clandestine operation, but as a cloak to veil a series of deceptions and outright lies on the part of some Pentagon and senior White House officials.

During the writing of this book, Gen. Colin L. Powell was formally contacted by Senators Mark Hatfield (R., Oregon) and Bob Packwood (R., Oregon) about the possibility of awarding an Armed Forces Expeditionary Medal to the veterans of El Salvador. On March 9, 1992, the chairman's office replied by saying, ". . . award of the Armed Forces Expeditionary Medal for service in El Salvador is inappropriate. The Armed Forces Expeditionary Medal is reserved for those U.S. military operations designated by the Joint Chiefs of Staff as involving a significant number of US Service personnel who encountered foreign armed opposition or for whom hostile action was imminent."

Clearly, whichever staffer was assigned the task of answering the senators' inquiry was not provided an appropriate amount of knowledge regarding both the AFEM and service in El Salvador by the chairman. Awarded twenty-one times to date, the AFEM has been given to operations lasting no more than one day (Cambodia, Mayaguez Hostage Rescue, May 15, 1975) and for operations boasting fewer than a handful of U.S. service personnel (Congo, OPERATION DRAGON RED AND BLACK. Rescue, November 23–27, 1964). The counterinsurgency effort in El Salvador utilized a minimum of 55 to an estimated maximum of 150 U.S. service personnel assigned to the U.S. MilGrp on a 180-day basis over the span of *twelve years* during the conduct of the war. Rough figures would then strongly indicate that over 3,600 advisers (including non-SF personnel) took part in Salvador's civil war. Fewer than five hundred SF advisers were assigned to Simons's White Star Project, yet the JCS then felt that was a "significant number" of U.S. service personnel, enough to warrant an AFEM.

The encountering of foreign armed opposition is testified to by Captain Morris's own personal record in 1981, and further documented by David Passage's eloquent narrative to the joint staff, which came on the heels of the first three Purple Hearts awarded to Special Forces advisers. In addition, the shooting of Lieutenant Commander Schaufelberger was proved to be the work of a guerrilla group sanctioned by the FMLN. These, and other recorded incidents, demand a definition of what General Powell considers such opposition to consist of when considering the authorization of the AFEM. If full-blown combat is the criterion, the chairman of the Joint Chiefs has apparently elected to ignore a memorandum authored by Gen. Maxwell Thurman, who was commander in chief of the U.S. Southern Command during the FMLN's unsuccessful final offensive of 1989. In his narrative—meant to support the recommendation for a *second* oak-leaf cluster to the Joint Meritorious Unit Award—General Thurman offered that "the Farabundo Marti National Liberation Front (FMLN) conducted the largest and most aggressive offensive in the history of the ten-year civil war. Throughout the country the FMLN used modern Soviet bloc weapons ranging from AK-47s to SAM-7 surface-to-air missiles during this large-scale operation."

Thurman, considered to be a heavy hitter at the Pentagon, went on to say that U.S. Military Group personnel directly supported Salvadoran combat, combat support, and combat service support operations. "They were constantly exposed to enemy fire and continuously executed their mission with such valor, professionalism, and dedication to duty that the Salvadoran Armed Forces were able to achieve a significant victory," wrote the SOUTHCOM CinC. The narrative goes on to describe the precise actions undertaken by U.S. advisers, ending with "The level of danger they encountered was consistent with what U.S. personnel with similar responsibilities have faced during recent periods of armed hostilities worldwide. There were countless incidents where U.S. personnel were taken under direct and indirect fire and where enemy troop units moved within meters of U.S. personnel."

As described above, U.S. advisers were authorized to draw hostile-fire pay as a result of congressional action in the mid-1980s. Clearly, General Powell has his reasons for denying the recognition due Salvador's veterans despite formal evidence which refutes the chairman's claims that none of the above ever took place to the degree such recognition would endorse. However, the JCS cover-up even extends to the denial of a shoulder sleeve insignia–Former Wartime Service (SSI-FWTS) or combat patch to Salvador's advisers.

When such a device was requested for approval in 1992, Brig. Gen. T. C. Jones of the Office of the Deputy Chief of Staff for Personnel wrote:

Army Regulation 670-1, paragraph 27-17, is very specific in defining requirements for the authorizing of wear of SSI-FWTS. Authorization may apply only to soldiers assigned to U.S. Army units. Those units must have been assigned to a theater or area declared a hostile environment by the Secretary of the Army or higher, or a Declaration of War made by Congress. The units must have actively participated in or supported ground combat operations against hostile forces

in which they were directly or indirectly exposed to fire or
threat of enemy action. The military operation normally
must have lasted for thirty days or more.

Again, the facts refute Pentagon smoke-and-mirrors explana-
tions regarding proper and appropriate recognition of adviser
efforts in El Salvador. For instance, the army is the only service which uses the SSI-FWTS to recognize wartime service.
Other adviser elements representing the army's sister services
would simply be required to rely upon their own versions of
the SSI-FWTS, such as the navy's Combat Action Ribbon, in
order to commemorate their advisers' service in El Salvador.

El Salvador was declared a hostile environment by the secretary of defense, per 37 U.S.C. 310 (hostile-fire pay), thereby
meeting the criteria for such an authorization as stated in General Jones's letter. U.S. Army units (the MilGrp and those assigned from U.S. Army units such as advisers from the 3/7th
Special Forces Group) clearly participated in or supported
ground combat operations, as attested to by formal embassy
and SOUTHCOM memorandums spanning the conflict. Again,
these personnel are officially acknowledged as to having been
directly or indirectly exposed to fire *or the threat of enemy action* by sources subordinate to the Pentagon and secretary of
defense's office. El Salvador's civil war lasted twelve years
with U.S. adviser involvement beginning in earnest in 1979,
thereby easily meeting the "normal" thirty-day requirement offered under Army Regulation 670-1.

When one considers other recent awards of the SSI-FWTS,
the general's attitude seems arcane. In the case of DESERT
STORM, the criteria for an SSI-FWTS "appl[y] only to soldiers
receiving imminent-danger pay and who are under command
and control of CENTCOM." Soldiers authorized to wear an
SSI-FWTS do not have to have come under enemy fire nor
taken an active part in ground or air combat. In the case of
PROVIDE COMFORT, a humanitarian operation in support of the
Kurds in northern Iraq, the criteria are even more liberal; soldiers are authorized to wear a combat patch "who received
imminent-danger pay and either deployed into Iraq or were
members of a unit that had elements deployed into Iraq who,
based on their mission in the deploying unit, did not personally
accompany the elements into Iraq." Such units include ground
crews supporting aviation operations based out of Turkey and

administrative/logistical commands supporting forward deployed PROVIDE COMFORT elements.

In a personal letter from one Special Forces communications sergeant assigned to the Salvadoran MilGrp from 1987–1988, the continued and escalating exposure to combat of U.S. advisers is described.

> I was attached to the Estado Mayor [Salvadoran version of the JCS] in support of all communications throughout the country. There were many instances of SF advisers having to fight their way out of engagements and although I'm not sure, a lot of these engagements were swept under the rug for fear of losing support for [El] Sal with the American Public. Congress did not want the public to know that their advisers were getting shot at (Vietnam Syndrome) and that is why they promised the public that there were only going to be 55 advisers, hence the "double nickel." The loophole with the 55 was that there were positions in-country which did not fall under the 55 rule and we could stock them with SF-qualified people. I fell under that rule. I would work in the Estado Mayor and after work would assist my peers in the field. From Chalatenango to CEMFA I have been in all the hot spots.

Even so, the Department of Defense still refuses to award even its most basic combat acknowledgment—the combat patch—to the veterans of El Salvador.

The State Department can also claim culpability for protecting its own interests in El Salvador. Under State Department rules and regulations, a member of State working in a declared danger zone draws an impressive form of "combat pay" in recognition of his or her exposure to untimely injury and/or death. According to a senior MilGrp officer, State Department employees serving in El Salvador drew "a huge extra pile of money for themselves [in danger-zone pay] and their families live in luxury." Obviously both the Department of Defense and the State Department considered El Salvador to be at war, and therefore a combat/hostile-fire/danger zone where their respective employees were being paid to serve. It is interesting to note that both State and the DoD are the most vocal (as well as evasive) when asked to formally comment on their roles where this issue is concerned. "You have to remember there was a lot of eyewinking going on between the Congress, the

State Department, and the Oval Office during that period," reminds Colonel (Ret.) Waghelstein. "Everyone knew what was really going on, but no one wanted to come right out and say it."

By the war's conclusion, fifteen American soldiers had died in El Salvador. This number almost equals the number of U.S. troops killed during OPERATION URGENT FURY, and exceeds casualty figures for twelve other campaigns where the AFEM was awarded by the JCS/Secretary of Defense. In a letter to the author regarding the Secretary of Defense's decision not to award an AFEM to U.S. military members who served in that conflict, Col. Kenneth Deutsch offered this:

> After an assessment of the situation in El Salvador, it was determined (e.g., scope of operations, etc.) did not warrant the award of the AFEM. This decision should in no way be considered as a lack of appreciation for the sacrifices of our U.S. military advisers who have served in El Salvador. On the contrary, commanders have had available and used a full spectrum of military awards and decorations to appropriately recognize individuals and units for outstanding achievements and conspicuously meritorious service.

Those who attempted to see Sergeant Fronius awarded the Bronze Star after his death in combat might disagree with the good colonel's assessment.

In June 1992, Maj. Patricia Sigle, chief of the army's Military Awards Branch, wrote an official reply to a letter inquiring why Salvador's advisers were not considered for the Combat Infantryman's Badge, or CIB. Major Sigle was replying for Secretary of Defense Richard Cheney, who despite his position as the SECDEF never served a day in military uniform. The gist of Major Sigle's response relies upon Department of the Army messages issued in 1963 and 1965, which pertain to the Vietnam War. These messages stipulated that the award of the CIB was authorized to otherwise qualified personnel "provided they are personally present and under fire." Despite her letter's very complete history of the CIB and the exacting criteria for its award, the device has been routinely given out since the invasion of Grenada where CIBs were deemed earned upon less than seventy-two hours in the combat environment. CIBs earned during OPERATION DESERT STORM were awarded en masse despite the fact that the majority of those authorized to wear the award never came under fire, fired a shot in anger, or even saw a single enemy soldier.

In her conclusion, the major appears to acknowledge that CIBs should have been authorized for service in El Salvador. Perhaps her observation is based on the ignored petitions of at least three former MilGrp commanders. "Soldiers who served in El Salvador know they have made a difference and should be proud of their service, regardless of whether formal recognition was received," offers Major Sigle. Would this staff officer feel the same way if she had served over 180 days in El Salvador as a combat adviser, considering that such awards have a direct and meaningful impact on future career progression? One MilGrp officer has already voiced his opinion on the subject. "No formal credit for a combat tour means no advancement. We're competing with the acknowledged veterans of Grenada, Panama, and the Gulf War, all of whom have in some way been given credit where wartime command experience is concerned. Without it, one's career is severely affected."

To its great credit, the Veterans of Foreign Wars voted to petition the Department of Defense (DoD) to award an Armed Forces Expeditionary Medal to the veterans of Central America's longest war. Resolution 427 was unanimously approved during the VFW's 93d National Convention in August 1992. According to Mr. Richard Kolb, executive editor of *VFW* magazine, the organization's official publication, the matter is a priority issue for the Veterans of Foreign Wars in 1993. The resolution was drafted by a veteran of El Salvador.

As for the war in El Salvador, it appears to have been won by both factions. "It [the war] ended in the best possible fashion for both sides," says M.Sgt. (Ret.) Bruce Hazelwood, who served seven years as Special Forces adviser to El Salvador. "Had the government won a military victory, the death squads would have run rampant, seeking revenge against the Left. Had the Communists won, the Right would have feared for their lives, and U.S. foreign policy would have suffered a black eye. A negotiated peace will allow the country to heal itself, with neither side able to claim victory or defeat. It was this kind of solution we were fighting for, and Special Forces advisers were critical to the success of the policy."

As of December 1992, Special Forces advisers were working closely with UN forces to effect the declared cease-fire then in force. Instead of bunkers they are rebuilding schools.

Rather than distributing cases of ammunition, they are handing out surplus DESERT STORM medical supplies. Still, the question of proper and appropriate recognition of their efforts remains unanswered. The war in El Salvador was neither a covert nor clandestine U.S. military operation. In fact, almost brutal media attention was given the conflict up until the doomed 1989 final offensive by the guerrillas. Why deny U.S. advisers and other military personnel assigned to the MilGrp in El Salvador recognition for their wartime service when—by all appearances—U.S. foreign policy goals were achieved?

The answer lies in the military/political arena of the conflict. Pentagon and State Department officials at all levels made promises to Congress and the American people that were neither kept nor enforced. In many instances, these same officials testified before congressional committees meant to oversee U.S. involvement in the conduct of the war. Today, the authorization of campaign medals and individual combat decorations by those who may have testified that no such activities were taking place could have a less than positive impact on their own careers. Serious questions remain unanswered regarding former presidents Reagan's and Bush's knowledge and actions where Central America is concerned. And the answers to those questions may point to a deliberate and active campaign to deceive Congress and the public on the part of the Pentagon and the State Department.

"The actions of our advisers in El Salvador are being confused with the policies and politics of the time," remarked a congressional aide to Congresswoman Pat Schroeder. "They are apparently being penalized for the questionable decisions and actions of their superiors."

"Civic action is the new war right now," wrote an adviser now serving in eastern El Salvador. When you look at a UN cease-fire, this one is the first that has held for over one-hundred days. . . . This is the first time SF has been an active part of a demobilization. I'm not saying I'm God's gift to El Sal or I'm doing great things. I'm just trying to help some people find peace for the first time in twelve years."

Indeed, in the case of special operations forces and how they affected the longest war in Central America, their performance and credibility clearly outshine that of their commanders and political leaders back home. In March 1993, to his great credit, Gen. Carl W. Stiner (Ret.) elected to confront the duplicity of twelve years of official cover-up and deceit by formally petitioning the army to acknowledge the combat service of special operations forces in El Salvador. Replying to a formal letter from the author on the part of the Veterans of Special Operations, General Stiner wrote, "I understand your concern regarding the issues surrounding the awarding of the CIB and CMB to those deserving military members and I concur with your proposal. Without the superb support of the special operations forces in El Salvador, the duration and intensity would have been even greater."

Stiner, then the commander in chief for all U.S. special operations forces (USSOCOM), was aided in his decision by the revelation of a formal military report ordered prepared by Maj. Gen. David Barato, a former SOCOM commander, in October 1992. Agreeing that SOF personnel should see combat recognition, Major General Barato commissioned his staff to prepare a paper that would document the year-by-year involvement of U.S. advisers in the war. In addition, overviews of the increasing combat involvement of SOF advisers were presented, along with recommendations of line-by-line changes to regulations affecting the award of the CIB, CMB, SSI-FWTS, and Armed Forces Expeditionary Medal. Finished after General Barato had left to take a command in Italy, the report was stonewalled by the Special Warfare Center's chief of staff because of reported personal bias against those who served in El Salvador.

Sent copies of the report, the Veterans of Special Operations forwarded the documentation to Secretary of Defense Les Aspin and the Senate Armed Services Committee chaired by the Honorable Sam Nunn. With formal support for combat recognition being given by California's congressman Robert Dornan and the additional weight of General Stiner's endorsement has lent new spirit to the fight for appropriate recognition of the veterans of El Salvador's civil war.

Perhaps the sacrifices of the dead will not have gone unnoticed by those responsible for sending them into battle.

As of September 14, 1993, the following has taken place with respect to the issue of formal combat recognition being authorized for the U.S. veterans of the war in El Salvador.

On July 15, 1993, congressmen Robert K. Dornan and Dan Burton formally pertitioned both Senator Sam Nunn (Senate Armed Services Committee) and Gen. Wayne A. Downing (current CinC, USSOCOM) for support in the awarding of various combat awards and decorations to both conventional and SOF participants in Salvador's civil war. Senator Nunn responded in a formal letter to the author on August 5, stating "I share your desire to ensure that all of the men and women who have risked their lives for our nation receive the respect and recognition that they deserve, and I commend the dedication of Americans who served as military advisers during El Salvador's recent civil war. Please be assured that I will remember your support for the awarding of these honors should this matter come before the Senate Armed Services Committee."

On August 13, Gen. Downing formally responded to Congressman Dornan's office that "It would be inappropriate for me, as Commander in Chief [USSOCOM], to comment when a decision has already been made by the U.S. Army Chief of Staff." Gen. Downing was referring to his service's continued efforts *not* to authorize combat awards and decorations to this group of veterans. Further, Downing failed to inform Congressman Dornan that while serving as commander of the Army's Special Operations Command at Fort Bragg he had ignored a March 1993 formal request from then CinC-USSOCOM Gen. Carl Stiner to "petition the service for support in this matter." Supporting Stiner by this time were former U.S. SOUTHERN Commanders Gen. Fred G. Woerner (Ret.) and Gen. John R. Galvin (Ret.).

In early September 1993, LTC Fausto H. Segovia, Defense Attaché to the Salvadoran embassy in Washington, D.C. confirmed "the Joint Command of the Armed Forces of El Salvador informed us that U.S. military advisers will not be awarded [a Salvadoran combat award designed specifically for such advisers]." Insiders with the JCAFES confided intense pressure had been placed upon them by both State Department and Pentagon sources to kill the recently proposed award, which had been worked out between the U.S. MilGrp El Salvador staff and the Salvadoran senior command. Ironically, Mr. Gilberto Osorio, senior adviser to the FMLN Central Committee and former Chief of Operations for the PRTC guerrilla commando, formally supported combat recognition for American service personnel during a July 1993 press conference held in San Francisco. According to Osorio, who fought for eleven years against both Salvadoran and U.S. forces, it was the armed American military adviser serving on the battlefield which turned the course of the war against the FMLN beginning in 1983.

With the FMLN's surprising endorsement, the Pentagon's continued attempts to conceal its true role in this war takes on new meaning. For example, during the November 1989 FMLN offensive (when the capital of San Salvador was partially occupied by guerrilla forces), then-Captain Nelly Aleman-Guzman was wounded in three locations by a sniper's round as she was attempting to seek cover in her medical team's safehouse. Despite being treated by Army physician Ron Tolls, also serving in El Salvador, and recommended for a Purple Heart, Captain Guzman was denied this award due to political concerns, namely, that the wounding of an Army nurse in El Salvador might upset the proverbial Reagan-Bush policy's apple cart. Today, Nelly Guzman is a major assigned to Walter Reed Army Hospital. She has never been formally acknowledged for her combat-related injuries, and had she been she would have been the first female military nurse to have been authorized such an award since the Vietnam War.

As further evidence of the Pentagon's duplicity in its conduct of the war in El Salvador, Army medical personnel assigned to El Salvador reported treating Special Forces Staff Sergeant Pisina in San Salvador on August 28, 1989, for a leg wound received during a brief firefight with FMLN forces while he was on patrol. SSG Pisina was ordered by MilGrp representatives to announce he'd accidently shot himself with his own weapon while in the secure confines of his base area. He, like Maj. Guzman, did not see a Purple Heart awarded for said injuries. In both cases, video and/or color slides were taken of the above individuals after their wounds were treated by Army physicians and nurses in El Salvador. The author has viewed this supporting evidence.

To his great credit, Congressman Dornan will be formally drafting and submitting a congressional amendment in a January 1994 session of the House. According to Dornan, Armed Services committee members support formal combat recognition. If the amendment is passed by the House, such recognition will be mandated by law. Both the JCS and Pentagon will have no recourse but to do what they should have done in the first place—to properly honor military personnel who fought, bled, or died in El Salvador. Should this occur, Mr. Andy Messing of the National Defense Council deserves great credit for his unswerving support of the campaign to see such service formally recognized. Without Andy's determination and skillful infighting in Washington, D.C., a great many heros would remain unsung.

Finally, those closely attuned to the war in El Salvador believe that the truth will only be fully presented for historical review when and if a formal congressional investigation is held into the conduct of the war. It would be most interesting to listen to senior military and political leaders testify under oath during such a proceeding, not to mention hearing the testimony of those who served on the ground and in the air during Central America's longest civil war.

CHAPTER
TEN

"Never send an honest man on a political mission. If you want political insight, send a State Department queer."
Old Navy SEAL Saying

Grenada is the most southerly island of the Windward group, its land mass measuring only 120 square miles. Discovered by Columbus in 1498, the island was originally named Conception. Ownership of Grenada was fought over by the British and French until the Treaty of Versailles granted all rights to Great Britain in 1783. Grenada did not become an independent state until February 1974.

With a population of just over 106,000 people, the island's economy depends primarily upon agriculture. Light industries include sugar mills, distilleries, and a brewery. What Grenada offers in abundance is education, with over sixty primary schools operating as of 1971. Of particular interest to those pursuing a medical education is the University of Medicine located at True Blue Point, on the southern end of the island. There students from around the world, including a high percentage of Americans, attend medical school.

Grenada also depends heavily on tourism. Clubs and hotels are scattered around the island, the best located along Grand Anse Road, which offers excellent beaches for swimming and sunbathing. Boating, skin diving, and fishing are favorite activities of those who visit this delightful Caribbean paradise. In 1983, some of the visitors included military advisers from Russia, Cuba, East Germany, North Korea, and Czechoslovakia.

To the north of Grenada lies the much smaller, less populous, and more isolated island Carriacou, known throughout the West Indies for its handcarved wooden boats. The next largest island nation is Barbados, another tourist attraction, which shares its visitors with Grenada's friendly shores. Those dwelling on Carriacou are content in their isolation, particularly those foreign advisers who were completing a major terrorist/guerrilla training center on the island in 1983.

On October 19, 1983, Prime Minister Maurice Bishop was executed by political rivals led by Gen. Hudson Austin. Bishop, who had encouraged close ties with the Soviet Union and Cuba, was seen by Austin's sixteen-man Revolutionary Military Council as becoming "soft" in his political views. After Bishop's first arrest by Austin, the prime minister was released from captivity by a crowd of over one thousand supporters. In a public attempt to win the release of a still-imprisoned coworker, Bishop was recaptured, then executed by the army. As public unrest grew over the incident, the United States voiced concern for the safety of Americans on the island, many of whom were medical students. Despite official communiques from Grenada, which assured the safety of U.S. citizens, a non-combatant evacuation operation (NEO) was hastily formulated at the Pentagon, and it was decided to use naval forces then en route to Lebanon as a possible means of intervention. By October 23, the decision to conduct an evacuation had been revised. Now the United States was considering an assault on Grenada in order to protect an estimated one thousand American citizens, of which six hundred were said to be students. When told that the naval evacuation operation was en route, General Austin responded that such an action would be treated by the armed forces of his country as an invasion.

Aboard the helicopter-assault carrier USS *Guam*, operations (S-3) offered three possible courses of action: assault the island using an all-air force; rely on an all-surface invasion; a combination of the first two. By October 24, it had been decided to exercise option three. The army became responsible for securing the southern portion of the island, with the Marine Corps charged with taking the northern end. The joint-service attack would commence on the morning of the twenty-fifth. A thirteen-man SEAL platoon would conduct a special reconnaissance mission at Pearl's Beach in support of the Marine effort. The army, having already infiltrated several small Ranger reconnaissance teams onto Grenada by parachute, was further tasked to rescue the American medical students who were believed to be concentrated at the True Blue campus at Point Salines.

Aboard the *Guam*, Vice Adm. Joseph Metcalf III, Task Force 120's senior commander, was struggling to bring the short-fuse operation into focus. At his side was Maj. Gen. Norman H. Schwarzkopf, who in June 1983 had assumed command of the 24th Infantry Division (Mechanized), based at Fort Stewart, Georgia. General Schwarzkopf had been named Metcalf's deputy for OPERATION URGENT FURY on October 26, the decision confirmed with Metcalf's commanders the following day. It was said that the senior army commander was deeply concerned about why the United States seemed so intent on mounting an attack against the tiny island.

Grenada had been a concern of the U.S. intelligence community for some time. Prime Minister Bishop's assumption of power occurred in 1979, about the same time as the Sandinista victory in Nicaragua. Bishop's New Jewel Movement conducted a peaceful coup against Prime Minister Eric Gairy's prodemocratic government, quickly establishing diplomatic relations with Cuba, North Korea, Vietnam, and the Soviet Union. Shortly thereafter, weapons shipments, East Bloc advisers, and construction specialists began arriving. The international airport at Point Salines was marked for expansion, allowing it to receive the largest civilian and military aircraft then operational. Bishop's government, which included dedicated leftist Bernard Coard, one of the coup's ringleaders, said that the airport's expansion was merely an improvement meant to encourage greater tourism. The United States wasn't buying, and intelligence overflights and agents on the ground were encouraged to gather more information regarding the military buildup.

By early 1982, intelligence reports showed U.S. concern was justified. A sophisticated military base was being constructed with the help of foreign advisers, who were also improving Austin's military and internal security services. But the buildup was taking place primarily on Carriacou, *not* Grenada. At Naval Special Warfare Group 2 (NAVSPECWARGRP 2), based at Little Creek, Virginia, exercises were developed which revolved around Soviet-supplied SA-2 missiles being deployed on Carriacou. SEAL platoons ran full dress rehearsals, using the latest intelligence developed by the CIA and the DIA. The SEALs were to conduct a night infiltration of Carriacou by combat rubber raiding craft (CRRC), moving inland to confirm and photograph the suspected missile facilities. Once that was accomplished, they would exfiltrate the area and return with their film to friendly waters. Upon the development and analysis of the pictures, then-president Ronald Reagan would be apprised of the operation and its findings. It was promoted the president would then contact the Soviets, presenting the SEALs' photographs as evidence of a second Cuban missile crisis being formulated in the Caribbean.

At Little Creek, the SEALs trained for the mission during 1982 and 1983, becoming familiar with Grenada and Carriacou. By October, with the violent overthrow of Bishop's government and the ascension to power of a far more radical element within the New Jewel Movement, the timing appeared perfect to "take down" the most serious threat to regional security in Latin America since the Sandinista victory in Nicaragua four years earlier.

Originally conceived as a twenty-four-hour-long operation, URGENT FURY evolved into one of the most chaotic military efforts ever mounted by the United States. No one service involved was fully prepared for the assault on Grenada, and premission preparation and planning were made unduly difficult due to the short-fuse nature of the invasion. Using the safety of the American medical students as a cover to dismantle the growing Soviet military presence on the two islands, the United States needed to move quickly before Austin's government gained control of internal dissent. Because of the tight deadline, up-to-date battlefield intelligence was severely lacking, and there were not even current maps of the islands. Admiral Metcalf would have to rely heavily upon special reconnaissance efforts provided by Detachment 3, SEAL Team 4, and its internal assets, which included SEAL Delivery Vehicle Team 2, Detachment 2, and Special Boat Unit 24. This special operations force was aboard the USS *Fort Snelling* (LSD-30), part of the larger MARG 1-84, which had been diverted from its original course.

On October 21, Lt. Michael J. Walsh was alone on the *Snelling*'s flying bridge. A seventeen-year SEAL veteran, Lieutenant Walsh had five tours of Vietnam under his belt, including one as an adviser to the South Vietnamese PHOENIX program. A highly decorated SEAL, Walsh had made the transition from enlisted man to naval officer, bringing a grass-roots understanding of naval special warfare with him. Taking his platoon to Lebanon for a six-month tour, the SEAL officer was concerned that nine of the thirteen SEALs in Detachment 3 were fresh out of high school and the difficult naval special warfare course at Coronado, California. He was also three SEALs short of a full sixteen-man platoon.

Daydreaming, Lieutenant Walsh noted the ship's compass. Its needle read 160 degrees, a deviation from the *Snelling*'s original course, which immediately caught Walsh's attention. "My internal map of the world went off," he recalled nearly ten years later, "because the heading we were on didn't point toward Lebanon." To search for the ship's captain, Lieutenant Walsh went belowdecks. "We ran into each other, and before I could say anything about our heading, the CO told me we had just been ordered to invade Grenada." On the morning of October 22, the SEALs said they needed to be on Grenada as soon as possible to begin sending back real-time intelligence. Walsh wanted to get from the *Snelling* to the island of Barbados so he could pick up the three missing SEALs, but the Marine helicopter pilots assigned to MARG 1-84 said they couldn't deliver his platoon to either Barbados or Grenada because they were too far away. By now, the SEALs were eight hundred miles away from their objective.

Concerned with the lack of information and growing confusion regarding URGENT FURY, the SEAL officer requested Admiral Metcalf to allow his platoon to reconnoiter the Point Salines airfield, Pearl's airfield, or the bay at the port of St. Georges no later than October 23. But plans were changing faster than the admiral could reasonably react to. With the entire task force now at full alert, a meeting between Metcalf, Schwarzkopf, and representatives from the Joint Special Operations Command (JSOC), the State Department, CIA, U.S. Army, USMC, and the Carrier Air Wing (CAW) was arranged for the twenty-third. The scope of the operation was growing, as were the problems involved. The group discussed communications concerns, to include net control, secure and unsecure voice, and the repeated use of call signs. The army wanted the SEALs to conduct reconnaissance from Point Salines up to St. George's in order to locate main-force Cuban units suspected to be in the area. Road mines were a concern, as well. No other information was available to Task Force 120 regarding the beaches or friendly units that might already be on the island.

Ordered to capture Grenada's sixteen-man military council as soon as possible, Metcalf assigned the mission to the SEALs as well as to 1st Platoon, A Company, 2d Marine Reconnaissance Battalion, a twenty-five-man element sharing bunk space on the *Snelling* with Walsh's sailors. The council's headquarters was reported to be located at Fort Rupert, which, for some reason, was also known as Fort George. The SEALs and the Marines worked together on an operations order until midnight of the twenty-third. Then, without warning, their raid was reassigned to the army's Delta counterterrorist force. First Lt. C. K. Dalgleish, the Marine recon platoon leader, later said, ". . . the Recon Platoon could have been employed as a raiding force if the need had arisen." Instead 1st Platoon would end up reconning Fort Rupert on October 26, in support of the Marines' push toward St. George's. On the twenty-seventh, Dalgleish would report finding General Austin's office at Fort Rupert "pretty well cleaned out" with the exception of mountains of classified documents detailing the extent of Soviet/Cuban involvement in Grenada.

Meanwhile, Walsh and Dalgleish were assigned to "free" Governor-General Sir Paul Scoon and family from the Governor's Residence. As Sir Paul was the queen's representative and still the *official* head of state on Grenada, the United States needed his support of its military decision to attack the island. Concluding that he could successfully assault the residence via helicopter, Lieutenant Walsh ordered his SEALs to carry three hundred rounds of rifle ammunition apiece, one antitank rocket, twelve rounds of 40mm high explosive ordnance for their M-203 grenade launchers, as many fragmentation grenades as possible, and at least one smoke grenade. "We had no idea what to expect on the ground," said Walsh. "In Vietnam I'd personally conducted over fifty snatch operations while with the PHOENIX Program. Better to go in heavy and fast, than light and fast, where firepower is concerned."

The SEALs outfitted the Marine recon platoon with LAAW rockets and blocks of C-4 explosive from their own plentiful supply aboard the *Snelling*. Lieutenant Dalgleish and his men would act as a blocking force around the Governor's Residence, tackling anyone foolish enough to attempt to interfere with Scoon's departure. Like the SEAL raiding party, the Marines were heavily armed and spoiling for a fight. But eight hours before they were scheduled to launch the attack, the plan was canceled. This time the order was said to come directly from the chairman-JCS, who wanted the newly formed SEAL Team 6 to be "bloodied." So a team from the army's Delta force was to snatch the Revolutionary Council at Fort Rupert, and SEAL Team 6 was to go after the governor-general. According to one interviewed senior SpecWar officer, "The special operations pie was getting sliced thinner and thinner, as each service bartered to get its special forces on the ground in Grenada."

Delta's operators would airmobile onto the island, successfully grabbing General Austin's henchmen and whisking them into protective custody offshore. They would also attempt to capture the Richmond Hill prison, but would be driven off during a daylight assault. SEAL Team 6 elected to conduct a static-line parachute drop from two thousand feet into the sea, their specially modified Boston Whalers air-dropped from the huge C-141, as well, but weather conditions were terrible, with ten-foot ocean swells complicating ST 6's efforts to marry up with their madly bobbing Whalers. Four operators drowned, striking the ocean's surface and going straight to the bottom due to enormous personal equipment loads. Once they'd managed to gain the shore, the commandos were forced to infiltrate through St. George's in order to assault the governor-general's compound. There the SEALs found themselves outnumbered, outgunned, and with nearly every man wounded by stubborn defenders of the "People's Revolutionary Army" (PRA) and the Marines had to send a force to relieve the lightly armed platoon; Walsh's "bluewater" SEALs were denied permission because "how would it look for the 'Jedi Warriors' to be rescued by your average fleet-supporting SEAL?" ST 6 operators did successfully capture Radio Grenada, using it to encourage PRA troops to surrender.

It soon became apparent that no one, from the JCS level downward, understood how to employ their special operations forces properly. A truly integrated Special Operations Command (SOCOM) was then several years away from reality, and Special Forces units owned by the individual services had received little attention since the end of the Vietnam War. Admiral Metcalf did attend a three-hour "seminar" on SpecWar delivered by Lieutenant Walsh, the SEAL platoon leader, but General Schwarzkopf paid little attention to the briefing, and according to Walsh, "He struck me as uninterested in special ops. I recall him making some rather critical comments while the admiral and I were meeting, and then it seems he left us alone entirely."

Metcalf ordered Walsh's SEALs to conduct a prelanding reconnaissance of Pearl's Beach, prior to the Marines attacking the airport located on the eastern side of the island. Aboard the

Snelling, First Lieutenant Dalgleish complained that it should be his platoon's responsibility to conduct such a mission, forgetting perhaps that it was the SEALs who possessed the transportation to get them from the *Snelling* to the beach, and back again. The SEAL 3rd Platoon had two sixty-five-foot Sea Spectre MKIII patrol boats, a 36-foot SeaFox as well as an MK8 and an MK9 swimmer delivery vehicle. It also had the only combat rubber-raiding craft (CRRC) to deploy combat swimmers or to slip ashore, as would be necessary at Pearl's. To the Marine officer's credit, he can only be accused of wanting to use his platoon's skills for the fulfillment of the mission at hand.

During the late evening of the twenty-fourth, 3d Platoon launched one SeaFox and a CRRC (this was the first actual combat deployment of the F470 Zodiac rubber boat) from the *Snelling*, then twenty miles from the Grenada coastline. As he was climbing down the ladder into the SeaFox, Lieutenant Walsh was informed by the ship's captain that the Marine barracks in Beirut had just been blown up. "He thought I needed to know," remembers Walsh, "but it was the last thing we needed to hear before going ashore at Pearl's." Deflecting his men's questions about the tragedy in Lebanon, the veteran SEAL cast off for Grenada.

Several miles off the island's coastline, the SeaFox was picked up by three PRA patrol boats. Walsh evaded their efforts to locate him by sliding his tiny fleet between the massive ocean swells that had earlier claimed four SEALs from Team 6. By gradually reducing his engines' RPMs, Walsh lowered the SeaFox's radar signature to the point where the PRA patrol boats simply lost him. But the evasive effort had cost the SEALs time. Instead of landing his platoon and conducting a patrol down the length of the beach, Lieutenant Walsh had to launch a five-man swimmer recon element to chart the beach from the sea. At the same time, two other SEALs were dispatched to conduct a scout-swimmer recon of the beach itself. This would require them to actually crawl up out of the water to search for obstacles and enemy positions. Leaving the SeaFox and transferring to the CRRC, the SEALs began running multiple reconnaissance efforts while the Marines at sea prepared for the assault.

Using a pair of night-vision goggles borrowed from JSOC, Walsh was startled to see numerous figures moving around the proposed landing area. Small bonfires became visible as the raiders got closer to shore; a light rain beginning to pelt the already wet SEALs. Walsh remembered his men reporting their AM-FM radios had been picking up broadcasts from the BBC as early as the twenty-second. "The BBC was broadcasting the fact an American task force was preparing to invade Grenada just twenty-four hours after we'd been notified ourselves. Now I was seeing hundreds of enemy soldiers working on the very beach we were supposed to be reconning. It was obvious they were prepared to take us on." But the BBC was not Grenada's first tipoff to the invasion. During a private conversation with Lebanon's CIA station chief William Buckley, held several months after OPERATION URGENT FURY had been completed, Buckley told Walsh that the U.S. State Department had notified the Soviet embassy on Grenada of U.S. intentions to attack the island almost seventy-two hours prior to D day. As the Russians prepared to leave, they passed State's warning on to the Cuban embassy, which sounded the alarm. Relying on an up-to-date military library, a Cuban colonel was flown immediately to Grenada where he swiftly outlined Marine Corps doctrine regarding amphibious assaults to senior Cuban/PRA officers. Under the colonel's direction, the Cubans and PRA began preparing positions at all the most likely landing sites. It was this effort the SEALs were observing from their CRRC during the wee hours of the twenty-fifth, as Cuban and Grenadian soldiers finished digging foxholes and camouflaging crew-served fighting positions. Shortly after his conversation with the young SEAL officer, William Buckley would be kidnapped and tortured to death by Islamic terrorists.

With daylight rapidly approaching, the SEALs finally received the recall signal from the scout-swimmers on the beach. Under the driving rain of a sudden squall, the CRRC headed for the shoreline. Walsh nearly ran over the two scouts as the Zodiac beached itself. The two SEALs were shaken, yet excited, about the Cubans walking within feet of them without discovering their presence. "The squall literally drove the Cubans off the beach," offers one operator. "Even as we were preparing to land, we could see their cigarettes being tossed into the sand. They just packed up and left, a single Soviet armored personnel carrier was the only thing hanging around, and it was on the end of the runway at Pearl's airport."

Walsh ordered the Zodiac pulled up into the dense foliage and its outboard engine dumped into one of the carefully dug Cuban foxholes. Collecting the information gathered by his re-

connaissance teams, the SEAL officer determined a beach
landing was out of the question. At 0200 hours, the SEALs
transmitted "walk track shoes" back to the *Guam*. At sea, the
Marines realized they would have to send their first wave of
troops in by helicopter since the surf zone was "marginally usable," but not for boat operations. Still, the 22d Marine Amphibious Unit (22 MAU) ordered a large contingent into the
waiting boats. For an unknown reason, the 142 Marines of
Echo Company were diverted to a landing zone (LZ) south of
Pearl's airport rather than the original LZ, the terminal itself.
Echo Company began its assault on the airport at 0520 hours,
nearly an hour and a half past their original time-on-target. Enemy resistance proved to be light at the airfield, the Marines
capturing it by 0800 hours.

As Echo Company was preparing for its airmobile operation, Walsh and his recon team remained hidden in the Cuban
foxholes until daybreak. Ordered to stay on the beach as a trip-
wire warning system, the SEALs hunkered down to await the
Marines. With the first soft light of morning making it possible
to see, Lieutenant Walsh began checking his men. "Everyone
was in pretty good shape, but I discovered my medic had
fallen asleep sometime during the night," remembers Walsh. "I
pulled my .357 Magnum and placed its barrel against his head.
That woke him up. His eyes got wide as I told him in no uncertain terms what would happen to his ass if I caught him
sleeping again! You know, I don't remember him dozing off
again until the war was over."

Voices drifted down from a small hill facing the beach.
Fearing an enemy gun position was just above them, the navy
officer ordered his men to stay put while he pulled a one-man
reconnaissance. Halfway up the hill, with dawn breaking,
Walsh stopped to watch a Marine Cobra gunship as it lined up
its electric Gatling gun on his exposed figure. "I couldn't do
anything but stand still, raising my weapon high overhead,
hoping the pilot would take a moment to ID the short little
bastard standing out in the open." The Cobra's crew did just
that, noting Walsh's distinctive face paint and U.S. weaponry.
As the Cobra passed over him, the gun position began firing,
its muzzle pointing straight up at the sky. Although the crew's
rounds missed the target, returning to earth they began impact-
ing directly on the SEAL platoon's position. Walsh, by then
running for his life, shouted for his team to "stay in the holes!"
Overhead, the Cobra made a tight turn, silencing the Cuban

position with a withering burst of 7.62 gunfire. Walsh later discovered that no one on the *Guam* had informed the Marines that SEALs were on the beach. Recovering its CRRC, the platoon made its way back to the *Snelling* as the battle for Pearl's airport finally got under way.

Third Platoon spent the rest of the twenty-fifth cleaning equipment and getting some rest while Lieutenant Walsh planned for the next reconnaissance mission. On the morning of October 26, the SEALs were ordered to the western side of the island where the Rangers and the Marines faced stiff enemy resistance, thanks in part to the State Department's courtesy call to the Russian embassy. Over the course of the next two days, the SEALs conducted three beach reconnaissance missions and one search and seizure. Sleep was at a premium, with Walsh eating only enough food to keep his metabolism going. It was during this time that the SEAL again came into contact with Major General Schwarzkopf.

"I was on the *Guam*, meeting with Admiral Metcalf and his staff about what we could do next in support of the operation. By now, URGENT FURY was as chaotic as it was ever going to get. I remember watching the admiral pacing the bridge, just walking back and forth. The information overload was enormous; it was mass confusion ashore." Walsh had been up for nearly forty-eight hours. His uniform was damp, his belly empty, and his face unshaved. Always at his side was the stainless steel .357 Magnum revolver. "General Schwarzkopf was looking at a map. He wanted some information about a specific area, and I remember him calling me over to where he stood. 'Hey, Boy. Come over here . . .' is how he put it." Walsh's hair stood up on the back of his neck. Assuming the most professional air he could, the lieutenant informed Schwarzkopf that "he could call me 'Walsh,' 'Lieutenant Walsh,' or 'Lieutenant.' I'd respond to any of those. But I was not his 'boy.' " The room grew quiet as the assembled staffs' mouths fell open. Admiral Metcalf offered a brief smile in support of his subordinate as Schwarzkopf mulled over what he'd just heard. "After a moment or two, the general nodded to me. 'Fine,' he said. 'Now would you please come over here and point something out to me?' After that incident, and based upon what we were providing to Admiral Metcalf in terms of hard intelligence, I got the distinct impression Schwarzkopf was beginning to look at special ops in a different light than I'd noted earlier."

So was Metcalf's immediate staff. The army's Delta effort was one-for-three, the capture of Austin's military council a success, but the counterterrorists' attempt to seize the airport at Point Salines as well as Richmond Hill Prison were both foiled. The Rangers who'd jumped onto Point Salines had faced stiff resistance and were burdened with the additional mission of rescuing Delta's pinned-down operators. SEAL Team 6 was assigned the Scoon rescue mission and the assault on Radio Grenada. Although the station was captured, ST 6's counterterrorists were bottled up by a determined, heavily armed reaction force before withdrawing to safety with Scoon. Unlike 3d Platoon's reinforced raiding force, Team 6's operators were lightly armed and few in number. Plus, their means of extraction was on the waterfront, as opposed to Walsh's plan to utilize helicopters, which would have landed at the governor's compound. Running out of ammunition and the team heavily wounded, it appeared the Scoon rescue attempt might fail. But, at 0300 hours on the twenty-fifth, Golf Company, 22d MAU, was ordered to break through to the SEALs, who they had just learned were at the Governor's Residence. Golf, taking only light fire from PRA stay-behind elements, rapidly cleared Queen's Park, with Dalgleish's recon platoon ordered to secure the high ground overlooking the park. As daybreak arrived on the twenty-fifth, Golf Company reached ST 6's SEALs. Scoon and the SEALs were evacuated by the rescue force, which formed a protective corridor back along the route just traveled. Meanwhile, First Lt. Dalgleish's Recon Marines reported driving off enemy gun crews from two 23mm antiaircraft pieces. Using several of the LAAWs provided by the SEAL 3d Platoon, Dalgleish destroyed the gun positions to prevent them being used once the area was abandoned. "They [ST 6] evidently had enough time to run a small, green cloth flag up the pole at Scoon's house," remembers one of 3d Platoon's operators. "It had the words SEAL TEAM 6 in white lettering sewn onto it. We later removed the flag."

Once again, U.S. special operations forces appeared to be falling flat on their collective faces. Those in the special operations community still do not understand why both Delta and ST 6 were assigned Ranger missions (the seizure of the airport at Point Salines) and conventional light-infantry missions (Richmond Prison). These same voices point out the rescue of the governor-general was a tasking fueled by the State Department's urgent desire to see Scoon safely off the island. The

United States needed to cultivate the governor-general's support of URGENT FURY, which he would communicate to the British government once free. Admiral Metcalf's SEAL platoon was easily capable of conducting the operation, and indeed was prepared to carry it out using a plan which integrated Marine ground forces as well as Marine air assets. In the end, lives were needlessly sacrificed, and special operations suffered yet another setback in the eyes of those who were skeptical of their worth to begin with.

By October 28, Walsh and his SEALs had conducted their second search-and-seizure operation, as well as the platoon's fifth beach reconnaissance. This time they were supporting the interests of the army's 82d Airborne Division, which was being flown in to support the embattled Rangers. Ironically, after conducting their beach recon of Grand Mal, Lieutenant Walsh and his men conducted a special reconnaissance mission of one of the campus areas where American students were said to be. "We'd been directed to see if there was any way we could secure the campus using a waterborne force, as the Airborne were still slugging it out with pockets of Cuban and PRA troops," Walsh said. "Sure enough, we found a way in and were seconds away from stepping off the boats when the word came down to abort the mission, ASAP. No one could believe what we were hearing, and I offered that we were right at their [the students] backdoor." Disregarding the SEALs' proximity to the stranded Americans, who were supposed to be the rationale for URGENT FURY to begin with, JSOC ordered them to withdraw. So, unseen by the occupants of the campus, the SEALs reversed direction and crept back out to sea. Another twenty-four hours would pass before the paratroopers could break through to the stranded students. Says one URGENT FURY veteran of the decision, "It was all interservice politics. The army was supposed to get the students, and it would be the army that accomplished the mission, period."

The morning of the twenty-ninth saw the SEALs once again on the move. They were beginning their sixth day of operations, and were feeling the effects of the killing pace. Walsh was rotating squads as best he could, giving his men whatever downtime possible. But because of their ability to move about the island's coastline collecting badly needed information, Task Force 120 was creating a steady stream of missions for the platoon. On that morning, only one squad would be conducting a search-and-seizure operation, using the one SeaFox patrol boat. Their comrades were getting what rest they could.

The primary outlaw figure, General Austin, had been on the loose since the beginning of the invasion. By October 27, eight key figures had been apprehended by URGENT FURY forces. These included Maj. R. Gahagan, operations officer for the PRA, and Lt. M. Bridgeman, head of the PRA reconnaissance detachment. On October 28, vital information was provided by a senior PRA captain who had been present during the execution of Prime Minister Bishop. The captain's information was further confirmed by two other sources possessing intimate knowledge of the same event. Later on in the day Hotel Battery, 3/10th, 22d MAU, reported capturing Bernard Coard and his wife as well as Lieutenant Colonel James (Ministry of the Interior) and Selwyn Strachan, the New Jewel Movement's executive assistant. All four were swiftly moved to the *Guam* as concern for their safety was expressed by U.S. intelligence officers.

Also aboard the *Guam* was "Andrew," a Grenadian citizen who was offering to lead the Americans to where General Austin was hiding. According to this informant, the general was "holed up in a house" located at the Westerhall Point housing area. Andrew gave an exact description of the dwelling, said to be "the fifth house from the entrance to Westerhall, on the left side of the road." There was a jetty at the back of the house, a rubber dinghy tied up alongside it. In addition, the informant advised his listeners there were possibly two Cubans holding hostages at another house in Westerhall. General Austin was said to have his wife with him and weapons close at hand.

Once again, Admiral Metcalf sent for his SEALs.

Lt. Michael Walsh was concerned. His men were holding up well under the pressure of their first combat deployment, but the platoon's morale had been badly affected by the canceled student rescue the day before. While other forces involved in the operation were "kicking ass," the SEALs of 3d Platoon had yet to fire their weapons in anger. Walsh kept hammering home the point that theirs' was a vital mission in support of Admiral Metcalf, and that successful reconnaissance meant getting in without being spotted, gathering the information required, and slipping away without compromise. So far, they'd done exactly that. It looked like their patience and professionalism were going to be rewarded.

The weary SEAL officer sat quietly through the briefing.

Studying the map provided, he knew the operation was possible, especially with a willing guide like Andrew going in with the platoon. Walsh needed a satellite communications radio, something not yet organic to SEAL platoons. A representative from JSOC, a Major Mataxis, mentioned that he had both a radio and an operator with him. He volunteered to accompany the SEALs on their snatch mission. "I told Mataxis he was welcome, but it would be my show," Walsh recalls. The major was more than happy to simply "straphang," the upcoming mission promising to be one of the most important of the conflict.

Before leaving the briefing, Andrew was introduced to Walsh. Having extensive experience with informants and intelligence agents after five successful tours of Vietnam, the SEAL laid all his cards on the table. "I pulled my .357 out and put it to this guy's head, right there in front of the ship's captain. The lives of my men were on the line, as was my own. I told Andrew that because he had told us he was a personal friend of Austin's, I was uneasy about why he'd want to turn his buddy in.

"No one moved. Everyone just stared at us. They couldn't know what I was thinking because they'd never been where we were planning to go with this guy. I told Andrew that if he was leading us into a trap, I'd make sure he'd be the first man killed . . . and that it would be me that pulled the trigger. He understood I was serious, and so did everyone else present."

The SEAL snatch team, supported by their transport personnel and accompanied by the two JSOC representatives, cast off from the *Snelling* and headed toward Hudson Austin's hideout. Walsh planned to slip in by water, the team taking over a house that Andrew had pointed out was across the street from the general's. They would wait until nightfall, taking advantage of the darkness to make their final approach. Austin was said to be armed with at least one AK-47 assault rifle and several hand grenades. Many close to him had described Austin as "crazy." Walsh was determined to take no chances.

As the raiding craft nuzzled up against the muddy bank, Mataxis's radio operator received an abort message. "I couldn't believe it," said Walsh. "We were *there*, we knew *he* was there. I told them how close we were. They didn't care. I begged them to let us put a surveillance on the house until whomever they wanted to do the mission could get there. Again, a negative response. It was a totally fucked up thing to do to the men, not to mention the tactical absurdity of leaving the most important guy on the island alone. But we did it, we left." The platoon would later discover the army's Rangers finally captured General Austin—forty-eight hours after their own attempt was aborted. Once again, military politics had intervened in how the war was being run. Austin belonged to the Rangers, not to the SEALs.

On October 30, Lieutenant Walsh was detailed to search for a downed Marine Cobra gunship that had flown directly into the line of fire of a Cuban antiaircraft gun during an attack on St. George's. The crew was believed dead, but no wreckage had been found in the waters below the AA gun's position. Walsh questioned locals living in the area and visited the abandoned gun's position. He was successful in his investigation, but turned the final recovery operation over to explosive-ordnance-demolitions (EOD) specialists after being notified of his platoon's final mission of the war.

With Grenada considered secure, Task Force 120's attention turned toward the island of Carriacou. Besides intelligence already provided by outside agencies regarding the buildup taking place on the island, the Marines had gathered real-time information from friendly locals, including former Prime Minister Blaize, Grenada's first elected prime minister. PRA forces on Carriacou were said to consist of one platoon of regulars, with a possible full company of militia to support them. Radio intercepts confirmed a Spanish communicator operating a radio from Carriacou, lending credence to the belief that foreign advisers might still be on the island. Returning to the *Guam*, Walsh was offered several possible missions by Admiral Metcalf.

"First, the admiral informed me there was a cable/wireless station positioned atop Mount Royal, which was damn near in the middle of Carriacou. The station was said to be run by North Korean advisers, and the admiral offered we could do whatever we wanted once we were at the objective. I asked how much time I had to put the mission together and was told only twenty-four hours. There was no way we could get in there unless it would be by air, and that wasn't possible." The reason the SEALs couldn't expect air support had to do with the Marines' intention to assault the island on November 1. The MAU, basing its plans on intelligence gleaned from its own sources, predicted the operation would take no more than forty-eight hours. The 82d Airborne would relieve the Marines once Carriacou was secured, hopefully no later than November 2.

Walsh begged off the North Korean site. Metcalf then suggested Camp Carriacou, a sophisticated military base, which boasted nine barrackslike buildings, a pier, an impressive headquarters area, and various other support buildings. The camp was far larger than anything needed by one PRA platoon. "We estimated the barracks alone could house up to five hundred troops," Walsh said. "I told the admiral there was no way my platoon would be able to take on one-quarter of what might have been there. We weren't going to walk up and down the aisles, throwing hand grenades and shooting people as they slept. It would have been suicide."

Finally, Walsh found his mission. He asked what the admiral most wanted to know, and Metcalf responded by pointing a finger at an intelligence photograph of the airfield on Carriacou. "That, is what I'm most curious about."

Back aboard the *Snelling*, Walsh issued an operations order. They would be going in "heavy" again, prepared to take on an unknown number of enemy troops. As per the platoon's standard operating procedure, every man carrying an M-16 would also have an M-203 40mm grenade launcher attached beneath its barrel. Once again, three hundred rounds of ball ammunition per man was required. Grenades, smoke, claymore antipersonnel mines, and the always-favorite LAAW rockets were readied. The SEAL lieutenant hoped they'd get to Carriacou before the East Germans, North Koreans, and whoever else was still there got the word to bail out. "The conduct of UR-GENT FURY makes a Chinese fire drill look organized," the SEAL commented privately. The platoon wanted a big score, and Carriacou could provide it if Murphy and his Laws didn't get in the way.

By the evening of October 30, the platoon was ready. They would infiltrate using the SeaFox, transferring to the CRRCs for their final approach to the island. Walsh had decided to patrol up a short stretch of improved road leading from the infiltration point to the airfield. His priority information requirements (PIR) included questions on runway conditions, building contents, armed enemy personnel, and the presence of communications facilities. Once the airfield had been reconned, the SEALs would patrol toward Camp Carriacou. Task Force 120 wanted surveillance on the target, and had additional PIR about the barracks, the number and nationality of personnel in the area, enemy defensive activity and communications, and potential helicopter landing zones.

It would be a hard two days' work for 3d Platoon, which was dog-tired and suspicious of receiving yet another abort command once they'd reached their objective. "Morale was the hardest thing to keep alive," Walsh said. "We'd run back-to-back missions with little time for rest. Despite the disappointments, the men did what good SEALs do, they drove on."

But there was an unexplained delay, and the SEALs remained onboard the *Snelling* until October 31, then given the green light, the platoon finally departed for Carriacou. As they approached under the cover of darkness, two civilian aircraft passed directly over their CRRCs. The planes dropped quickly onto the airfield, taxiing to the terminal area. Inside, Walsh knew they were too late. The day's delay had prevented the SEALs' reaching the airfield in time to set up a reception party. Had someone tipped the foreign advisers off? If so, who? Better yet, why?

The platoon rapidly headed for the airfield. One end of its runway was under four to five feet of water, which explained the curious "haze" appearing on the FIST photograph studied aboard the *Guam*. Turning on his night-vision goggles, Walsh watched in dismay as figures hurried around the waiting planes. "There were quite a few people moving around, some loading the aircraft, others standing a nervous guard. We were too far away to properly identify them, so firing from our position was out of the question." The deep water on the runway made rapid movement impossible, and before the platoon could come up with an alternate plan, the planes were once again airborne. "They got out, pure and simple," says Walsh. Later, Hawkeye surveillance planes would report they'd picked up no such aircraft activity on Carriacou that night and it was claimed that the SEALs were lying about their observations. After hearing the conflicting reports, a senior naval commander aboard the *Guam* angrily responded that "Lieutenant Walsh doesn't lie!"

Ordered to place surveillance on the airfield, Walsh took his men back to the far end of the flooded runway, ordering each SEAL to tie himself to the trunk of a tree in order to avoid drowning should he fall asleep. "We were exhausted by this time," recalls Walsh. Exfiltration was planned for the next evening, after a full day of reconnaissance work. Sometime during the night, Chief G. R. Davis was bitten on the leg by an unidentified snake. Davis toughed the mission out, but nearly lost his leg.

The next morning, the SEALs untied themselves and moved to higher ground. Taking a brief rest, they were startled by a barking dog, which had discovered their perimeter. The animal's owner, apparently out for a walk, stumbled into the heavily armed SEALs moments later. Since the platoon was compromised, they departed the area, leaving behind a curious hound and badly frightened local. The SEALs patrolled for the remainder of the day, uncovering a white-slavery ring staffed by runaway European girls. "They appeared to be thirteen to sixteen years old," one SEAL remembers. "They told us they provided pleasure for the Cubans and other soldiers on the island. We told them they were free, that we'd get them out to one of the ships on our helicopter. But they didn't want to leave. I guess they were happy where they were."

On November 1, the Marines assaulted Carriacou. Their only resistance was a single PRA soldier, who surrendered when faced by the combined firepower of Fox Company. The rest of the man's platoon had run off, melting back into the population and hoping to be overlooked. Carriacou's populace welcomed the Marines with flowers and flags. Locals pointed out PRA platoon members masquerading in civilian attire, and the unit was ordered by the Marines to assemble at 0800 hours on the morning of the second. Aboard the *Snelling*, Walsh's freshly exfiltrated SEALs were cleaning their equipment and preparing to continue the journey to Lebanon. Since the beginning of hostilities on October 24, they had carried out eight special-reconnaissance missions, four search-and-seizure operations, two aborted rescues, one aborted POW snatch, one aborted raid. And Walsh had investigated the missing gunship.

Third Platoon, SEAL Team 4, would receive the following awards for their efforts in both Grenada and Lebanon:

> The Navy Expeditionary Medal (Lebanon)
> The Armed Forces Expeditionary Medal (Grenada)
> Humanitarian Service Medal (NEO, Lebanon)
> Combat Action Ribbon (Grenada)
> Navy Unit Commendation (Grenada and Lebanon)
> Sea Service Deployment Ribbon (MARG 1-84)
> Combat Action Ribbon (Lebanon)

In addition, a Navy Commendation Medal was awarded to Chief G. R. Davis for his actions on Grenada and Carriacou. Navy Petty Officer First Class W. E. Atkinson was awarded the Navy Achievement Medal for actions on Grenada and Carriacou, as well. Lieutenant Walsh received a Bronze Star for bravery. Neither he nor his platoon were ever formally debriefed by the navy about their actions during OPERATION URGENT FURY.

Of their performance during URGENT FURY, the message sent back to NAVSPECWARGRP 2 at Little Creek from the *Snelling*'s captain stated that "SEAL Team 4 was repeatedly placed in situations of intense preparation, constantly changing tasking and sometimes frustrating cancellation. They never flagged." If anything, this is one of the greatest understatements of the entire campaign.

CHAPTER
ELEVEN

> I needed a Deputy Commander . . . I assembled my subor-
> dinate commanders and told them that Major General
> Schwarzkopf was my Deputy and that his authority ema-
> nated from me . . . He was a principal element of the com-
> mand, and a key to both the decision process and the
> ultimate success of the mission itself.
>
> VICE ADMIRAL METCALF
> *Ambiguity and Command*

The attachment of Schwarzkopf to Vice Admiral Metcalf's
immediate staff was also a sign of the army's concern about its
ground forces being under the command and control of a navy
officer. Indeed, Metcalf's assignment to oversee Task Force
120 was based primarily on his previous experience as commander of surface warfare forces that covered the evacuation
of Saigon at the end of the Vietnam War. Originally seen as a
non-combatant evacuation operation (NEO), Grenada very
quickly became a fast, furious, free-swinging battle rather than
a twenty-four-hour walk in the park.

Today a retired lieutenant commander from Naval Special
Warfare, Michael Walsh remembers seeing the admiral's staff
"running around like bumper cars" on the bridge of the *Guam*
during the first forty-eight hours of the campaign. "They were
pinging off the walls," he recalls. "There was no plan. War is
chaos, but at Grenada no one knew what they were doing or
what they were supposed to be doing." Schwarzkopf, who was
formally introduced as Metcalf's deputy two days after the invasion was under way, began working immediately to restore
control over the confused ground situation. The challenges
were enormous. During the first forty-eight hours of the battle,

many senior commanders ashore were unable to pinpoint the locations of their forces at the company level and below. Battlefield intelligence was poor, worsened by the complete lack of reliable, secure, and interoperable field communications. Making matters worse was the task force's inability to accurately estimate the enemy's strength and where he might be found.

It was at Grenada that Schwarzkopf first applied his low-profile approach to war-fighting, an approach cultivated by his experiences in Vietnam and further honed by a series of demanding assignments leading up to command of the 24th Infantry Division (Mech). Working diligently behind the scenes, the army commander offered critical advice to Metcalf's staff, advice that allowed a handle to finally be gotten on an operation many felt was running amok. Says one officer of the overall command situation at Grenada, "He [Schwarzkopf] stayed in the background quite a bit. He didn't detract from the admiral's position as the task force commander, but it was clear he didn't particularly want to be too greatly associated with URGENT FURY's execution, as well."

It is impossible to gauge what the general's final thoughts were as to the employment of special operations forces during the brief campaign. But given the wide margin of error experienced by every component sent into battle, special ops appears to have done no better or worse than anyone else involved.

Until now, the highly successful special reconnaissance operations conducted by the fleet's lone SEAL platoon have never been examined. With effective ground reconnaissance lacking during the operation, it is baffling that TF 120 also failed to utilize the SEAL platoon deployed at Roosevelt Roads in Puerto Rico. This sixteen-man element had been on alert since October 20, five full days before the war began. It's assigned mission was to infiltrate Point Salines "to collect information on AAA [antiaircraft] sites and to be prepared for follow-on taskings." It is important to recall that Walsh's platoon successfully infiltrated Pearl's Beach on the eastern side of the island, conducting essentially the same mission. On the morning of the twenty-fifth, the Rangers jumped from five hundred feet onto the Salines airfield, barely escaping slaughter because the Cuban-operated AAA guns were unable to deflect their barrels low enough to engage the paratroopers' C-130s. Had this second SEAL element been infiltrated into

Grenada aboard the USS *Portsmouth*, a nuclear attack submarine then in Puerto Rico on training exercises, the platoon could have reconned the airfield at Salines well in advance of the planned airdrop. It could have supplied real-time intelligence about the condition of the airstrip and its defenses, and then directed air assets against those targets before the Rangers arrived over the drop zone.

On October 22, Naval Special Warfare Group 2 was prepared to deploy an additional two platoons to "augment the MARG 1-84 SEALs involved in URGENT FURY or to conduct preemptive operations elsewhere in the Caribbean." On that same date, two NAVSPECWAR officers, involved in the planning of contingency operations for URGENT FURY, were prepared to link up with the advance forces on the scene via parachute drop. They would have carried with them badly needed intelligence such as up-to-date maps, charts, and imagery. But they were never called upon to deliver their materials to Metcalf's staff.

The failure to utilize the navy's very capable SpecWar assets at Grenada blunted Task Force 120's intelligence gathering efforts and denied the forces ashore information about enemy activities and about targets which presented "a threat to the fleet or amphibious task force." One such target was the AAA at Fort Fredrick which downed two Marine Cobra attack helicopters during an attempt to relieve the trapped ST 6 counterterrorists at Scoon's residence. When the gun was finally destroyed, it was discovered that Fort Fredrick was the Cuban command-and-control center. With its demise, all organized resistance on the island fell apart. A coordinated reconnaissance could have identified the important tactical installation prior to D day, allowing for its early destruction.

Although an unclassified report on the conduct of OPERATION URGENT FURY has never been prepared by the joint services, Admiral Metcalf has offered a list of "lessons learned." One of these has to do with the proper employment of forces. According to the admiral, "The lesson here is, use forces as they are trained to fight. Do not try to invent something different for them to do."

At Grenada, highly trained counterterrorist forces (Delta, SEAL Team 6) were used as light infantrymen on badly chosen operations. The results were predictable, but each unit was successful in accomplishing at least half its assigned missions. The Rangers, who since the mid-1970s have conducted the bulk of their training during darkness, were parachuted onto Grenada during the early hours of morning when they were most visible to defenders ready to shoot them out of the air. Since 1986, the Ranger regiment has been able to field regimental reconnaissance teams, capable of deep-penetration missions like those offered on Grenada. During wartime, those special reconnaissance teams can be subordinated to work for a task force such as Metcalf's TF 120. Both HALO and SCUBA qualified, Ranger reconnaissance operators could have deployed from Fort Stewart, Georgia (where the 1st Ranger Battalion is colocated with the 24th Infantry Division, then General Schwarzkopf's command). The teams could have infiltrated Grenada via a high-altitude parachute insertion, using C-141 aircraft. Indeed, the small number of Ranger elements reported to have done exactly this were most likely from the Rangers' reconnaissance arm.

If a truly organized joint forces effort had been undertaken, an eyes-on-the-ground intelligence gathering effort could have been forged between the army's Ranger reconnaissance teams and the navy's on-call SEAL platoons. Had that option been explored, the quality of real-time battlefield intelligence would have been greatly enhanced. As it turned out, too little was deployed too late. That one lesson was apparently not lost on General Schwarzkopf, who would rely heavily on special reconnaissance during the months leading up to OPERATION DESERT STORM.

CHAPTER
TWELVE

Friendly fire isn't. The only thing more accurate than incoming enemy fire is incoming friendly fire. Also, radios will fail as soon as you need fire support desperately.
Murphy's Laws of Combat

On December 19, 1989, the United States launched OPERATION JUST CAUSE fifteen minutes ahead of schedule. The target this time was the Republic of Panama, a small Central American nation of tremendous strategic value to American national interests. Gen. Manuel Noriega, Panama's dictator, was implicated in drug smuggling, money laundering, and a host of other activities that put him at odds with the United States. Further, Noriega was becoming unpredictable as a political/military force in Panama. There was strong evidence that Panama was deeply involved in the smuggling of weapons from Castro's Cuba to the Communist regime in Nicaragua, where the weapons shipments were broken down and sorted out to guerrilla movements in El Salvador and Honduras. Noriega was dealing in intelligence, as well. His agents and spies were collecting valuable information regarding U.S. military operations throughout Latin America. The dictator's high stakes dabbling in espionage was cause for considerable concern at the Pentagon.

In addition, General Noriega's Panama Defense Force (PDF) was growing increasingly more bold about harassing U.S. service personnel and their dependents. Tensions had become stressed beginning in 1985, with no easing of the situation as Noriega increased his control over the country, often challenging the United States in open forums across the country. According to the Torrijos-Carter Treaty of 1979, by 1999, the operation and total control of the Panama Canal are to be turned over to the government of Panama. If Noriega were to hold power for another decade, he would own one of the most vital waterways in the world. Panama's leader had already offered that there could be no U.S. military presence in his country after the canal's turnover.

Then on December 15, 1989, Noriega declared to the Panamanian Legislative Assembly that "a state of war existed with the United States." The next day, First Lt. Robert Paz was killed by PDF forces. Later on that same evening, a U.S. Navy officer and his wife were detained and abused by other PDF forces. By December 17, President Bush ordered that Panama be attacked before further violence against U.S. citizens could take place.

The invasion of Panama marked two milestones in special operations/reconnaissance. The first was the highly successful integration of "special operations forces" (SOF) on the conventional battlefield. Lessons had been learned, many being heeded. With over four thousand SOF troops being deployed, SOF would play a vital role in JUST CAUSE.

The army's Special Forces (Task Force Black) undertook several high-priority missions. Capt. Luis Berrios, from Bravo Company, 3/7th SFG(A), conducted a site surveillance mission on Tinajitas, where a PDF company was established. The Special Forces officer would later direct fire onto the site, which he had reached thanks to five rental cars coordinated for by S.Sgt. Maj. Leo Rabago.

At 0100 hours on December 20, a small Green Beret force disabled the single television transmission tower on Cerro Azul, preventing Noriega from broadcasting to his scattered forces and outposts. Led by Maj. Kevin Higgins, a blooded veteran of El Salvador's war, Company A of the 3/7th made a mad midnight dash via helicopter to the Pacora River bridge. An important link between the Tocumen/Torrijos Airport and Fort Cimarron, the bridge would allow Noriega's elite Battalion 2000 to engage U.S. troops as the war unfolded. Major Higgins's small force landed at the bridge just as the lead elements of a PDF convoy began crossing it. For the next several hours the Green Berets held the bridge, with close fire support provided by AC-130 gunships. By morning's light the weary defenders were augmented by elements of Company A, 1st Battalion, 7th Special Forces. Meanwhile, SF special reconnaissance teams charged with relaying information about specific targets and PDF movements were roving throughout Panama.

Task Force Green consisted of an army Delta squadron, charged with the capture of Noriega as well as with the release of an American prisoner Kurt Muse, who had been active in radio propaganda supported by the Central Intelligence Agency. Delta conducted a spectacular raid on Muse's prison, but was unable to locate General Noriega despite hundreds of tips and long hours in the air, courtesy of Task Force 160.

Task Force Blue reflected the navy's SEAL Team 6. Working in conjunction with Delta and TF 160, the SEAL counterterrorists also took part in the search for Noriega. Together, the two units combed private homes, offices, known civilian hangouts, and military backwater posts to which Noriega might have run.

The Rangers, having perfected the art of airfield seizure, jumped onto the tarmac of the Tocumen/Torrijos Airport at 0045 hours on D day. Leaving their C-130 aircraft at a mere five hundred feet above the earth, they had secured the airport within hours.

At 0105 hours, a Ranger force left the safety of its aircraft just 480 feet above the dark drop zone. The PDF forces at Rio Hato were considered some of Noriega's best, and as such were selected to be humbled by the army's light infantry force. After a sharp, decisive fight the Rangers secured Rio Hato. The Ranger regiment had possessed a third seizure operation, but early on in the planning of JUST CAUSE that mission was passed along to Task Force White, made up of SEALs from SEAL Team 4, located at Little Creek, Virginia.

What took place at Paitilla would influence the conduct of SEAL operations in another war yet to come.

CHAPTER
THIRTEEN

Where the fuck is that gunship?
Unidentified SEAL
Paitilla Airfield

OPERATION BLUE SPOON was planned for nearly two years before being retitled JUST CAUSE. Unlike Grenada, the invasion of Panama would be meticulous in preparation, precise in execution. Originally conceiving the operation as an amphibious assault, the navy offered to land Marines on both sides of the country, to include putting troops ashore via the Panama Canal itself. The Panamanian Defense Forces (PDF) would be unable to monitor such a task force steaming up over the horizon, and by the time an alert could be sounded, U.S. heliborne forces would be landing at selected targets across Panama City. The army's Rangers had been quietly practicing the seizure of the canal's lock system since 1984. Their expertise would be required to thwart dynamiting of the locks during the invasion.

The army had opposed the navy plan, and after much debate the army's plan was the one adopted. There would be little navy or Marine involvement; army airborne and light infantry forces would be airlifted into Panama through Howard Air Force Base. Special operations forces would undertake specific missions, and some of the units would already be in country before the invasion. At the Pentagon, Adm. William J. Crowe said he wanted specific navy involvement in a joint operation. Crowe, the chairman of the Joint Chiefs of Staff, was someone BLUE SPOON's staffers had to listen to if they expected smooth sailing during the plan's approval phase.

Later, when Admiral Crowe asked just how the navy had been worked into BLUE SPOON's scheme of maneuver, he found it hadn't been, at least to the satisfaction of the chairman. According to sources familiar with what took place during the meeting, Crowe was uncommonly adamant about seeing the SEALs "getting a piece of the action." BLUE SPOON's planners got the message, and the SEALs got their mission.

By June 1989, the assault plan for Paitilla Airfield had worked its way down to NAVSPECWARGRP 2, at Little Creek. The mission had two objectives. Manuel Noriega maintained a private Learjet at the airfield that could take him anywhere in Latin America. Paitilla, located in the southeast portion of Panama City, would offer the dictator a swift means of escape if he was able to reach the airfield and make use of the aircraft. Noriega's capture was of the utmost importance to the Bush administration.

Commodore John Sandoz, commander of Naval Special Warfare Group 2, elected to use BLUE SPOON as a vehicle to demonstrate his SEALs' ability to move four complete platoons and all their operational equipment from Little Creek to Panama, using only two C-141 cargo aircraft. SEAL Team 6, not under Sandoz's command, was only able to lift out two of its platoons with equipment, using the same number of 141s. It would be an impressive accomplishment if the bluewater SEALs could outload the Jedi Warriors.

Sandoz, a naval ROTC graduate of the University of Washington, possessed excellent naval special warfare credentials. He'd graduated Basic Underwater Demolition/SEAL school (BUD/S) in June 1968, going from there to Vietnam where he served several combat tours. One of his more memorable missions took place in November 1970, when his squad assisted fellow SEAL officer Dick Couch in the rescue of RVN POWs held captive in a Viet Cong prison camp. After Vietnam, Captain Sandoz commanded Underwater Demolition Team (UDT) 21, and SEAL Team 4. In 1989, he was the commodore of NAVSPECWARGRP 2. His competition with SEAL Team 6 may have stemmed from the fact that the Jedi Warriors—as the SEAL community referred to the counterterrorists—were not under the commodore's command at Little Creek.

BLUE SPOON's planners envisioned the SEALs conducting a night assault from the Bay of Panama, using one riverine patrol boat (PBR) towing a "lizard line" of combat rubber raiding craft to a release point just off Paitilla. ST 4's operators would land on the airfield, moving swiftly up its 3,500-foot length until Noriega's private hangar was reached. One squad would then disable the aircraft by slashing or shooting out its tires while another squad would drag light aircraft from adjoining hangars onto the runway to block air traffic. The remaining squads would maintain a tight security perimeter around the runway, just in case the PDF got curious. Overhead, the air force would provide an AC-130 gunship. If things got too rough for the SEALs, they could rely on their attached AF combat control team (CCT) to call for fire. It was estimated that the mission would take no more than six hours.

On paper, it looked pretty good. SEAL Team 4 was selected by Commodore Sandoz to provide the necessary manpower and equipment. Then, during the early summer of 1989, Sandoz directed his most combat experienced SEAL to review the final plan. With five tours of Vietnam behind him, the week of hell at Grenada, and a highly successful tour of Lebanon, Lt. Comdr. Michael Walsh was easily the most qualified SEAL officer Sandoz could turn to for a professional opinion. So much so that in February 1992, Walsh's former commanding officer would write, "LCDR Walsh is an outstanding naval officer . . . Walsh knows Naval Special Warfare thoroughly. He is highly regarded and well respected throughout the community and military at large as the consummate professional." In addition to his experiences in Grenada and Lebanon, Walsh had just completed three and a half years in Panama, where he'd carried out both clandestine and covert intelligence gathering operations for the Southern Command (SOUTHCOM). He was intimately familiar with the country. And he knew how the airfield at Paitilla was laid out.

When he reviewed the proposed assault, Walsh was stunned at how the SEALs were to be employed at Paitilla. Though they had been trained to fight as eight-man squads, ST 4's operators were expected to function as a rifle company at Paitilla. Worse, they were being ordered to advance over barren ground that was brilliantly lit by the airfield's lights and those of the surrounding city. It was so absurd that Walsh was sure an alternate plan wouldn't be turned down. After all, that's what they were paying him for.

Just five minutes from the Panama Hilton, Paitilla's hangars hosted not only Noriega's personal plane but others belonging to the country's rich and powerful. Skyscrapers stood around the airfield, their balconies offering spectacular views of the bay and equally clear observation of the runway and its facilities. A number of important PDF officials lived high there, above the busy downtown avenues, their persons and property guarded by specially selected PDF soldiers.

From the south end of the runway looking north, the airfield had a series of open-front hangars running along its left flank. Paitilla's terminal, administrative offices, cafeteria, and parking area were strung out along the right flank of the airstrip. Helicopters could land at the helipad located at the northern end of the field, and road access was available from the nearby highway. A poorly maintained security fence ran along the rear of the hangars. Between it and the hangars was a narrow ditch, which could be easily crossed during the hours of darkness. On the other side of the fence lay the barrios of Panama City, a sprawl of urban clutter, which could provide easy access as well as cover to a small team of commandos intent on infiltrating Paitilla's tranquil confines.

Approaching Sandoz, Lieutenant Commander Walsh described the plan as fatally flawed. The SEAL officer explained his personal recollections of how Paitilla was laid out, pointing out the structures on both sides of the runway that would allow for a murderous crossfire to be initiated against anyone caught in the open. Reaction time for a PDF relief force was too short, given the high-speed avenue of approach provided by the highway outside Paitilla's gates. An attacking force coming up the runway would have no cover from incoming fire, nor was there concealment available to hide behind. Running up the airfield's center strip would be like taking the field in an empty football stadium. If confronted by angry, well-armed PDF soldiers, the SEALs' only way out would be a long retreat back down the airstrip, where only the empty sea awaited them.

"It was a bullshit op," says Walsh today. "What was the tactical priority of Paitilla anyhow? Forty-eight SEALs to flatten a tire? The airfield couldn't have been used to reinforce the PDF because they hadn't that kind of lift capability to begin with. Would the Israelis have committed three platoons of their best commandos for this kind of operation? No way!" As Sandoz listened, Walsh submitted three alternative plans for his consideration.

The first plan revolved around a regulation eight-man SEAL squad. Coming from the highway in a truck disguised to look like one of Panama's many Canal Zone inspection vehicles, the SEALs would enter Paitilla's barrio late at night. Tourists, American military personnel, and Canal Zone employees were a common sight on the streets of the capital, and the presence of several prestigious clubs nearby would offer a reason why these particular "zonies" were out so late.

Parking the vehicle along a side street, two operators would act as vehicle guards. The remaining six, carrying their weaponry in gym bags and dressed in dark clothing, would move to the fence line separating the city from the airfield. This group would locate one of the many openings in the fence that had been pinpointed by earlier reconnaissance, four SEALs slipping inside the lightly guarded perimeter while the remaining two became fence guards. Crossing the shallow ditch, the assault group would locate Noriega's private hangar and make entry.

Inside, the team would dispose of any PDF guards, using silenced H&K MP-5 submachine guns. The silenced weapons were standard inventory by then, due to Walsh's memorandum after his platoon's operations in Grenada. The guards down, it would be a simple matter to damage the Learjet's tires so that it couldn't take off. The SEALs would leave the aircraft in the hangar, as there was no reason to risk compromise by pushing it onto the tarmac. Their mission accomplished, the assault team would rejoin the two-man security element waiting at the fence, moments later linking back up with their escape vehicle. The next stop would be the Rodman Naval Station, just outside Howard Air Force Base, only twenty minutes away.

Plan two was simpler, utilizing a smaller SEAL force. Infiltrating from the highway, a two-man SEAL sniper team would cross the airfield's parking lot, climbing onto the roof of the cafeteria, which was located on the terminal side of the complex. From this vantage point, the shooters would have an unrestricted view of the Lear's open hangar. Using a .50-caliber sniper rifle with night optics and silencer, the SEALs could disable the aircraft with several well-placed rounds fired into its tires and/or cockpit. The specially designed round contained a heavy explosive head, easily capable of grounding the plane. This plan employed only four operators: one two-man team which would only fire on the plane if it attempted to leave Paitilla, the remaining SEALs positioned nearby as the shooters' security element. In essence, the airfield would be under passive surveillance by the SEALs until either the plane was moved or General Noriega showed up to claim it. It was a textbook SEAL operation.

Plan three required even fewer operators. Surrounded as it was by tall apartment buildings, Noriega's hangar was clearly visible from a number of balconies. Walsh proposed renting one of the many apartments offering a view of the airfield, placing a two-man SEAL team with the massive .50-caliber inside to interdict the Lear should it be rolled onto the tarmac. The closest such building (which was reported to have just such a series of apartments available) provided an easy six-hundred-meter shot directly into the hangar's bay. SEAL marksmen could hit targets at a measured *mile* with the weapon system (one sniper had placed five rounds within a seven-inch circle at that distance). Punching the aircraft's tires out from six hundred meters would be routine.

Of the three plans, the last one held the most promise. A minimum of operators would be employed. Security of the team was as near airtight as could reasonably be expected, and Paitilla would be under constant surveillance during the first few hours of the invasion. As the SEALs did not have to seize the airfield, the presence of a sniper team would accomplish the second mission statement, as well. Using the .50-caliber, for a brief period the SEALs could easily prevent anyone or anything from using the landing strip. As for Noriega, if the general appeared, it would simply be a matter of making a call to Task Force Green.

There is strong merit to Walsh's last concept. The army's Special Forces had been operating just such an apartment as a safehouse in downtown Panama City for some time. "It was the 1990s, and we were supposed to be conducting special operations missions," Walsh says. "We needed to be smart."

His briefing finished, Walsh was told that the original plan would be executed by ST 4's platoons. The commodore had not been moved. On at least one more occasion, Walsh would raise the issue of Paitilla. He would be rebuffed. Only wanted from Walsh was yet one more signature on the prewritten, preapproved plan. His mark would add another layer to the diffusion of responsibility should things go sour on the ground. Sandoz knew of Walsh's expertise in planning. In his own words, Sandoz said that Walsh's "detailed planning, foresight, and attention to detail resulted in his Logistics Directorate meeting every commitment, in what was more often than not a confusing situation complicated by real world crises."

Shortly after his refusal to bless Paitilla, Walsh was removed by Sandoz from operations and made the ST 4's logistics officer, responsible for pulling together the equipment and load plan which would put the team in Panama. It was an enormous challenge, but the SEAL officer accomplished what was believed to be impossible: he safely loaded four SEAL platoons with all their equipment and necessary ammunition aboard two C-141 Starlifters. That was of little comfort to Walsh. "Those men didn't have to die," he would tell those around him in the aftermath of Paitilla. The majority of the ground operators agreed with him.

December 19, 2000 hours

It was time to go. Their faces heavily smeared with camouflage paint, the SEALs began loading their CRRCs with the evening's "toys." They were heavily armed, carrying AT-4 antitank rockets, fragmentation grenades, smoke, and claymore antipersonnel mines. Individual weapons included the new squad automatic weapons (SAWs), lightweight machine guns, which fired the same 5.56 round as the M-16 battle rifle. The system's firepower was awesome in the hands of a trained operator. Many of the SEALs were carrying M-16/203 systems. The 203 was a grenade launcher attached beneath the M-16's barrel. It fired 40mm grenades with deadly accuracy, a superb weapon for putting people's heads down—or taking out parked aircraft. There were M-60 machine guns present, as well. The M-60 fired the heavier 7.62mm round and had been in the SEALs' inventory since its successful introduction during the Vietnam War. The 60 could provide covering fire for the length of the runway at Paitilla or punch through unreinforced structures with ease. Two sniper rifles were also present.

Many of the commandos carried personal sidearms—.357 Magnum revolvers, .45-caliber automatics, and the issue Beretta 9mm pistol. Combat knives were present, as well. The SEALs were unhappy at their lack of up-to-date intelligence about the airfield's security, despite an attempted "soft" recon of Paitilla the day before. One SEAL had even rented a hotel room overlooking the target, hoping to gather as much information as he could about its activities. The SEALs weren't taking any chances. If need be, they would be ready to take on a small army.

Their gear stowed and secured to prevent loss during transit, the men took their places in the tiny boats. Fourteen "rubber ducks" would be used, each carrying a four-man team. Special Boat Unit 26 would support the operation. This unit provided similar services for the rotational SEAL platoon colocated with

SBU 26 at Rodman. Concerns about using the in-country SEALs had been raised by mission planners, worried there might somehow be a security leak if the Panama SEALs learned too much. This fear was as unwarranted as well as it was insulting.

Aboard the PBR was Comdr. Thomas McGrath. A longtime member of the naval special warfare community, McGrath was one of many UDT operators who found himself reclassified as a SEAL in 1983. At that time, the decision was made to deactivate UDT Teams 11, 12, and 21 due to the increasingly similar missions and training UDT and SEAL operators were conducting. SEAL Teams 4 and 5 sprang up overnight, the core of their personnel coming from the deactivated UDT teams. Although graduates of the same arduous BUD/S selection course at Coronado, California, operators electing to become UDT frogmen did not receive the highly specialized training given to SEALs. McGrath fell into this category. Originally appointed to lead the assault team ashore at Paitilla, Commander McGrath was personally replaced by Commodore Sandoz on December 14, after the final successful rehearsal exercise was conducted at Eglin Air Force Base in Florida. No official explanation for the last-minute change of command has ever been offered; most likely it stemmed from McGrath's not being considered a "real deal SEAL" by those he was supposed to lead into combat, most of whom would be going to war for the first time themselves. Sources also point out the commander possessed "zero operational experience" on the ground. Lt. Comdr. Patrick Toohey, a mustang officer who'd served with ST 6 in Grenada, was assigned to replace McGrath.

The PBR would tow the CRRCs to within roughly a mile of Paitilla Point. McGrath would confirm their location, then release the task force under Toohey's command. Remaining at sea, the PBR would monitor the mission by radio. It would also be the SEALs' means of emergency extraction should the attempt be unsuccessful. Advised that all was ready, the black patrol boat cast off from the aging wooden pier at Rodman. It would be a cold, wet trip for the raiders, dressed in only the camouflage-pattern cotton battle-dress uniforms issued them for over-the-beach operations.

H hour was set for 0100 hours. Just south of Paitilla, the Rangers would begin tumbling out of their C-130s, striking hard and fast at the international airport. At Rio Hato, the same manner of attack would be taking place, the Rangers again on point. Task Force Green's attempt to rescue Kurt Muse would also be under way, as well as a second SEAL mission targeted at Noriega's private yacht moored in nearby Balboa. In short, the invasion of Panama would commence with simultaneous attacks all across the country, each meant to contribute to the swift collapse of the PDF.

At 0045, Commander McGrath was informed by radio that H hour had been advanced by fifteen minutes. Fighting was breaking out in downtown Panama City between PDF forces and American units attempting to reach their final lines of departure. High overhead, an AC-130 Spectre gunship was preparing to lay down a barrage of fire for troops assaulting the PDF's headquarters. Elsewhere in the capital, Delta's hostage rescue team was shooting its way into the prison where Muse was being held. The element of surprise had been lost.

SBU 26 reached its release point on time. After sharing a few words with Toohey, McGrath released the lizard line, and the CRRCs were under their own power. Laying low atop the inflatable boats' sides, the SEALs pounded through the choppy waters toward the single red light positioned at the end of the runway. Aboard one of the craft was the air force element, which was responsible for communications with the AC-130 assigned to protect the SEALs as they made their assault. Despite the specific rules for premission checks, the combat control team had yet to establish communications with the airborne gun platform. Just minutes from the shoreline, the air force operators were still frantically attempting to reach "Air Papa," the gunship's nom de guerre. Until communications were established, there would be no overhead cover.

The AC-130 was an integral part of the operation and had been requested early on by planners at NAVSPECWARGRP 2. The variety of weapons aboard the Spectre gave the SEALs great latitude in choosing the means of close air support or target interdiction. The AC-130 Spectre was a converted C-130 cargo aircraft equipped with advanced fire-control systems, sensors, side-firing weapons, aircraft defense systems, electronic warfare systems, an air refueling capability, and secure and unsecure communications systems. The Spectre was the most accurate weapons system in the air force inventory. Originally developed for close air support missions in Southeast Asia, the AC-130 was considered especially effective in the roles of close air support, air interdiction, and armed reconnaissance. It was exceptional as a point defense option and was equally superlative for air-to-ground surveillance. In short, a coordinated effort between the highly experienced gunship crew and the equally well-trained SEALs should have ensured a high degree of mission success. But the two elements needed to be able to talk to each other, first.

Onboard the gunship were five individual radio systems: UHF secure, FM secure, HF secure, SATCOM, and VHF. All monitored by a trained operator who was a permanent part of the fourteen-man crew. Visual contact was provided by two means. The first was the forward-looking infrared (FLIR) surveillance system, which relied on either radiated or reflected heat to locate and track both friendly and enemy forces. Featuring two angles of view (narrow and wide), the FLIR could also be used to identify friendly elements if—like some Green Berets—they were wearing a tiny strip of specially developed thermal tape on their uniforms. But for some reason, the SEALs had not taken advantage of this identification system. In addition to FLIR, a low-light-level television (LLLTV) system, which also offered two angles of view, used ambient light to provide a black-and-white image of what was taking place on the ground. Both the FLIR and LLLTV systems were monitored by trained operators.

The AC-130 also offered a laser target designator/range finder and a laser illuminator. Had the SEALs on the ground been equipped with handheld laser target designators (LTDs), they could have "painted" specific areas of resistance for the gunship's firing officer who, in turn, would have selected the proper weapons system to deal with the threat.

The Spectre's arsenal included two 20mm Gatling guns mounted aft of the forward crew entrance door. Firing a 1,565-gram projectile at 3,300 feet per second, the guns were capable of providing pinpoint accuracy at the rate of 2,500 rounds per minute. The guns were meant for use against small vehicles and personnel under light cover. Under combat conditions, the guns were supposed to be fired no closer than within five hundred meters of friendly troops. In reality, gunships supporting Special Forces operations had fired the weapons within *ten meters* of friendly forces, with mind-boggling accuracy.

Located aft of the left wheel well is the Spectre's 40mm Bofors cannon, a trainable gun, which fires a clip-fed two-pound projectile at three thousand feet per second. Used against light armored vehicles and personnel under medium cover, the Bofors was the primary weapon of choice to be used against any fortified PDF personnel inside hangars or other administrative buildings at Paitilla. Like the Gatling guns, danger close range is five hundred meters.

Finally, located in the left paratroop door of the aircraft is the impressive 105mm howitzer. Manually loaded, the single-shot weapon flings a thirty-three-pound projectile downrange at 1,620 feet per second. Considered the ultimate weapon to use against personnel under heavy cover or medium to heavy armor, the 105 was not to be fired closer than 650 meters to friendly positions.

But none of those systems was available to Lieutenant Commander Toohey, just seconds away from his objective.

One by one the rubber boats bumped up against the shorefront's rocks. Clambering ashore, the platoons spread out along the end of the runway. There was no cover anywhere. Worse, the entire northern end of the airfield, including the hangar and administration buildings where PDF guards were reported to be, was brightly lighted. Even more illumination was provided by the glow of the surrounding city, which bathed the entire airfield. Toohey passed the word to his subordinate officers, reminding them that strict rules of engagement were to be followed: minimum force, and only that level which would decide the issue; civilians were to be treated with kid gloves, if at all possible; minimal collateral damage was to be inflicted upon the aircraft and facilities. Uncle Sam didn't want to buy Noriega and his cronies brand-new Learjets once everything was said and done.

It was a hell of a way to fight a war.

The word was given to move out. Golf Platoon, under the command of Lt. Tom Casey, headed for Noriega's hangar. Casey's two squads would split the chore of securing the north end of the airfield while also disabling the Lear. Despite their heavy loads, the SEALs moved swiftly down the tarmac toward their objective. Bravo Platoon, led by Lt. John Connors, provided further security and was also to drag light aircraft out onto the runway to prevent the landing of PDF reinforcements. At the first of the hangars, Connors's men encountered several armed civilians, thought to be security personnel for drug lords who parked their planes at Paitilla. The men were rapidly disarmed, then handcuffed. Out on the tarmac, one squad was hurriedly dragging the first obstacles onto the runway.

Lieutenant Commander Toohey remained at the infiltration

point. Several SEAL corpsmen were setting up an emergency aid station, in case of injuries or wounded. The young officer kept the air force team with him, ordering them to continue their efforts to establish a ground link with Air Papa. But at least one of the CCT operators should have been working his way up the airfield with Golf Platoon so that he could be immediately available to Casey for fire-support requests. Such missions could not be coordinated from Toohey's position, where his platoon was acting as both a rear guard and emergency reaction team for the two platoons disappearing up the runway. Overhead the AC-130's engines could be heard, while in the distance the bright flare of tracer ammunition could be clearly seen, the din of automatic weapons fire growing louder with every passing minute. On the ground, Toohey received a situation report over his handset. A helicopter was reported to have left the city of Colon, on Panama's Atlantic side. If Noriega was one of its passengers, he might have been heading for Paitilla. Flying straight across the country, it would take the chopper at least twenty-five minutes to reach the airfield. The SEALs were under the gun to get the job done.

Golf Platoon reached its objective. A radio transmission noted that several PDF armored cars were possibly en route to the north end of the airfield. This report may have come from a rented apartment occupied by a SEAL surveillance team earlier that day, as there was still no commo between the AC-130 and Task Force White. Casey's men could see Noriega's Learjet in the hangar, its gleaming white nose poked just forward of the cement threshold. Using his radio, Toohey ordered Casey's squad to intercept the armored cars should they become a threat. Golf's second squad, led by Lt. Mike Phillips, would cover their sister squad's dash past the open hangar. Second squad would then disable the Lear using the best means possible. Connors, whose Bravo Platoon was nearly finished at the civilian hangars, was ordered up to support Casey. The PDF vehicles were known to mount 90mm guns. If they could get onto the tarmac, there would be no place for the SEALs to run to or hide. Toohey wanted Bravo's complement of AT-4s to reinforce what Casey's SEALs were already carrying. Between the two squads, the armored threat could be dealt with.

But without the element of surprise, the odds against the SEALs had risen dramatically. Curious about the growing intensity of gunfire in the city, out onto the balconies came armed PDF house guards, who quickly spotted the SEALs running hell-bent-for-leather up the airfield. Grabbing handheld portable radios, they issued the alert, then snatching up assault rifles, they took aim on the men below. Inside Noriega's hangar, the guards were also up by then, grabbing clothes and retrieving weapons. More PDF soldiers could be seen making their way toward the administration buildings on the right side of the runway. The cross fire Lieutenant Commander Walsh had warned the commodore about was quickly becoming a reality.

Casey's squad was less than one hundred feet from the hangar's entrance when they went to ground. The SEALs tried stuffing themselves behind a row of light aircraft parked on a grassy portion of the field, but their lower legs and feet were left exposed and clearly illuminated by the hangar lights. Phillips's men were off slightly to one side and behind Casey's squad. Weapons ready, the SEALs prepared to cover the last rush necessary for Casey to get his people to better concealment. Still no shots had been fired by either side. From inside the hangar came a shouted demand for the SEALs to surrender. PO Carlos Moleda responded, demanding that the PDF surrender to the SEALs. To get out of the PDF's line of fire, Casey's squad began moving. In an instant, the battle was on.

From the hangar, the Panamanian soldiers let loose with long bursts of automatic-rifle fire. As the SEALs were attempting to gain their feet, they were struck down like ducks in a row. All but one were wounded. From where he lay, Lieutenant Casey attempted to return fire, even as Phillips's squad was rushing forward to lay down a protective base of fire for their wounded teammates. Both sides were now shooting furiously at each other, with additional enemy rounds coming from the administration buildings on the opposite side of the runway. The SEALs were caught in a cross fire, whose fury was supplemented by rounds from apartment buildings within rifle shot of the airfield. Several SEALs lay dead, and the seriously wounded were incapable of defending themselves. The less seriously injured were trying to shuck themselves out from beneath the weight of their rucksacks, while at the same time firing at the pinpoint flashes that seemed to be coming from all around them. Mixed between the staccato reports of automatic weapons fire and exploding hand grenades were the audible sounds of men in pain, anger, and disbelief.

Lieutenant Phillips keyed his handset. "Heavy wounded!" he

shouted. "Bravo, get up here!" Watching his squad attempt to find cover, Phillips heard one man shouting about the Spectre. "Where the fuck is that gunship?" Phillips was wondering the same thing.

Three thousand feet above Paitilla, the technicians assigned to "the booth" watched in horror as the SEALs fought for their lives. Relaying what was going on to the crew on the flight deck, the airmen wondered why they hadn't received a call for fire from the combat control team. Capable of placing accurate fire from three thousand feet, the Spectre could easily have engaged targets had they been given some. Another problem which prevented the gunship becoming involved was its crew's inability to identify friend from foe. Although the Spectre's systems could have distinguished the SEALs from the PDF, no one on the ground was wearing the required special reflective tape. Neither was the SEALs' overall position identifiable, the action on the ground too furious for the naval commandos to regroup and form a tight perimeter. Even an emergency strobe light aimed skyward would have done the trick, had the SEALs had time.

Lieutenant Toohey heard Phillips's request for Bravo Platoon to move forward. Knowing Connors would already be heading toward the firefight, he also ordered his remaining SEALs forward. The corpsmen would stay behind, ready to receive the wounded Golf's junior officer had announced were somewhere up front. At a run, Toohey and his men hurtled toward the ghastly scene at the far end of the runway. As the SEALs disappeared, Toohey heard one of the CCT operators yell that they'd made contact with the gunship. He was not impressed.

Lt. John Connors rushed in behind Phillips's squad. Taking in the enormity of the disaster facing him, the SEAL officer ordered his squad on line and began advancing toward the primary PDF positions. Firing his M-16/203, Connors hoped his people could put enough suppressive fire downrange to buy some time. The wounded were being shot to pieces, spinning bits of shattered concrete and wildly dancing ricochets causing secondary wounds as they struck unprotected bodies.

Moving forward, Connors was suddenly punched backward several steps. He'd been struck several times, but his 40mm grenadier vest and load-bearing harness had taken the brunt of the bullets' impact. Regaining his balance, Connors continued his advance at an even faster pace, firing from the hip as he moved to close with the enemy. With one of Bravo Platoon's squads acting as a shield between the PDF fire and SEAL wounded, Mike Phillips ordered SEALs Chris Tilghman and Alfredo Morino to begin dragging their teammates out of the kill zone. The intensity of the PDF's outgoing fire was not decreasing, despite Connors's squad's continued display of raw courage and firepower. Phillips could see that, despite their serious injuries, two wounded SEALs from Casey's squad were still firing. Successfully dragging one wounded commando to cover, Alfredo Morino was returning for a second SEAL when he was struck in the head by a bullet. Seconds later, Tilghman appeared to be struck from behind by a burst of fire. He collapsed under the weight of the wounded SEAL he'd hoped to carry to safety.

The night's humid air was now filled with thick clouds of cordite. Connors was now down, mortally wounded while he was attempting to fire a grenade into one of the PDF's defensive positions. Seeing his teammate slump backward, Phillips raced to his friend's side. Ignoring the bullets skipping around both men, Phillips began dragging Connors away from the fight. Several more SEALs appeared, lifting the wounded officer and moving him quickly to forward corpsmen. Phillips watched Connors die on Paitilla's grassy field, then raced back to the raging battle.

As he advanced, Phillips began consolidating the remaining SEALs. Soon the heavy firepower carried by the men was coordinated against the remaining PDF positions. As the SEALs poured fire into the hangar area, Phillips ordered an AT-4 to be fired at Noriega's still-standing Learjet. The antitank rocket struck the aircraft cleanly, its impact making a mockery of the State Department's concern about excessive battle damage. Within minutes the fight for Paitilla was over. Scattered sniper rounds continued to impact against the remaining buildings, some bouncing off the tarmac then whining off into the night. SEAL firepower soon brought an end to even that sporadic resistance.

At the aid station, Lieutenant Commander Toohey was demanding immediate medical evacuation for his dead and wounded. A voice crackled over the radio that help was inbound, but ninety minutes passed before a medevac helicopter was released from Howard Air Force Base, only a ten-minute flight away from Paitilla. On the ground lay Lt. John Connors, PO Donald McFaul, Torpedoman's Mate 2d Class Isaac

Rodriquez, and Boatswain's Mate 1st Class Chris Tilghman, all KIA. Rodriquez had been released from his SEAL probationary period on the flight from Little Creek to Panama. He'd worn the gold Trident marking him as a SEAL for less than a week. The dead commando was the nephew of former Green Beret and Medal of Honor winner Roy P. Benavidez.

Those SEALs still alive held Paitilla for far longer than six hours. Reinforced by a fourth platoon at first light, it wouldn't be until much later in the day that the 82d Airborne choppered in a relief force. The specter of Grenada still hung heavy over the SEALs. A persistent rumor was still making the rounds about those SEALs involved in the rescue of Governor-General Scoon. It was said the SEALs had claimed casualties which didn't exist in order to jump-start the Marine reaction force which finally broke through to the surrounded men. "That's bullshit," states Mike Walsh. "Every one of those operators had been hit. They were low on ammunition, and their first priority was to get Scoon clear of the island." Had someone at Hangar 3 on Howard Air Force Base discounted Toohey's urgent requests for medevac and reinforcement on the basis of a rumor started six years earlier? The SEALs would never know. Finally relieved by the army, the wounded and those who'd managed to escape unscathed returned to Rodman. For them, the war was over.

In the spring of 1990, Commodore John Sandoz briefed Admiral Carter and his staff on the SEALs' involvement in OPERATION JUST CAUSE. According to one eyewitness, the naval officer never once mentioned the dead SEALs or their wounded comrades. Also in attendance were CDR Norm Carley and CDR Tom McGrath, both veterans of JUST CAUSE. The two SEAL officers sat stony-faced through the entire proceeding. Several months later, he would give the same briefing to the assembled body of the Fraternal Order of UDT/SEAL at the Little Creek, Virginia. Along with several hundred former and active duty UDT/SEAL operators were Adm. George Worthington and Lt. Comdr. Michael Walsh, then the national president of the organization. According to Walsh, Sandoz was literally booed off the podium at the end of his speech. "Everyone there knew the truth," recalls Walsh. "It was like we were expected to forget that four good SEALs had died, and eight others had been seriously wounded. We weren't the kind of crowd you could bullshit about the stupidity of how that operation was conceived and carried out."

Mike Walsh retired as a lieutenant commander from the navy in February 1993 after being passed over for commander. John Sandoz was then shaping policy in the Office of the Secretary of Defense as the director for requirements under the assistant secretary of defense for special operations and low-intensity conflict, where he couldn't hurt anybody.

CHAPTER
FOURTEEN

The SEALs were not really spread out the way they should have been to fight ... Even well-trained units make some tactical mistakes every once in a while.

Unidentified SpecWar Commander
OPERATION JUST CAUSE

I didn't want my people to get their ass shot off for nothing. That's what leaders were for, to not let that happen ... kill the other sonofabitch, not your own people.

COL. (Ret.) Arthur "Bull" Simons
The Raid

No amount of finger-pointing or official investigations could wipe away the nightmare of Paitilla for the SEAL community. Special warfare as a whole was again on the spot, their successes (Task Forces Green, Black, and Blue all accomplished their missions; 50 percent of JUST CAUSE's U.S. casualties were suffered by special forces operators, who carried out harrowing raids, ambushes, special reconnaissance missions, and POW snatches) were dramatically overshadowed by the tragedy suffered by ST 4's operators. As happened after Grenada, the conventional military either failed to promote the positive contributions rendered by its services' SpecWar units, or exploited the negative results. In the SEAL community's case, the diffusion of responsibility was finally laid at the doorstep of the unfortunate men assigned to carry out the mission's operations order. The official view was that they hadn't done it right and had paid the price for their inexperience and poor battlefield tactics.

The air force went on record saying the AC-130 never had

radio contact with the ground forces at Paitilla, and that the absence of communications was the fault of the SEALs, who were reported to have been fumbling through their frequencies during the heat of battle. In short, had the assault force been more experienced with their communications equipment and procedures, Air Papa would have provided the necessary support needed that night. However, at least one air force source added that the Spectre "wasn't really the proper platform" to support the SEALs at Paitilla, pointing out that the wounded SEALs were too far inside the safety fan. In short, according to this source, even if Lieutenant Commander Toohey had made commo with the gunship, it couldn't have fired because of the small distance between the SEALs and PDF.

In truth, it was the air force that had insisted its combat-control operators be assigned to special operations units relying on AF Spectre aircraft. Like Grenada, the theme of joint-service interplay was a predominant factor in the SpecWar equation, with everybody wanting a slice of the pie in order to prove their worth. Major Higgins, whose Green Berets crushed the PDF convoy at the Pacora River bridge, was also assisted by an on-loan combat controller. In Higgins's case, the threat on the bridge was so high that the Special Forces officer asked for fire support well within the established safety fan. AF Staff Sergeant Ecklof, Higgins's single-man CCT, accepted responsibility for the mission and relayed the request to the gunship overhead. The ensuing 20mm fire, which the Spectre's crew laid down with exceptional accuracy thanks to Ecklof's blow-by-blow calls, smashed the PDF assault within minutes.

At Paitilla, it was not the SEALs who were responsible for their radio link with Air Papa, but the air force. Clearly little or no premission coordination was accomplished by their CCT element, or reliable communications would have been ensured prior to the platoons' leaving Rodman for Point Paitilla. In addition, it appears that the air force team was using just one single radio to communicate with their assigned aircraft; Spectre could have been reached by at least four other communications systems. If so, the absence of a secondary, or reserve, radio system denotes a severe lack of experience on the part of whoever was directly responsible to Lieutenant Commander Toohey for his air-link with the gunship. Finally, where Staff Sergeant Ecklof was at Major Higgins's side during the most intense moments of Task Force Black's battle for control of the bridge, Toohey's CCT element is reported never to have left the southern perimeter at Paitilla airfield. If so, it would have been impossible for Toohey, Casey, or Connors to coordinate gunship support in the SEALs' defense without a CCT "shadow" at their side.

Perhaps the single most glaring indictment of the joint-service "collaboration" between the army's Special Forces, navy SEALs, and air force CCT assets during JUST CAUSE was that it was unnecessary. The Green Berets and SEALs were fully capable of coordinating their own gunship support. It is not difficult, and has been taught by the air force to those sister service units requiring this capability, for years. The SEAL mission statement includes calling in naval gunfire, fast-attack air support, and indirect fire support such as mortars and artillery. To say that they were incapable of directing overhead gunfire reveals ignorance of their very intense and specialized training in this area.

Critics of the SEALs' small unit tactics at Paitilla fail to fully appreciate the configuration of the killing ground and those events that placed the platoons within its boundaries. Those who say inexperience at both the practical and leadership levels led to the slaughter at Paitilla, should ask why more experienced men were not present and just who decided on the assault force's personnel roster. Finally, we can disregard the inane reasoning put forth by the mission's planners, who assigned Paitilla to the SEALs to begin with. Apparently, because the airfield was colocated near a body of water, they concluded that the airfield was naturally a SEAL undertaking. All special operations forces train diligently in small-boat operations, which was the selected method of infiltration. Anyone from the special operations fraternity, including the Marines' Force Recon platoons, could have landed at Paitilla Point.

The core of the problem lies not with the mission itself—disabling Noriega's Learjet and contaminating the airstrip were missions which the SEALs were certainly capable of carrying out. The emphasis needs to be redirected to how the mission *was to be executed*. Certainly the alternative plans offered by Lieutenant Commander Walsh six months earlier bore the mark of experience mixed with firsthand knowledge of the objective. Why weren't those options explored more fully?

Even more troubling to many SEALs is the question of how some of their teammates were wounded and killed. Firsthand accounts strongly indicate that at least two SEALs were killed by friendly fire, with several of the wounded injured in the same manner. At Rio Hato, the Rangers suffered two KIA due to friendly fire. To its credit, the army was prompt to confirm that fact when questions were asked.

One navy source, who requested anonymity when discussing the subject, says the topic of friendly fire casualties at Paitilla is "taboo." "No one is saying anything," he offered. "Hell, the operators knew how fucked up the whole thing was, and it's been them that have had to take the blame." This same source confided it is possible that photographic medical evidence supporting the possibility of friendly fire "was shredded at NAVSPECWARGRP 2 by a senior staff officer." Others sharing his views point to the dead men's pathological reports presently stored at the Bethesda Naval Hospital in Maryland. These documents, sources say, will resolve the controversy if and when the reports are reviewed by a responsible, independent investigative body whose findings are made public. "The story is 'they' want the dead to be remembered as heroes, killed in combat by the enemy. That's a joke! Those men's actions have been second-guessed at every turn. Somebody is just covering their ass because the operation was so screwed up to begin with."

In memory of his slain teammate, Lt. Mike Phillips and his wife named their first child Connor.

CHAPTER
FIFTEEN

I remember you guys [Special Forces] from Vietnam ...
you couldn't do your jobs there, and you didn't do your
job in Panama. What makes you think you can do your job
here?

GEN. NORMAN SCHWARZKOPF
CINCCENT, Saudi Arabia

Gen. Normal Schwarzkopf received his marching orders after Saddam Hussein's successful occupation of Kuwait. Of the
many combined services units which he ordered to Saudi
Arabia, special operations forces were to be among the first to
arrive in country. While their employment under Schwarzkopf
would evolve as OPERATION DESERT SHIELD gained momentum,
the impending Gulf War marked the first time since Vietnam
that a united special operations command was to be integrated
onto the conventional battlefield.

Schwarzkopf's first priority was to defend Saudi Arabia
against a continued Iraqi thrust. By August 1990, it was clear
to Central Command (CENTCOM) that a mechanism was
needed to assess the capabilities and limitations of all those
forces being drawn into the Gulf. To integrate the multiforce
Coalition with its different tactics, procedures, weapons and
communications systems, and cultures, General Schwarzkopf
realized he'd need to rely on his special forces assets. Because
of the average SOF operator's high level of education, training,
language capability, and diverse tactical and technical expertise, it was concluded that Special Forces and the navy's
SEALs were the proper vehicle for CENTCOM's requirements.

At the direction of Schwarzkopf, CENTCOM assigned Special Operations Command Central (SOCCENT) to manage the effort. SOCCENT turned to the army's Green Berets, navy SEALs, and air force's Combat Control and Pararescue teams to meet the growing mission requirements represented by the Coalition forces.

Special Forces was to provide the entire 5th Special Forces Group, which would deploy from its new headquarters at Fort Campbell, Kentucky. The 5th responded immediately, complemented by the 3d Battalion of the 160th Special Operations Aviation Regiment (SOAR). Initial mission requirements for OPERATION DESERT SHIELD included:

> Chemical warfare training (NBC)
> Weapons training (light infantry)
> Close air support (familiarization)
> Maintenance (operator training on weapons, vehicles)
> Defensive tactics against armor/infantry/air threat
> Offensive training (urban warfare, desert warfare)
> Mobility and countermobility operations
> Communications (secure and unsecure)
> Medical (combat lifesaving)

Specific battalions, companies, and teams were attached to Arab Coalition units at the division, brigade, battalion, and company level to assess their ability to perform on the battlefield, then to provide training to improve those areas found lacking. The Green Berets would also provide radio communications between the Coalition forces and CENTCOM. Additional teams would work alongside all the other Allied forces.

One of the most important missions assigned Special Forces was that of "ground truth." General Schwarzkopf knew he'd need real-time intelligence about the location of his forces and what they were doing if he was to successfully maneuver the Coalition. Through the 5th Group, he was able to assign Special Forces ground-truth teams to each unit on the battlefield. These teams maintained constant communication links with CENTCOM, reporting on their unit's location, activities, intentions, and capabilities. The teams also provided close air support for their unit commanders, and coordinated with units adjacent to their own to avoid "friendly fire" incidents. During the war, not one Coalition unit possessing a ground-truth team suffered injuries or death from friendly fire. In addition, 5th Group also offered a special operations coordination

(SOCOORDS) link at the division and corps level. These links were self-sustaining, possessing their own transportation and communications systems. They were operational twenty-four hours a day, and provided real-time information for the 1st and 2d Marine Divisions, 7th Corps, 18th Airborne Corps, and the 1st Armored Division (United Kingdom).

Joining with Special Forces were the navy's SEALs. OPER-ATION DESERT SHIELD was the first time an entire naval special warfare group (NAVSPECWARGRP) was deployed overseas. The SEALs would be the first special operations force on the ground in Saudi Arabia, followed by the army's Special Forces. During DESERT SHIELD, SEALs provided Saudi person-nel with training in close air support, SEAL/Marine operations, and special reconnaissance. Operators also conducted night se-curity patrols of the harbor at Al-Jubayl and checked selected ships' hulls for mines. Special reconnaissance missions in-cluded beach surveys along the occupied Kuwaiti coastline in preparation for possible Marine landings, agent infiltrations, and deception operations. Finally, the SEALs carried out nu-merous visit, board, search-and-secure (VBSS) operations in the Gulf and elsewhere to help enforce the United Nations' blockade of Iraq.

Of the missions given to special operations forces, that of supporting the Coalition was the most vital. Without SOF inte-gration, it would have been impossible for these forces to have received close air support or naval gunfire. In addition, the links provided CENTCOM with a force that was capable of conducting tactical operations with the other Allied forces on the ground.

One of the most critical of the Coalition assistance efforts was the reconstruction of the decimated Kuwaiti army. It was felt that, with sufficient attention paid to its rebuilding, the Ku-waiti army could be a viable force, so Special Forces assigned teams to train the available Kuwaiti military and civilian refu-gees. Against all odds, the Green Berets accomplished their mission and accompanied six brigades of their counterparts into Kuwait City during its retaking. Schwarzkopf would later offer his opinion that the Coalition warfare effort was easily the most vital mission performed by SOF during the conflict.

The first mission assigned to the SEALs and Special Forces was border surveillance. Early on, roving Green Beret recon-naissance patrols discovered that the entire border between Saudi Arabia and Kuwait had been abandoned by the Saudis, who felt such a demonstration would assure Saddam Hussein that his invasion of Kuwait would not be contested by Saudi Arabian forces. Along the frontier a few scattered outposts were held by Saudi border police; other outposts were occupied by Iraqi forward units. After hurried consultations with the Saudi government, accompanied by Saudi military forces, U.S. special forces elements began retaking the occupied outposts by force. Once the border was stabilized, Green Beret and SEAL teams conducted static reconnaissance from these outposts, every so often sending mobile reconnaissance teams into Kuwait to ferret out the locations of Iraqi troop and armor formations. This information allowed CENTCOM to predict possible Iraqi intentions during OPERATION DESERT SHIELD. The outposts were also an early warning system meant to provide Schwarzkopf's staff with at least six hours' notice of any major Iraqi buildup along the border or of an outright attack over it. In many cases, the SOF special reconnaissance teams pinpointed Iraqi efforts to reinforce the frontier area, then directed Allied air and artillery attacks against them. The result was a buffer action, which kept the Iraqi army off guard and on the defensive during the massive undertaking being coordinated by CENTCOM in Saudi Arabia.

The routing of information and intelligence was completed by an intelligence handling system called Socrates. Deployed by USSOCOM at CENTCOM's request, Socrates greatly improved the management of the huge amounts of information being generated and sent to Saudi Arabia. This information was then coded, and made available to consumers within the theater of operations. Socrates allowed immediate access to real-time information (such as that provided by the border surveillance units), national data bases, situational assessments, and worldwide connectivity with similar Allied systems.

At 0238 hours on the morning of January 17, 1990, a combined task force of air force MH-53J Pave-Low helicopters and army AH-64 Apache attack helicopters flew the first air attack mission of the ground war. Their objective was two Iraqi radar installations, which were networked to four Iraqi fighter bases, which were further controlled by an air defense control center located in southern Iraq. In order for the air force to successfully get its aircraft over Baghdad, a blind corridor would have to be created through the Iraqi air defense system.

The emphasis on mission rehearsal was great. Intelligence provided on the installations was so accurate that the pilots even knew the exact ground distance between the two facilities. Details such as refueling and the precise order of which munitions would be fired from the helicopters were worked out, the final plan approved by Schwarzkopf, who demanded a "100 percent" chance of success from air force colonel George Gray III.

The mission had originally been presented as a ground operation by SOCCENT's commander, Col. Jesse Johnson. In his scenario, helicopters from the 160th SOAR would infiltrate western Iraq, fast-roping Special Forces teams into the desert near the installations. In unison, the Green Berets would launch two attacks, taking down the radar sites minutes before the air war began. General Schwarzkopf was uneasy about such an operation.

"Schwarzkopf was concerned about tipping his hand," says one source. "He didn't want anyone on the ground that early in the game, and he was alert to the possibility of compromise where such a mission was concerned." The CENTCOM commander was also sensitive to the very real possibility of the enemy's capturing SOF operators inside Iraq. Hussein's propaganda machine would make good use of commando POWs.

For Schwarzkopf, the record spoke for itself. He had not been impressed by Special Forces or their operations since his first tour as an adviser to the South Vietnamese Airborne. During that period he'd had to send his "little people" into battle to pull the Green Berets out of the fire when one of their base camps was overrun. The cost to the Vietnamese paratroopers had been high. Later, the political fallout from the Son Tay raid had been embarrassing to Gen. Creighton Abrams, then the MACV commander in Vietnam. Abrams had known nothing about the special operations raid until after its apparent failure. With egg on his face, all the general could do was privately express his distaste for anything having to do with Special Forces. For Schwarzkopf, to whom Abrams was a highly respected role model and personal friend, the lesson was clear.

After Vietnam, Schwarzkopf witnessed the aborted rescue attempt of American hostages in Iran. That effort had also been a joint services operation which offered the most talented and battle-proven SOF assets then available. Schwarzkopf knew that his SOF commander at SOCCENT had been one of the participants at DESERT ONE. Col. Jesse Johnson had been with Delta then, when, as a major, he was directly responsible for the roadblock forces at the final landing site deep within Iran. It was Johnson's teams that had been forced into contact with wandering Iranian trucks and buses at the landing site, contacts which resulted in several one-sided firefights and the capture of forty-four frightened Iranian nationals. After the decision to abort the mission was made, the major's Ranger teams were to destroy the helicopters which were to be left behind. But the destruction never took place, resulting in the Iranian discovery of classified documents detailing the rescue operation aboard the RH-53s. It would later be claimed that not enough ordnance had been available to carry out the destruction. But the LAAW antitank rockets, which Johnson's motorcycle teams had strapped to their handlebars, would have vaporized the aircraft had they been fired directly into the choppers or rigged with detonation cord and C-4 plastic explosives. According to retired air force colonel James H. Kyle, the on-scene commander for the operation, "We never seemed to know what the roadblock team was doing . . . especially when we needed them." In any event, Kyle made the ultimate decision to leave the grounded helicopters intact, although he was not informed that they hadn't been searched and sanitized by Johnson's ground teams prior to the task force's hasty departure.

No one involved with *that* special operation had come out smelling like a rose, including its overall commander, army general James Vaught. Johnson's penchant for getting into trouble continued. As a colonel he'd become embroiled in a shootout between the State Department, the JCS, JSOC, the U.S. European Command (EUCOM), and Delta itself during the 1981 kidnapping of Gen. James Dozier by the Italian Red Brigades. Sent by the Joint Special Operations Command (JSOC) to support Italian antiterrorist forces in their efforts to free the American officer, Johnson's mission became a military and political nightmare as misread signals and unclear command authorities turned the rescue operation into a massive confrontation between all those involved. Johnson is reported to have fired the first round by telling the on-scene deputy EUCOM commander, Gen. W. Y. Smith, that he (Johnson) worked for JSOC not EUCOM, which had claimed overall responsibility for the operation from the beginning. From there on, things went rapidly downhill. Dozier would finally be freed by Italy's antiterrorist squad with minimal assistance from Delta, which suddenly had become a very high-profile presence. According to one former Delta operator, privy to Johnson's career with the counterterrorist unit, "He [Johnson] did not impress those of us in Delta as much as he did those outside of the unit. He was always felt to be looking out for number one, looking for how a situation could benefit his own agenda." Now Colonel Johnson was outlining to Schwarzkopf a special operations raid into Iraq, whose personnel would probably be coming from Delta's ranks because by then the unit had a war-fighting mission in addition to its counterterrorist activities.

At Grenada, Vice Admiral Metcalf had to bear the brunt of misguided and mishandled SOF missions when both the navy's and the army's most touted special operations units (Delta/ SEAL Team 6) appeared to fall flat on their collective faces. From his position as Metcalf's deputy, Schwarzkopf had quietly watched the ensuing media attention and the military fallout which seemed to follow botched special operations.

Following on the heels of OPERATION URGENT FURY was OPERATION JUST CAUSE, where the catastrophe at Paitilla overshadowed those other successes enjoyed by Delta, SEAL Team 6, Special Forces, and SEAL Team 4. That time Lt. Gen. Carl Stiner took the hits. Further influencing Schwarzkopf was his former roommate at West Point, Maj. Gen. Leroy N. Suddath. Suddath had been given the task of cleaning up Special Forces when he'd taken command of the newly formed Special Operations Command (SOCOM) in the mid-1980s. Suddath, also a strongly conventional officer, was determined to bring the Green Berets in line with the rest of the army. Ranger qualified but possessing no experience in commanding special operations units, Suddath made no bones about where his priorities lay concerning Special Forces. There is little doubt he shared his opinions about the organization with his old friend, Norman Schwarzkopf.

Schwarzkopf, who, after his tour with the 24th Infantry Division, had served at the Pentagon, then went to Fort Lewis where he was the commanding general of I Corps. From there he returned to Washington as deputy chief of operations and plans, finally assuming command of CENTCOM in late 1988.

Now faced with what could become World War III, the CENTCOM commander was reminded that the special operations community had not delivered since Vietnam. The war with Iraq would be a conventional conflict, dependent upon air power, air mobility, armor, and mechanized infantry. There would be damn few roles for special operations in such an arena, and those that did exist would need to be carefully monitored to avoid "getting out of control." To Schwarzkopf, relying upon Special Forces operators to start the ground war with a raid was simply too risky. Certainly the mission fell into the special operations category, but there had to be a better way of accomplishing it. SOCCENT was tasked to come up with an alternate plan, and air force colonel Gray, commander of the 1st Special Operations Wing (1st SOW) did so.

The plan worked. Guided to their targets, the Apaches launched twenty-seven laser-guided Hellfire missiles. Teams White and Red struck individual objectives thirty miles apart from each other in western Iraq. Their timing was perfect, the Hellfires destroying the radar sites within seconds of each other. The result was a twelve-kilometer corridor through which the Allied air forces could fly undetected into Iraq's heartland. No Apaches or Pave-Lows were lost during the fifteen-hundred-mile round trip.

Unreported to the media was the ground involvement of Special Forces just prior to the helicopter task force entering western Iraq. Flown to the border by the 160th SOAR, several small teams of Green Berets fast-roped onto the desert's surface. Their mission was to place beacons that would act as reference points for the corridor to be flown by the combined army–air force strike force. Those same beacons would continue broadcasting their signals to the oncoming flights of stealth fighter-bombers and other aircraft assigned the night's bombing missions over and around Baghdad. The operators assigned that critical mission remained on the ground to monitor their equipment until ordered to exfiltrate via airframes from the 160th. Special Forces had helped to open the door to Iraq. Throughout OPERATION DESERT SHIELD, the CENTCOM commander had come to rely more and more on his SOF assets. Now they had opened the door to Iraq, doing so without mishap or loss. For special operations, it was a new beginning on the conventional battlefield.

CHAPTER
SIXTEEN

Captain—now Admiral—Ray Smith was the best possible guy to take the SEALs into the gulf. The one thing he didn't want was to be remembered by the SEAL community like John Sandoz was after Panama ...
FORMER SEAL RICHARD COUCH

The impressive accomplishments attained by SEAL operators during DESERT SHIELD/DESERT STORM are rooted in the tragic events of Grenada (OPERATION URGENT FURY) and Panama (OPERATION JUST CAUSE). In contrast, five SEAL platoons of sixteen men each conducted 270 missions during the Gulf War with no casualties. They were the first ground force to:

Deploy to Saudi Arabia (August 10, 1990)
Request close air support to suppress Iraqi artillery
Effect the one (and only) pilot rescue at sea
Capture Iraqi military oil platforms
Recapture Kuwaiti soil (Qaruh Island)

Before going any further it is important to understand just exactly what SEALs are and what they do. The Korean War gave birth to a navy land capability, underwater demolition teams (UDTs) conducting limited over-the-beach operations along the coast of North Korea. Termed special operations groups (SOGs), the UDT raiders carried out raids against bridges, tunnels, and railway lines vital to North Korea's supply efforts. Disbanded after the war, the SOGs gave way to a new unit which mixed the proven UDT mission with ground operations. Of considerable interest to the Central Intelligence Agency, who had utilized navy SOG teams in Korea, the new unit was buried within the existing UDT organizations. They were titled SEAL teams, because of their ability to be inserted behind the lines by Sea-Air-Land means.

In January 1962, the first SEAL team was formed in direct response to President John F. Kennedy's interest in unconventional warfare. Special Forces had been active since 1952, but it was Kennedy's fondness for the army unit's distinctive green beret which brought them into the limelight ten years later. The SEALs did not have a nation-building mission as did Special Forces. Rather, they were responsible for the following missions:

Direct action (DA)
Special reconnaissance
Unconventional warfare (UW)
Counterinsurgency
To provide guides for intelligence agents during infiltration/ exfiltration
To service escape-and-evasion networks set up behind enemy lines

Later on, counterterrorism would be added to the SEALs' mission statement. Many of their earliest such missions were conducted against the Viet Cong infrastructure during the Vietnam War. In the 1980s, the SEALs were tasked to field specific teams to specifically target international terrorists. These will be discussed in the next chapter.

To accomplish their missions, SEALs most normally operate at platoon strength. Each platoon consists of two squads, each squad made up of eight operators. The reasoning behind this number has to do with how many operators each CRRC can accommodate. Therefore, a platoon of SEALs can deploy over water using two CRRCs. Two such craft make up one boat detachment. Further, the platoon can be split so that each CRRC can undertake an individual mission or sub-mission requiring eight operators. Normally SEALs operate as four-man teams when they are in the field. A SEAL "team" can consist of a single operator, although the smallest operational element is normally two SEALs.

Eight platoons make up a SEAL team, which numbers 30 officers and 180 enlisted men. Today there are two naval special warfare groups based in the United States, each consisting of four teams. Odd-numbered teams (1, 3, 5, and 7) and their support units are at Coronado, California; the even-numbered teams (2, 4, 6, and 8) are located at Little Creek, Virginia. Additional forward-deployed platoons are stationed in Scotland, Puerto Rico, and Panama. In 1987, the Naval Special Warfare Command was established to oversee and direct all NAVSPECWAR assets and training. This command is based at Coronado, California, along with the Basic Underwater Demolitions/SEAL (BUD/S) qualification course. By Easter 1991, NAVSPECWAR was nearing its goal of having sixty operational platoons available for worldwide deployment.

Each team is supported by special boat squadrons, these consisting of two rigid hull inflatable boats (RIBs), two Setton craft (high-speed attack-delivery boats), and two Fountain craft (high-speed attack-delivery boats). Additional support is provided by swimmer delivery vehicle teams (SDVTs), using the Mk-9 and other classified midget submarines for infiltration/exfiltration missions.

From January 30 to February 15, SEALs conducted six mine-hunting missions in the Gulf using SCUBA gear and SDVs. Each operation required ten hours of dive time, with onboard sonar used to locate Iraqi underwater mines. All were conducted in hostile waters, with the SEALs clearing twenty-seven square miles of water. Possible mines were spotted from the air as SEALs covered assigned grid areas in SH-3 and SH-60 helicopters. These flights went from dawn to dusk. Ninety-two such sorties were flown, with twenty-five floating mines discovered and destroyed after SEAL operators placed explosive charges directly on the devices. Even so, the mining effort was so persuasive that amphibious operations were deemed to be too high of a risk to conduct, although small-boat operations continued.

The evolution of a unified special operations command, jump-started in the mid-1980s, proved to be beneficial to the individual SOF commands because they received better guidance and mission orientation. The SEALs were no more army Rangers than the Rangers were Marine Recon. Clearly, NAVSPECWAR needed to define *how* their commandos would be employed in the Gulf, and under what circumstances. Leading this effort was Rear Adm. George Worthington (Ret.), who assumed command of Naval Special Warfare in August 1989. Admiral Worthington was especially stung by the tragic events at Paitilla. A 1965 BUD/S graduate, Worthington served as both a UDT and a SEAL officer in Vietnam. In 1972, he assumed command of SEAL Team 1, based at Coronado, California. He strongly supports continued improvement and refinement of the SEAL program. At the onset of OPERATION DESERT SHIELD, Worthington emphasized the importance of NAVSPECWAR's six-point "mission assessment loop." The criteria were first used during OPERATION DESERT SHIELD. These were:

1. A high probability of success
2. Operations in a maritime environment or within one day's patrol from the water
3. Operations in support of the central command and/or its components
4. Missions that contributed to the overall war effort
5. Missions which required no more than a full platoon to undertake successfully
6. Taskings which assured high survivability of the operators involved

Under the command of Capt. Ray Smith, SEALs and their support units conducted over 270 individual missions in support of Gen. Norman H. Schwarzkopf's Central Command. By war's end, not one SEAL had been lost to injury, accident, or combat. To many, Worthington's criteria were the only good thing to have come out of the conflagration at Paitilla. One SEAL commander said, "The SEALs lost during the raid on Paitilla airfield were lives wasted, in the sense that the operation was flawed to begin with. What we learned form Paitilla was this: We needed to redefine how SEALs would be deployed in future conflicts, so the mission(s) would be accomplished, yet SEAL lives would never again be needlessly lost.

"Our successes in the Gulf demonstrated the validity of the emphasis. Not one SEAL killed, not one operator injured. This is how we honored our teammates lost at Paitilla."

A graduate of the naval academy in 1967, Smith attended the BUD/S course two years later. He graduated with Class 54 in January 1970. Assigned to UDT Team 13, the young officer served in a number of capacities, including platoon commander, in the Republic of Vietnam. A flurry of assignments after Vietnam ended with Smith serving as the executive officer for UDT Team 12. In July 1981, he returned to Coronado as director of the Naval Special Warfare Training Department, at the Naval Amphibious School. Further assignments within the community served to move Smith into the enviable position of commanding SEAL Team 1, in August 1989. A year later, Captain Smith deployed to Saudi Arabia as commander of Naval Special Warfare Task Force, Central. In December 1991, Captain Smith became Rear Admiral Smith.

Welcome to Saudi Arabia

It was a come-as-you-are war, according to DESERT STORM SEALs assigned to Naval Special Warfare Group 1 (NSWG-1) in Coronado, California. Platoons from Teams 1, 3, and 5 were ordered to begin loading their equipment during the first week of August 1990; flights to Saudi Arabia were scheduled for the tenth. "We worked day and night," recalls one operator. Equipment included diving apparatus, parachutes, rubber raiding craft, engines, ordnance, rappelling lines, high-speed boats, thirty-seven-passenger buses, forklifts, and communications gear. In addition, elements from SEAL Swimmer Delivery Vehicle Team 1 (SDVT-1) and Special Boat Units 11, 12, and 13 were hurriedly assembling their assets to support SEAL OPs in the Gulf. It would be the first-ever combat deployment of an entire naval special warfare group.

Landing at the Saudi airbase in Riyadh, the SEALs were stunned by the fierce heat. "It was 125 degrees," one commando remembers. "We were told to just grab ground and begin setting up our gear until a more permanent base could be located." That base would be "Half-Moon Bay" on the Saudi coastline, a harbor town better known as Ras Al-Mishab. Once there, the SEALs set up a defensive perimeter, manning it with their own people. The threat of terrorist attack was considered a priority concern, and the SEALs did not want to suffer the same fate as the Marine barracks did in Beirut.

DESERT SHIELD—as it was then known—saw the SEALs handed the following missions:

> Saudi close air support training
> Royal Saudi SEAL/Marine training
> Strategic recon/early warning on the Kuwaiti border
> Reconstruction of the Kuwaiti navy

The naval commandos were also to provide night patrols of the Al-Jubayl harbor, hull searches, hydrorecons of beaches, and inspections of freighters for illegal cargo and/or personnel.

The DESERT SHIELD period was critical to the SEALs as it allowed them to adjust to the harsh desert environment and to prepare for the coming war. "Hussein missed his chance by not coming over the border during the first thirty days of our deployment," offers a decorated SEAL officer. "His forces would have rolled through whatever we had along the border, and our fins would have been in the Gulf heading for oil platforms. We perfected our operations during that period and continued training."

It was during DESERT SHIELD that the SEALs used the mission-assessment loop.

Following the criteria during the course of the war, the SEALs conducted 13 harbor patrol missions, 92 helicopter reconnaissance missions, 118 combat search and rescue (CSAR) sorties, 1 platform seizure, 1 vessel seizure, the capture of 1 island, and 3 enemy prisoner of war (EPW) recoveries for a total of 229 combat operations. An operations officer for the SEALs recounted his rejection of numerous other missions handed the platoons. "There was one where a suspected amount of high-priority electronic equipment was deemed a viable target. They wanted us to snatch it, but time after time, we couldn't get verifiable information that satisfied our mission requirements. In the end, we rejected the mission, and I later found out the target was a dry hole."

While Operations sifted through mission demands, the platoons were diligently working in the field. Training of the Saudis was considered a political necessity, small-unit tactics and weaponry being the primary classes. SEAL operators also worked closely with the newly formed Saudi SEALs, although those never saw deployment during the ground war. "Most of the Saudi SOF types drifted back to the rear once the shit hit the fan," said one SEAL. "They used them as border guards, I think. Their SEALs were too new to have a particular mission, but they were very good, as I remember."

As the army's 5th Special Forces Group arrived in country, this training was turned over to the Green Berets, freeing SEAL assets for other, more-pressing activities.

Fast Attack in the Desert

Originally developed and tested by the army's 9th Infantry Division in the mid-1980s, one "fast attack vehicle" (FAV) detachment was deployed to Saudi Arabia. It was the first time such a detachment had been deployed in a real-world situation. Low-slung dune buggies, featuring high-impact suspensions, massive firepower, and satellite communications, the FAVs had long been a part of the SEAL inventory. Assigned to operate up to fifty miles inland, the SEALs required ground transportation that would allow them to reach that limit within one night. The FAVs gave the naval commandos just this capability.

Initially assigned to the combat search-and-rescue effort in the western Saudi desert, the FAV detachment perfected its tactics (such as desert land navigation) while awaiting word of a pilot's going down within their reach. None did. "The FAVs were to support planned air strikes in case a crew had to punch out. They would race in and get the pilots out, often traveling at eighty-plus miles per hour over the desert. As it turned out, they weren't needed in that capacity," said an officer in the SEAL command. The FAV teams worked closely with the 160th SOAR, which was responsible for all combat search-and-rescue missions (CSAR) associated with the Gulf War. In some cases, a FAV would be loaded aboard a 160th airframe and flown to within striking distance of the downed aircrew. The helicopter would land at a designated point and off-load the FAV, which would then go to the assistance of the downed pilot. Once recovery was made, the FAV team would then move to a designated pickup point to be met by its air support. All such tactics were developed during DESERT SHIELD, with SOF elements working side by side to accomplish the mission.

What these high-speed, low-drag desert racers also did was assist in the retaking of Kuwait City. FAV teams (there were four such vehicles deployed along with replacement parts and engines) acted as scouts, point vehicles, and perimeter security around the U.S. embassy when it was being retaken. Further, they escorted the American ambassador upon his arrival in newly liberated Kuwait, and generally seemed to be every place at once. It was the first time the FAVs had been tried in battle, and by all accounts they performed to the SEALs highest expectations. Operating along with the SEALs was Maj. Gary Utterback, a Green Beret exchange officer. Utterback was incorrectly identified as a SEAL when reporters snapped the now-famous picture of his FAV team outside the U.S. embassy in downtown Kuwait City.

One of the SEALs' primary missions during the war was the boarding and searching of hostile vessels, for which the SEALs developed an on-call capability to support CENTCOM's maritime interdiction operations. The VBSS task force was made up of one SEAL platoon, four snipers, and a command-and-control element. Four MH-60 Blackhawks, owned and operated by the 3/160th SOAR, transported the platoon to its target vessel. One Blackhawk transported the sniper elements, the others the assault teams. Overhead and on-call was an AC-130 gunship. The Spectre was available to engage the ship, should it prove hostile, and to prevent Iraqi surface vessels' coming to the assistance of the vessel being searched. In addition, the gunship could monitor the seas around the boarding party, using its sophisticated electronics package. At sea, the navy provided surface ships for prisoners or illegal cargo once the SEALs had control of the objective. The SEALs were also charged to look for suspected terrorists or Iraqi personnel seeking to infiltrate Saudi Arabia via the Gulf.

SEAL border reconnaissance missions were conducted along Kuwait's southern border with Saudi Arabia. It was a platoon of SEALs that first noted the armed advance of Iraqi armor and mechanized infantry toward the border town of Khafji, Saudi Arabia. Dug in, the operators were equipped with SATCOM radios, laser targeting designators, laser range finders, and superior night-vision and daytime observation optics.

Beginning on January 29, a combined-arms Iraqi force approached the deserted town with their tank turrets pointed rearward, a recognized signal for surrender. Saudi and Qatari ground troops left the cover of their foxholes to accept the Iraqi offer, only to be gunned down as the ground infantry and tanks opened fire. Streaming into Khafji, the Iraqi force occupied its streets, unaware of the SEALs still hidden nearby. Relying on their superior equipment and training in call-for-fire, the operators began sending detailed messages to the rear, where appropriate action was begun. They were soon coordinating air support and naval gunfire onto Iraqi positions. During the battle, SOF suffered its first casualties when an AC-130 Spectre aircraft was shot down, all fourteen crewmen lost.

The bunker protecting the platoon soon came under heavy fire, then ground attack by the Iraqis. Holding out until the last possible moment, the SEALs then hastily packed what equipment they could take with them, destroying what was left behind with thermite grenades and other destructive means. Laying down a base of fire, the SEALs evacuated their command position and withdrew, suffering no wounded or dead.

"The platoon leader was fairly new," remarked one lieutenant commander who served in the Gulf, "but he did a superb job of getting his people out of there and not leaving anything behind that the enemy could have recovered."

Khafji would be retaken by a combined Arab force, an effort which proved the mettle of the Arab Coalition. But the battle also demonstrated the Iraqis' inability to mount a coordinated offensive operation which could take and hold ground.

Crucial to the air war was CENTCOM's ability to recover its downed aircrews before they could be captured and exploited by the enemy. General Schwarzkopf assigned combat search and rescue (CSAR) to SOCCENT, as the air force could not offer a tangible and effective program to support the effort. Originally not an SOF mission, CSAR demanded trained aircraft, security, and medical crews. Further, the mission required specialized equipment and tactics.

The Special Operations Command assigned CSAR to the air force Special Operations Command Center, which would control all necessary aviation assets. Made up of army, air force, and navy aircraft and crews, CSAR would respond around-the-clock in Iraq and Kuwait. Because of the distances involved, CSAR in the northern portion of Iraq was assigned to SOF forces operating from bases inside Turkey.

SEAL CSAR teams were responsible for pilots and crews forced to ditch into the Gulf. Supported primarily by navy and air force rescue helicopters, the SEALs would be present on every alert flight staged in anticipation of a planned air strike. A total of 118 sorties were flown in support of these strikes, with mine destruction or aerial reconnaissance missions often assigned as follow-on missions. The SEALs would effect the first successful CSAR rescue on January 23. Two SEALs assigned to the frigate USS *Nicholas* entered the water to pull out a USAF F-16 pilot forced to eject over the northern Arabian Gulf. The rescue team was in the water less than five minutes, and all concerned were transported back to the *Nicholas* via a navy SeaHawk SH-60. By the war's end, seven actual CSAR missions had been launched with three successful "saves." The SEALs were responsible for one pilot making it home for dinner.

Also in the North Arabian Gulf were seven oil platforms, all occupied by Iraqi forces. After two OH-58 spotter helicopters were fired on by these elements, the decision was made to attack and capture the platforms. In a joint operation, the USS

Nicholas and the Kuwaiti *Istiglal* collaborated in shelling the platforms with naval gunfire. OH-58D Little Birds, armed OH-58s, then attacked the Iraqis from the air. Pilots from the 160th SOAR were reported to be flying these nimble aircraft in support of the SEALs. The helicopters fired missiles at the platforms, which provided little cover to their occupants.

After the first attacks against them, enemy personnel were seen moving about the platforms. A platoon of SEALs then conducted a VBSS of the platforms, taking twenty-three prisoners. In addition, numerous weapons were seized as well as intelligence documents and demolitions, which were to have been used to destroy the platforms if they had to be abandoned. Five Iraqi soldiers were killed in action. No SEALs or other U.S. personnel involved in the attack were wounded or killed. The Durrah Oilfield operation was the first face-to-face confrontation between Coalition forces and the Iraqi army. It also marked the first time enemy prisoners were taken in the conflict.

Also occupied during the invasion of Kuwait was Qaruh Island, just off the southern coastline. OH-58 spotters first flew over and drew gunfire from its defenders. Then Little Birds from the USS *Curtis* suddenly appeared, returning fire with their miniguns and launching missiles at Iraqi positions. After a brief period, white flags sprouted on the island. Navy SEALs inserted onto Qaruh and captured twenty-nine prisoners as well as weapons and equipment. Qaruh Island was the first Kuwaiti soil to be liberated after Hussein's march into that country.

SEALs aboard the USS *Curtis* also took part in a rescue-and-recovery operation in the north Arabian Gulf. The USS *Nicholas* and the USS *Curtis* were used as "special taskings" vessels, seagoing launch sites for "black" SEAL missions along the Kuwaiti and Iraqi coastlines. Black operations are missions conducted under strict security, most often revolving around direct-action missions, personnel and equipment recovery, POW snatches, and preemptive strikes.

SEALs aboard the USS *Curtis* were preparing for a direct-action mission just off the coast of Iraq, in the north Arabian Gulf. Just prior to launch, a number of Iraqi Zodiac CRRCs were encountered, heading out into the Gulf on an unknown mission. Manned by Iraqi sailors and commandos, the Zodiacs were taken under fire by the *Curtis*, and many of the small craft were sunk. Those rescued were taken aboard the navy ship, where they were secured then wrapped in blankets to fend off the ocean's chill. The SEALs were forced to cancel their operation because of the unexpected contact at sea, but more than twenty prisoners had been captured and a number of Iraqi Zodiacs sent to the Gulf's bottom.

The success of such missions was directly tied to unbending adherence to the criteria established by NAVSPECWAR Command. In addition, the SEALs were properly equipped with the latest technology, including optics, night-vision equipment, and weaponry. Employed at platoon strength and smaller, the operators were charged to carry out only those missions for which they were trained. Of their many forays against the Iraqi-held coastline, perhaps the most influential was Schwarzkopf's deception operation, which was meant to convince Hussein's forces that the Marines were preparing to land south of Kuwait City.

Beginning with DESERT SHIELD, Smith's frogmen prepared to conduct coastal reconnaissance against targets in Kuwait and Iraq. Coastal reconnaissance is the bread and butter of SEAL operations and, indeed, is their birthright, stemming from the efforts of navy scout-swimmers during World War II. "Beach recon is the least glamorous thing a SEAL can do," says one twenty-seven-year veteran of the teams. "It is cold, dirty, nerve-racking work. You have to be alert to your surroundings, to what's going on above, below, and around you. The SEALs perform some of the best beach reconnaissance in the world, and we have the charts to prove it!"

Eleven swimmer-recon missions were performed in the Gulf. SEAL teams were infiltrated by high-speed boats towing RIBs, and CRRCs launched from MH-47 SpecWar helicopters. Under the cover of darkness, swimmers would make their way to the shoreline, then begin the laborious process of conducting a hydrographic survey. Other information sought included beach defenses in place, visible weaponry, bunker systems and wire, and guard rotations. More than once, SEALs lay in inches of water as Iraqi patrols sauntered by, so close the operators could clearly hear the men talking.

"We never ordered the swimmer-recon teams to go ashore," says one naval commander. "The beaches were heavily mined, and there was no purpose in getting people injured or killed just to prove what was already known." Still, the SEALs made every effort to get as close as they could without being compromised. Armed with stainless steel .357 Magnum revolvers and knives, many swimmers also carried H & K MP-5 submachine guns as well. The high-speed boats that delivered them were more heavily armed, sporting 40mm grenade launchers, .50-caliber heavy machine guns, and M-60 light machine guns mounted on 360-degree rotating rings inside the boats' hulls. In a lesson learned from Grenada, the swimmers were allowed more than enough time to complete their mission safely. There would be no more beaches held until the Marines landed, as was seen at Pearl's Beach in 1983.

As part of a much larger plan, CENTCOM was giving every indication through the media and other information outlets that a beach landing by the Marines was being seriously considered. Full dress rehearsals were held for the benefit of the Iraqis, who were getting their best overhead satellite photography from the Soviets. Schwarzkopf needed to keep as many Iraqi divisions as possible looking out into the Gulf. With the SEALs' help he would do so.

The Mother of All Deceptions

Perhaps the most important SEAL operation of the war took place along the Kuwaiti coastline, just below Kuwait City. SEALs were assigned a number of missions in support of the ground war, but deception operations were new to them. Essentially a means of deceiving the enemy as to what was happening (or not happening) in a theater, the SEAL deception operations of DESERT STORM proved to be the testing ground for a concept, which, until then, had existed only on the books.

Deception operations by themselves were not new to the U.S. military. Such things had been carried out in other conflicts, although they were few in number. The conventional military tended to look at deception in terms of smoke screens to hide the advance or retreat of friendly forces. And in their most elementary sense, such methods of deception were both proper and useful.

Deception ops are intrinsic to the conduct of unconventional warfare by Special Forces. As SpecWar involves small groups taking on much larger adversaries, fooling the enemy by any means possible is a necessity. The manipulation of the enemy by good use of deceptive tactics is a highly sought after goal of local partisan units and their advisers. Better yet is the deception of the enemy's commander, who is charged with making good decisions. The key to a credible deception operation is how it nullifies the enemy's advantages on the battlefield.

Surprise is the key element in deception ops, both at the scene and in the mind of the individual responsible for responding to the deception.

At 0100 hours on the morning of February 24, 1991, a platoon of SEALs from ST 5 commanded by Lt. Tom Deitz, married up with high-speed delivery boats from their support element. The SEALs were armed with silenced H & K submachine guns, grenades, a variety of handguns and knives, plus demolition packages. Their mission was to place twenty one-pound charges along a two-hundred-yard stretch of previously reconned beach on the southern coast of Kuwait. Facing them was a host of Iraqi troops, heavily dug in and armed to repel an expected Marine landing. Deitz's platoon had visited the Iraqis on several occasions previously, sizing up their defenses and plotting bunker positions while lying in less than a foot of Persian Gulf surf. "We were never spotted," recalls the SEAL officer. "My men performed exceptionally well."

Slipping onto the coastline after being dropped well into the Gulf by their boat crews, the platoon fixed preset charges just below the water's surface. The beach was heavily mined, strands of barbed wire ran its length, and patrols made their rounds constantly. Iraqi bunkers were positioned along an enormous trench line, and the sounds of men eating and moving about could be clearly heard by the SEALs as they worked just off the beach in less than a foot of water. Since the tide would go out soon after they'd left, the commandos were certain the charges would make a lot of noise. Their charges in place, the platoon anchored blue-and-white buoys just offshore, as if they were marking lanes for Marine landing craft. According to Deitz, the purpose of the deception was to draw Iraqi units to the coast three hours prior to the start of the ground war. "We knew it was an important mission," says Deitz, "but it was something new to us, and we didn't know how effective it might be. Our job was to get it done, which we did."

After the SEALs' stealthy return to their infiltration craft, a single boat raced toward the shoreline, peppering it with .50-caliber fire and 40mm grenades. For five minutes the crew hammered at the Iraqi positions, then it headed back to sea. At the same time, air strikes were called in to support the facade. Jet aircraft hammered away at the Iraqi beachfront defense, and there are reports that a circling AC-130 gunship gave additional support. At 0400 hours, February 24, 1991, Schwarzkopf ordered the ground war to commence. Lieutenant

Deitz's platoon was safely back at its base, having breakfast, as the first tanks were breaching the berms and mine belts meant to keep the Coalition out of Kuwait.

"We were happy to pull the op off," recalls the SEAL officer. "But when the word came down the Iraqis had immediately ordered elements of at least two Iraqi armor divisions into the area we'd just left, well, that news made our day!" Indeed the Iraqis were completely unnerved by the massive explosions, air attacks, clearly marked boat lanes, and furious machine-gun and cannon fire that had been directed against them.

With the ground war under way, the SEALs began carrying out additional missions, many of which were direct action. Although the details of most such missions remain classified, one operator confirmed that targets were often radar and communication sites. Resistance forces operating inside Kuwait were also delivered needed supplies and weaponry, often from boats offshore. "We had a forty-eight-hour planning schedule," one SEAL planner said. "We'd get a mission request, which, if it passed our criteria for SEAL ops, would then go into the planning and support stages. Forty-eight hours later it would be carried out." But the pace of the ground war came as a surprise. Missions were bumped forward time and again, until the war simply pulled so far ahead that the SEALs and other SpecWar units were executing tasks as they came up. "It was crazy," remembers the same officer. "The war just ran right past us, and it was all we could do to just catch up."

Aftermath

The SEALs performed over 270 missions during their deployment to the Gulf. Captain Smith returned his task force to its base at Coronado on March 11, 1991. For NAVSPECWARGRP 1, it was a crowning achievement, which fully endorsed the viability of SEAL teams when they were utilized properly.

What was the difference between DESERT STORM and earlier, less successful engagements? "We learned from our mistakes and were smarter this time around," says a senior enlisted SEAL. Comdr. Tom Campbell, an experienced and respected officer in the SEAL community, offers this insight. "The admiral [Worthington] demanded SEALs be used as SEALs, in a maritime environment with land-based operations well within the criteria set. We demonstrated there is no better maritime/riverine special warfare package available than ours, which I believe is a priority consideration for the future of SEAL operations within USSOCOM."

Despite setbacks in earlier campaigns, and in spite of often inaccurate assessments and attacks by media military "experts" on their credibility, the SEALs proved their worth in the SpecWar arena of DESERT STORM. "We're not resting on our laurels," comments an operator from ST 5. "To us, the only easy day was yesterday. Once we got back from Saudi it was business as usual. The teams have gotten better, smarter, more effective. It's good to be a winner again."

CHAPTER
SEVENTEEN

Refuting another report, (Colonel) Johnson also denied that
the top secret Delta Force counter-terrorism team had been
used in the gulf war.

Defense Week
April 8, 1991

Recruiting for the 1st Special Forces Operational Detachment (Delta) began in early June 1977. The unit's formation
was the result of a study prepared by Col. Charles Beckwith
and Gen. Robert Kingston, both strong advocates of a special
force that would be capable of undertaking especially difficult
assignments. In 1962, Beckwith had served as an exchange officer with the British Special Air Service, SAS. He had returned to the United States convinced the British were on to
something where a truly elite force was concerned. Beckwith
would pursue the idea of a similar organization becoming part
of the U.S. special operations arsenal, refining his perceptions
during the Vietnam War where he became something of a legendary figure. Still, nearly fifteen years would pass before
DELTA became a reality.

Delta Force, as it became known as, developed exceptionally high standards for its operators. Each candidate had to be
in superb physical condition. He was required to possess a
deep understanding of his military occupational speciality
(MOS). He needed to be curious, as Delta's training program
would offer a wide variety of new skills which would have to
be learned to perfection. In short, to be an operator in Delta,
one would have to excel beyond anything the army had required of him previously.

Officers and enlisted personnel undergo the same selection

process, and take training together; the "natural" superiority of the commissioned officer is not assumed within the unit. Potential candidates must volunteer to attend Delta's assessment-and-selection course, which is held at Camp Dawson in the mountains of West Virginia. Volunteers undergo a complete screening of their records and must possess the necessary prerequisites before being granted the opportunity to attend selection.

General prerequisites for assignment to Delta are fairly straightforward. The volunteer must be a male*, who is a citizen of the United States, and can be no younger than twenty-two years of age. He must pass a modified HALO/SCUBA physical and eye examination, and be either airborne qualified or prepared to attend airborne training. The candidate must pass a background investigation and possess a minimum of a secret security clearance. There can be no pattern of behavior problems in the volunteer's past, and a minimum of four years' service is required to establish both a military background and personnel record.

Noncommissioned officers make up the enlisted corps, beginning with the rank of buck sergeant, or E-5. A volunteer cannot hold rank above sergeant first class (E-7) when applying for selection. NCOs must be qualified in their primary MOS and possess a GT score of 110 or higher. Officers who volunteer must be captains or majors who have graduated from college with either a BA or BS degree. They must also possess twelve successful months of command at the company level.

During the assessment and selection phases, Delta candidates are spared harassment. There is no need for such activity as the demands of the course are more than enough to qualify who will become an operator with the unit. A prephase testing period is held in West Virginia, where medical and psychological evaluations are conducted as well as refresher classes in land navigation. Candidates are watched closely from the moment they arrive in order to begin establishing individual profiles. One of the first trials undergone is the surprise twenty-mile road march with weighted rucksack, which must be performed within a specified but unannounced time period. This begins the weeding-out process.

Essentially, the selection phase examines the individual's

*As of 1993, DELTA now fields female operators. This is the first SOF unit to employ women in a combat role.

depths of internal motivation, "guts." Run through a series of land navigation exercises in full equipment, including the M-16 battle rifle, each candidate must successfully complete the required evolution within an unannounced period of time. The volunteers compete only against themselves, running the evolutions alone and at all times of the day or night. Those who are injured or quit are quietly removed from the selection process, although some injured personnel may reapply once they are physically able to reenter the course.

Once a candidate has proven himself to be physically and mentally tough enough for Delta, he then undergoes a rigorous psychological examination. After that is completed, the candidate's performance during selection and his personnel record are reviewed by a special board. Only then will the volunteer find out if he has made the grade. Initial assignment to the unit is for three years. Delta operators may stay with the unit as long as their performance meets the requirements for such extensions. Only two assessment and selection courses are conducted each year. Volunteers may apply from the active army, active reserves, or National Guard.

In its early days, the organization consisted of only seventy operators, whose headquarters was the old stockade at Fort Bragg, North Carolina. Delta's first break came after the successful release of hostages from a German Lufthansa jet by that country's elite GSG-9, one of the first counterterrorist units formed to combat international terrorism in Europe. President Jimmy Carter had to prod the JCS about a similar U.S. capability because Beckwith's struggling unit was almost unknown at the Joint Chiefs' level. Because of the president's interest in counterterrorism, Delta received a behind-the-scenes go-ahead to expand and recruit with all due haste. A nearly forgotten parallel organization was Col. Robert Mountel's "Blue Light," a counterterrorist unit, which was drawn internally from volunteers in the 5th Special Forces Group. Mountel believed such a unit could be more easily formed from existing talent and resources, perhaps basing his philosophy on the Vietnam-era special projects which had operated under MACV-SOG. Blue Light had been formed and trained and was operational by the time the JCS learned of Beckwith's Delta project. With two counterterrorist units to choose from, the JCS went with Beckwith's Delta because it had formal authorization, Blue Light did not. Mountel was ordered to disband his organization, leaving Beckwith holding the counter-terrorist ball.

Delta's mission statement includes the following taskings:

POW recovery operations during wartime
Counterterrorism operations both inside the United States and abroad
The recovery of stolen nuclear devices, or as a response to terrorist activities involving such devices
Special reconnaissance in denied or hostile areas

Today's organization has an estimated three squadrons, plus support and headquarters elements. Each squadron is made up of a classified number of troops, with sixteen operators assigned to each troop. One squadron is always on alert, while the others are in their training or support phases.

Unlike Special Forces, Delta uses detachment designations D, E, and F. The D detachment provides command and control. E detachments handle communications, intelligence, and administrative support. F detachments are the operational arms of Delta. The sixteen-man troops are broken down into four four-man squads, in the tradition of the British SAS. Each squad is color-coded for organizational and control purposes. Each Delta operator attends a nineteen-week training course upon successful graduation from selection. It is here that he studies the theory of terrorism, hand-to-hand combat, marksmanship, advanced demolitions and communications, advanced intelligence operations, and the other skills expected of Delta operators. Once back at the unit, the operator is assigned to an F detachment, where he will be on probation for an unspecified period of time. His probation passed, the new Delta soldier continues his training as part of the squad.

Delta personnel are permitted relaxed grooming standards so that they may fit into the everyday civilian world, and each carries a pager by which he can be summoned at any hour of the day or night. Operators are always armed and are issued federal concealed-weapons permits, which allow them to travel anywhere in the country with a side arm.

Often misunderstood about both Delta and its navy counterpart SEAL Team 6 are the roles of the organizations in counterterrorism. Antiterrorism is those *defense* measures taken to reduce the vulnerability of individuals and property to terrorist acts. Delta and ST 6 operators are not antiterrorists, whose personnel train selected subjects the skills required to avoid or escape the terrorist threat. Rather, a counterterrorist applies *offensive* measures to prevent, deter, and/or respond to terrorism. That is where the Delta Heads and ST 6's Jedi Warriors enter the international picture in support of U.S. policy and national interests.

With formal authorization granted on November 28, 1977, Delta began training in earnest. In 1978, the army was sending letters to personnel whose records reflected possible status as a candidate in the organization. In the meantime, Beckwith was making the rounds of foreign counterterrorist units he felt it necessary for Delta to train with. Equipment and funding were more than adequate for the new unit's needs, and improvements were constantly made to its procedures as the capabilities of terrorists became better understood. By late 1979, Delta operators were asked to prove their abilities. In a full-blown exercise designed to test the unit's every capability, Delta assaulted an aircraft and building at the same time. They were successful in "saving" the hostages involved, with little collateral damage suffered by the those taking part in the exercise. Delta was certified to be combat ready.

The unit's first real-world assignment was to be the 1980 rescue of hostages taken from the U.S. embassy in Iran on November 4, 1979. The operation was code-named RICEBOWL, but became better known as DESERT ONE when the assembled joint task force met with disaster deep within Iran. As the mission's ground commander, Beckwith had to shoulder the responsibility for failure, and Delta got its first black eye, despite the fact the mission's failure had nothing to do with the operators themselves. For Delta, it was back to the drawing board.

The introduction of the AirLand Battle doctrine in the early 1980s brought Special Forces once again to the forefront because, under the new doctrine—which was meant to counter the Soviet plan for war in Europe—Special Forces units would be infiltrated far behind Soviet lines to conduct special reconnaissance and sabotage missions in support of NATO forces. This began a slow shift in SOF development and training, with counterterrorist units such as Delta being looked at as to what role they might present as war-fighters under the AirLand concept. Nearly all terrorist activity was taking place overseas. Delta teams were either acting as observers while their European peers handled the problem, or serving as support elements in selected joint operations such as the previously discussed kidnapping of Gen. James Dozier in Italy.

Because of Delta's huge demands on funding and personnel, the highest levels wanted to know whether forces like Delta could be integrated into the battlefield if the need arose. And if not, what would be their fate should support falter or funds become more restricted? It was eventually decided to fold counterterrorism into the much larger and more diverse special-operations mix. Soon after the election of Ronald Reagan, the concept of low-intensity conflict (LIC) began to be explored by the army Training and Doctrine Command (TRADOC). The precepts of low-intensity conflict further emphasized special operations and those who were to carry them out. TRADOC planners offered that the 1980s and 1990s would see conflicts which would include "coercive diplomacy, special intelligence operations, psychological operations, terrorism and counterterrorism, various levels of guerrilla warfare, and Soviet-proxy limited conventional war." This last category would take place in primarily Third World countries found in Central and South America, Africa, and the Middle East.

Steaming up alongside the army's effort to establish a credible counterterrorist response in 1980 was the navy. As the only uniformed services to offer a true special forces capability, both were in constant competition to maintain such a presence within their spheres of influence. Oftentimes their training and wartime capabilities overlapped, with the Green Berets offering a maritime/riverine option to the army and the SEALs offering over-the-beach operations including ambushes, raids, escape-and-evasion support, and POW and sensitive equipment recovery. In other words, operators from both SOF organizations were capable of doing each other's jobs in many cases, although in specific instances each was clearly more effective than the other. "There are no better force multipliers than the army's Special Forces," says one senior SOF officer of this situation. "And there is no better violent response to direct-action situations than the navy's SEALs. The challenge is to keep everybody happy with their identified and proven areas of responsibility. That's why a unified special operations command was established."

One of the primary obstacles faced by Delta was deciding who actually issued the unit its orders. After much wrangling, a joint task force (JTF) was established for special operations regarding terrorism. All the services would be involved, but they would report to an army general who would be the JTF's overall commander. The only service not involved in the JTF was the Marine Corps, which although wanting to share in the SOF arena, was unwilling to give up Marine forces to another command. Says one SOF naval commander of this situation, "The Marines want to play at special ops, but they don't want to salute the army while doing so. Many believe their approach detracts from the unified effort taking place within the SOF community-at-large."

The JTF would ultimately determine the operational fates of both Delta and ST 6, which Beckwith himself spawned more by accident than intent. In preparing his input for the task force, Beckwith noted that a maritime counterterrorist capability was needed to complement Delta's ground presence. Beckwith referred to a "SEAL element," as maritime operations were clearly their territory.

Also involved with preliminary JTF planning was navy commander Richard Marcinko, a SEAL whose force of personality and fiery character was equal to that of Charlie Beckwith's. By his own admission, during a review of the colonel's proposal, Marcinko changed Beckwith's original wording from SEAL *element* to *command*. No such SEAL command existed at the time, which meant one would have to be established if Marcinko's sleight of hand slipped by those charged with the final review and approval of the JTF plan. To the SEAL officer's great delight, his "correction" was overlooked, and SEAL Team 6 was approved.

Like the army's Special Forces, the navy's special warfare community had already been experimenting with counterterrorism. On the West Coast four SEAL platoons were trained in basic counterterrorism techniques and tactics, although a formal unit had not yet been designated as a counterterrorist force. On the East Coast such an organization was already in effect, thanks to the chief of naval operations (CNO) Thomas Hayward and the Holloway Commission.

Determined to understand international terrorism, the Holloway Commission had recommended that study of the issue be undertaken overseas. As a result, a platoon of SEALs from Naval Special Warfare Group 2 was sent to Britain, at the direction of Comdr. Thomas Lawson, to study with the SAS's maritime counterparts, the Special Boat Service (SBS). The British had long recognized the need for an effective multiservice special operations command, and the SBS was responsible for the protection of English oil platforms, tankers, and other seagoing vessels that might become targets of terrorism.

Deployed to Britain during the spring of 1980, the SEALs were commanded by Lt. Comdr. Norm Carley, who in 1989 would personally command the SEAL element responsible for the successful sinking of Manuel Noriega's yacht in Balboa Harbor during OPERATION JUST CAUSE. Carley's platoon spent several months with the SBS, learning the tricks of the trade from the masters themselves. Upon returning to Little Creek, Carley's platoon was formally recognized as NAVSPECWARGRP 2's counterterrorist response team. The original terrorist action response team (TART) was soon afterward retitled MOB 6, as Carley's counterterrorists trained up another five platoons. MOB stood for MOBility, six being the full complement of platoons that could carry out counterterrorist actions. MOB 6 reported to NAVSPECWARGRP 2, but the JCS oversaw counterterrorist deployments.

Thanks to heavy inside support from the deputy chief of naval operations for plans and policy, Adm. Bill Crowe, Marcinko was selected by the CNO to command ST 6. Crowe had the inside track to CNO Hayward and was a believer in special operations such as those promoted by Marcinko and Carley. MOB 6 was absorbed into the new command, and Carley came aboard as Marcinko's executive officer. ST 6's early history resembled Delta, taking on seventy-some operators and offered the dregs of what facilities were available from NAVSPECWARGRP 2. Nevertheless, Team 6 soon became a proficient counterterrorist unit, which specialized in maritime operations, any over-the-beach missions that they might be tasked with.

In June 1983, Dick Marcinko was replaced as the commander of ST 6 because he'd been too abrasive, too radical, and too unconventional for even the navy's unconventional community. The navy's counterterrorist force was turned over to Comdr. Robert Gormly, a respected SEAL officer who was given the task of correcting the "bad habits" cultivated under Marcinko's regime. Gormly was the officer on deck when his team's first real-world mission took place on the tiny island of Grenada. Working alongside the Jedi Warriors would be Delta. Both units were about to be tested for the first time in a warfighting role, a role they had not trained for or been expected to become involved in by Beckwith or Marcinko. As we have seen, their performances were not top-notch.

After OPERATION URGENT FURY came a series of counter-terrorist actions for both Delta and ST 6. Each unit was becoming progressively more mature, with greater assets made available as their covert roles were defined by what was now called the Joint Special Operations Command, or JSOC. Supported by the army's 160th Special Aviation Task Force during OPERATION JUST CAUSE, Delta and ST 6 carried out specific war-time mission's such as the pursuit of Noriega and the freeing of American prisoner Kurt Muse from Modelo Prison in down-town Panama City. Although much of what both units accomplished remains classified, the general opinion of those in a position to judge was favorable toward the war-fighting abilities demonstrated in Panama. A senior officer with specific knowledge of U.S. counterterrorism said, "Today both Delta and SEAL Team 6's mission statements have been expanded to include wartime missions as they might be identified by JSOC."

Detachment Delta continues to be the army's primary counterterrorist unit, although certain Special Forces elements have been identified as pinch hitters should Delta be otherwise employed. These elements actively train in counterterrorism and are considered fully capable of being deployed in limited situations. In 1987, the navy commissioned SEAL Team 8 as a second counterterrorist force. Since then, ST 8 has seen its mission statement changed to reflect the conventional SEAL role with a specific regional area of responsibility. On the West Coast there are no formal counterterrorist SEAL teams, although rumors of an ST 7, specializing in black operations, have been common over the last several years. Such a development would seem natural as the organizational charts of both NAVSPECWARGRPs tend to emulate each other, and the dissolution of ST 8's role as a counterterrorist unit might imply that the West Coast SEALs were developing an organization to parallel ST 6. In any event, America's formal counterterrorists would soon be going to war in uniform as Saddam Hussein's forces occupied Kuwait.

By all accounts, operators from ST 6 were not deployed to the war in the Gulf. How they may have been used is open to conjecture, but it seems reasonable that the navy's counterterrorist force was most likely engaged in actions against known terrorists. Even though Saddam Hussein's call for a holy war against the non-Arab members of the Coalition was discounted by many senior Islamic leaders, the Coalition's most powerful members were nations that had spent millions of dollars on counterterrorist programs, and there can be little doubt that life for the professional bomb thrower was made as uncomfortable as possible while the war in Kuwait was being conducted. Intelligence agencies from around the world pooled information on the whereabouts and intentions of international terror figures, and it can be speculated that a close watch was maintained over the worst of the lot.

In the past, a small number of specific terrorists have been the subject of preemptive strikes by counterterrorist forces. These are normally sanctioned only when hard evidence indicates that a major terrorist operation is under way. Great Britain, Israel, and other nations have opted for the preemptive strike, and it has been offered by one high-ranking member on the secretary of defense's staff that the United States does not disallow such a strike being carried out by its own forces.

Contrary to Col. Jesse Johnson's impromptu interview with *Defense Week* in early April, JSOC deployed at least one Delta squadron to Saudi Arabia for the war. Supporting Delta were its assigned 160th SOAR aircrews and aircraft, as well as dedicated C-130 Combat Talons. General Schwarzkopf was shadowed by Delta operators who served as his personal bodyguard, and a command aircraft stood by to whisk him to safety if he or his command headquarters was attacked. There was also intelligence information about an Iraqi special forces mission to be conducted against the general and his staff in Saudi Arabia. Supposedly the unit was trained by Russian *Spetsnaz* advisers.

Of the many intelligence shortcomings noted during the Gulf War, the most explosive was the gross undercounting of Hussein's SCUD missile inventory. The SCUD is a ballistic missile, which can be fired from a fixed facility or a mobile launch site. Like the World War II German V-2s launched against England from across the Channel, the SCUD was not very accurate. Its most effective use is when several SCUDs can be directed at one time against massed military forces. Iraq was said to possess less than fifty SCUD launchers before the invasion of Kuwait, later figures put the number of launchers at over two hundred.

While the SCUD never amounted to much as a weapon of mass destruction against Coalition forces, it was a very effec-

tive weapon of terror to the civilian populations of Saudi
Arabia, Israel, and Bahrain. The most distressing attacks were
against Saudi Arabia and Israel. By firing the missiles at Saudi
cities, most notably the capital Riyadh, Saddam Hussein was
punishing the ordinary Saudi citizen for his government's support of the Coalition effort. The reader should recall that the
Saudis had originally abandoned their border with Kuwait as a
means of appeasing Saddam Hussein. It was only through
skillful diplomatic efforts and hard reasoning by Western diplomats that the Saudis were convinced that their appeasement
would only backfire once Hussein had consolidated his hold on
Kuwait. Of course, by hosting the forces rallied against Iraq,
the Saudi government was inviting retaliation, and Saddam
probably hoped that if enough damage could be done with the
SCUDs, the Saudis might evict the Coalition.

Israel was a different story. If Hussein could provoke Israel
into mounting a reprisal against Iraq, he would be successful in
splitting the already fragile Arab Coalition. Israel depended
upon her air force for such retaliations, and to reach Iraq, she
would have to overfly Jordan. Jordan, not a member of the Coalition, remained loyal to Iraq but provided only clandestine
military support to Hussein. If Israel violated Jordan's air
space, the act would be enough to bring the tiny country into
the war on the side of Iraq. Should that happen it would further widen the rift between the Arab nations of the Coalition,
none of which would support a war being waged by Israel
against an Arab neighbor.

Adding to the SCUD threat was the news that chemical
weapons could be delivered by the missile. The use of such
weapons against Israel would invoke memories of the gassing
of Jews by the Nazis during the Second World War, and no
amount of diplomatic hocus-pocus would be able to restrain
the Israelis. The United States knew this, and the introduction
of the Patriot missile-defense system on Israeli territory helped
ease Israel's concerns, but SCUDs continued to fall, and Israeli
patience grew thin. General Schwarzkopf, who had already
mounted an impressive air effort to locate and destroy the
launch sites, was faced with poor weather conditions, which
hampered electronic intelligence gathering and accurate air
strikes. The continued SCUD attacks added fuel to the growing
political fire.

Under the direction of Maj. Gen. Wayne Downing, overall
commander of U.S. counterterrorist forces, a joint operation

was mounted, which involved operators from Delta and the British SAS. Since the majority of the fixed launch sites had already been destroyed, the numerous mobile launchers would have to be located, targeted, and then destroyed. Assigning grid areas in western Iraq to his operators, Downing ordered Delta teams to work night and day until the mission was complete.

First, the most likely areas in which to hide a launcher were researched. Mounted primarily on long truck beds, the SCUD launch platforms were restricted to road systems that allowed speedy access to hardened missile resupply "farms." Further, the trucks needed places to hide during the day. The best such sites were provided by the bridges, tunnels, and dry culverts, which were part of the road systems. After a successful launch, the platform would have to move swiftly out of the area as the missile's firing signature would immediately be recorded by spy satellite, the information then sent directly to CENTCOM for targeting purposes.

With all of this in mind, Delta's teams began looking at the most likely spots on the map. Flying at less than fifty feet above the sandy earth, MH-60 and MH-47 helicopters flew the counterterrorists deep into western Iraq. After off-loading desert mobility vehicles, the operators began a painstaking search of the desert. They were aided by the latest electronic intelligence, but only real-time intelligence provided by the field forces would begin killing SCUDs. Delta's commandos hid by day under camouflage nets, resting until nightfall when they could continue their reconnaissance efforts. Soon their persistence paid off.

Western Iraq was plastered with search teams so that the missiles and their launchers could be located in time to pacify Israel. As each special reconnaissance team confirmed a launch platform or missile storage facility, the air force prepared to launch aircraft to engage the target. Using handheld laser target designators (LTDs), the operator would "warm" or "paint" the impact point for whatever ordnance the aircraft might be delivering. This method of destroying SCUDs proved extremely accurate and also preserved the lives of the operators on the ground.

When, in some instances, aircraft were not available, Delta engaged SCUD sites in a more direct fashion. One of the more favored techniques was the use of the .50-caliber sniper rifle with its RUFUS and other specialized rounds. Using suppres-

sors, which eliminated the report of the heavy rifle from five
hundred meters outward, Delta snipers successfully punctured
SCUD fuel tanks on mounted missiles and those found hidden
in supply dumps. Iraqi missile crews would only discover the
damage during the firing sequence, when a SCUD exploded on
the platform. Missiles damaged in storage were useless and
were normally destroyed by Coalition aircraft called in later to
strike the marked sites. SCUD crews without available missiles
were also engaged by Delta sniper teams, which could knock
over their targets from distances as far away as three thousand
meters.

For direct-action attacks, the teams were provided with AT-4
antitank rockets and other munitions capable of destroying the
platforms and their deadly cargo. Delta suffered three casualties during its SCUD-hunting missions, the men killed when
their MH-60 Blackhawk crashed into a sand dune after picking
up the team from where its Humm-V was wrecked.

In addition to killing SCUDs, Delta operators also provided
invaluable intelligence about what was happening on the
ground in western Iraq. The unit daily proved its war-fighting
capabilities, scrambling to waiting helicopters any time a
SCUD launch was announced to search for the offending vehicle and its crew. On February 27, the final day of the ground
war, Hussein tried one last time to provoke Israel. Moving
twenty-six mobile launchers to the border, the Iraqis prepared
to fire one massive sortie into Israel's cities and towns. Spotted
by a reconnaissance aircraft, the missile launchers were responded to by numerous Delta teams. Shortly thereafter, all
twenty-six SCUDs were located and destroyed, and no missiles
were fired. Schwarzkopf sent a personal message to the force:
"You guys kept Israel out of the war."

For Schwarzkopf, Delta's lackluster performance in Grenada
was forgotten. The contributions made by the counterterrorist
forces were further evidence that special operations had a place
on the conventional battlefield. He'd had no other force capable of undertaking such a sensitive mission, and Delta had
done it with minimal support and information. Delta had rescued Israel from the threat of Hussein's SCUD forces. It was
perhaps the greatest counterterrorist mission ever undertaken
by any such unit in the world. "They [Delta] were owed one,"
said one Special Forces operator. "They're very dedicated to
their mission, and the past always seemed to haunt whatever it

was they were handed after Iran and Grenada. No one doubts their abilities now, not after what happened in Iraq. No one."

For Detachment Delta the war in the Gulf vindicated the unit. "They did a lot of heavy stuff over there," offered one pilot from the 160th SOAR, responsible for flying the black SOF missions Delta was sent on. "Stuff no one will hear about in this century."

Today Delta continues to train at Fort Bragg, where it has recently moved into a multimillion-dollar facility called "The Wall." A professional relationship exists between the army's most elite counterterrorist unit and ST 6, and many of the two units' operators are close friends. Firmly under the command of JSOC, both units train with other counterterrorist forces around the world.

CHAPTER
EIGHTEEN

We wanted aces. Daredevils, barnstormers, hot rodders,
guys (pilots) who could pick it up, turn it around on a dime,
and put it back down with a flair.

CHARGIN' CHARLIE BECKWITH
Former Commander, Delta

The advent of today's special operations aviation (SOA)
forces sprang from the womb of OPERATION RICE BOWL, the rescue attempt that evolved into the mother of all military disas-
ters on the hardpacked sands of the Dasht-e Kavir in Iran.
Although a tragic blow to our national pride, DESERT ONE
proved to be the fire from which a determined SOA phoenix
arose.

The January 1979 ousting of Shah Mohammad Reza Pahlavi
from Iran's Peacock Throne was followed by the assumption
of power by Ayatollah Khomeini, a radical fundamentalist. In
November 1979, the American embassy in Tehran was overrun
by Khomeini's militants, sixty-six hostages taken to the
world's horror. The mass abduction and violation of international law was broadcast worldwide, a strident political message from Iran's revolutionary government announcing its
independence from the "Great Satan."

At Fort Bragg, North Carolina, Col. Charles Beckwith stood
ready to deploy to Iran with his newly activated Delta Force.
Authorized to form an antiterrorist unit, Beckwith had begun
screening potential operators' service records in 1977. By late
1979, the initial unit was certified as fully ready to undertake
hostage-rescue operations. Less than a month later, Delta received the green light to begin preparations to rescue the
Americans in Iran.

In its infancy, U.S. counterterrorist operations were based upon the operational doctrines and histories of its European counterparts. In most instances, that meant joint cooperation for transportation and other support services. But the situation in Iran demanded strictly unilateral action; the entire burden of mounting a global rescue mission fell upon the resources of the United States military. The most critical asset was specialized air support and personnel.

The planners for RICE BOWL had one technically successful rescue operation from which to take pointers. The Son Tay raid (OPERATION IVORY COAST-KINGPIN), mounted in late 1970, was a treasure trove of long-distance planning and execution methods. The major advantage of KINGPIN was the ready availability of experienced assets due to the Vietnam War, including battle-tested special-operations air capability. Although no American POWs were found at Son Tay, the mission demonstrated that the United States could operate deep within the enemy's backyard.

KINGPIN relied upon six helicopters, five of them being HH-53 Super Jolly Greens, then the air force's primary rotary air-rescue platform. The sixth was the H-3, a lighter version of the Jolly Green. In addition, HC-130 tankers acted as airborne refueling stations while the helicopters were en route the target. Two MC-130 Combat Talons using the then-new forward-looking infrared systems (FLIR) guided the assault force through the North Vietnamese radar belt and back. Of the six choppers, four were used in the actual assault and two as backups. Four spare HH-53s were in place at the air base at Udorn. As KINGPIN unfolded, some of the finest AF aircrews were assembled to ferry the raiders into Son Tay. Over 1,000 flight hours and 268 training scenarios were spent preparing the air component for its mission. Senior KINGPIN planners gave the operation a 95–97 percent chance of success by the time final briefings were in order.

The aftermath of KINGPIN proved its planners correct. Returning POWs confirmed hearing about the rescue attempt and being heartened by its execution. For twenty-six minutes (actual ground time) the Son Tay raiders controlled a portion of North Vietnam. They returned with no losses, although the HH-53 was destroyed on the ground, and one A-1 fighter-bomber was shot down over Laos, its crew rescued under fire by the Son Tay raiders.

In contrast, OPERATION RICE BOWL's organizers and operators

were forced to rely upon outdated rotary aircraft, inexperienced helicopter crews, and lessons not learned from the Son Tay experience. The navy's RH-53D Sea Stallion was selected as the primary rotary rescue platform. An airborne minesweeper, the Sea Stallion could be transported aboard aircraft carriers, the launch platform for RICE BOWL. The eight aircraft thought necessary for the mission would be refitted with advanced navigation systems aboard the USS *Kitty Hawk*. The 53Ds were five years old by the time they were commissioned to take part in RICE BOWL; they were not SOF aircraft as defined by today's standards.

Initially, navy and Marine pilots were assigned to fly the rotary-wing mission. The navy pilots soon proved to be unable to adapt to the special skills and daring required of special operations flyers. The air force had no unit that could support the mission with pilots. The job fell to Marine aviators who, to their credit, accomplished what the navy or the air force could not.

But finding suitable pilots was only the beginning of the air-asset nightmare. Due to in-flight refueling problems, the helicopter force would have to land at a site (Desert One) where fuel bladders transported by C-130 aircraft would await them. Further, the choppers would fly as an independent force from the C-130s, carrying Beckwith's Delta/Ranger/Green Beret assault teams. No Combat Talon aircraft would guide the Sea Stallions to Desert One as was done for the Jolly Greens en route to Son Tay. In the end, problems with the rotary-wing aircraft scrubbed the mission, due to pilot fatigue, mechanical breakdowns, overly restricted interforce communications, and pure bad luck. The choppers were to have transported Delta from Desert One to the daytime hide site outside of Tehran. The 53s were also to recover the hostages once the assault on the embassy had gone down, transporting both the raiders and the freed prisoners to an airstrip thirty minutes south of Tehran, where two C-141 transports would be standing by to fly them to safety. The airstrip was to have been seized by a seventy-five-man force of army Rangers during the second night of the operation. The C-141 Starlifters would evacuate everyone involved, air cover provided by AC-130 gunships and on-call tactical air support.

Tragically, Desert One became an inferno when one of the helicopters, attempting to reposition itself after the mission was scratched, tore into the C-130 carrying Delta's Blue team. In the resulting conflagration, Beckwith ordered all the 53s abandoned, their crews moved to the remaining C-130s. Due to the presence of innocent Iranian nationals captured at Desert One, no air strike was sent to destroy the abandoned aircraft, and the ground teams responsible for on-site demolitions failed to accomplish their mission. Eight operators were killed, and over $72 million worth of equipment lost. It was the blackest day in America's special operations history, but one destined to give birth to a new breed of SOA aviators.

The army moved quickly, establishing Task Force 158 in 1980 as a direct response to the events at Desert One. Crews and airframes were drawn from the 158th Aviation Battalion, of the 101st Airborne Division based at Fort Campbell, Kentucky. By 1982, TF 158 had been redesignated Task Force 160, fielding two companies from the 158th, one company from the 159th, and elements from the 229th, which formed up the attack side of the house. A highly classified unit, TF 160 trained hard to remedy the problems spotlighted by the Iran disaster. Unfortunately, a series of fatal accidents brought the unit to the media's attention, and particular attention was focused on TF 160's use of night-vision aids. As 160's survivability depended upon the effective use of darkness, night-vision equipment was experimented with by the army to a degree unheard of by the other services. Soon, the problems were ironed out, and media attention drifted elsewhere.

In 1983, then air force chief of staff Gen. Charles Gabriel and his army counterpart Gen. John Wickham, agreed that the army would assume all rotary-wing special operations missions. The agreement included missions assigned to the AF's Air Rescue Service, which was considered for disbandment in anticipation of such a transfer taking place. Within the air force, strong reservations were voiced, so the air force attempted to combine combat search-and-rescue units with its special operations assets. Apparently, that solution did not work out and the Air Rescue Service was reactivated in 1989 as an individual command. Strangely enough, the ARS was not deployed to Saudi Arabia in support of CENTCOM's combat search-and-rescue mission. That failure shifted combat search and rescue to the special operations forces under SOCCENT's control.

In September of 1984, Lt. Gen. David Nichols, deputy chief of staff plans and operations, voiced his opinion of the floundering pace of the transfer procedure in an air force memo.

"The working group [Joint Working Group] appears to be making the transfer too hard . . . Dedicated AF rotary wing SOF currently consists of 8 HH-53Hs, 6 CH-3s, and 9 UH-1Hs. Only the Pave Low HH-53Hs have sophisticated avionics."

General Nichols went on to state it was his observation that the army's ultimate avionics solution could evolve from a series of enhancements to its existing airframes, with the AF Pave-Lows "on call to provide support" until the army was fully operational in fiscal year 1989. These enhancements began with the UH-60 Blackhawks and CH-47 Chinooks. Army airframes became MH model 60s and 47s as special operations aviation took the lead from the air force in developing its rotary-wing capabilities.

The army's Task Force 160 soon became the 160th Special Operations Aviation Group. In that configuration, it was able to field two attack companies, two lift companies, a Chinook company, and support companies (including the headquarters element). In May 1990, the 160th was reorganized as a regiment, becoming the sole command assigned to manage all special operations aviation assets and capabilities. Incorporated into the regiment were the army's active component Special Forces group aviation detachments. Today, the 160th SOAR is staffed by 1,396 personnel divided among three battalions and support units. Its headquarters and first two battalions are located at Fort Campbell. The 3d Battalion is located at Hunter Army Airfield, where it supports the 1st Ranger Battalion.

First Battalion, 160th, is composed of thirty MH-60s, eighteen AH-6s, and eighteen MH-6s. The mission is classified as the 1st flies support for primarily "black" SOF operations.

Second Battalion, 160th, is composed of twenty-four MH-47s. The 2d flies support for both black and white SOF operations, acting primarily as infiltration/exfiltration platforms.

Third Battalion, 160th, is composed of ten MH-60s and eight MH-47s. The 3d flies all white SOF support and was the announced battalion deployed to OPERATIONS DESERT SHIELD/STORM.

Finally, the regiment has a forward deployed detachment that supports army SF assets in Panama and a National Guard battalion located in Tulsa, Oklahoma.

Col. Joseph Fucci possesses precisely the personality one

might expect in an SOF aviator. He is conscious of the media's interest in his organization, realizing that too much secrecy tends to prevent proper appreciation of the unit. We met early one morning in his office for one of the colonel's first interviews in the aftermath of DESERT STORM. "Pilots undergo a formal selection process," Fucci said. "They have to pass a swim test, PT test, our aviation written test, then take a checkride at night where they have to navigate without aids. After that, there's our board." Upon acceptance by the board, the pilots are required to complete an eighteen-week formal training program conducted at Campbell by Fucci's very capable instructors. The average 160 pilot comes to the unit with fifteen hundred flight hours, plus three hundred to four hundred additional hours using night-vision equipment. Commissioned officers stay with the unit about four years, warrants are permitted to remain until they desire to leave. "We have some warrants who were here when the task force was activated," offers Colonel Fucci.

Enlisted personnel undergo a similar screening process. Their records are examined for all the required schools and professional development programs, and a four-to-five-week train-up program must be completed before assignment to regimental duties. All those assigned to the regiment have an identifier code annotated on their records. This allows the regiment to locate and retrieve critical manpower assets throughout the army if required.

What's it really like to be a part of the 160th SOAR? "Special ops means longer hours, harder work, and more frequent separations from the families than normal aviation requirements," Fucci warns. "We train worldwide, as opposed to training primarily on the post one's unit is located at." Others interviewed agreed, adding that unlike the air force, *all* 160th SOAR personnel are volunteers.

Does that make a difference. "Yes, most certainly," said a senior 160 pilot. "The people we support know we volunteered for special operations just as they did. We live in the field with them, train alongside them, get dirty and tired and worn-out, just like they do. We're not 'pretty boys' with fancy scarves. Our customers know we'll come and get 'em, regardless of the situation." Special Forces ground operators who counted upon the 160th for black and for white SOA support, agree. "They're the best," exclaimed a young SF NCO who served in the Gulf. "No one flies like the 160th. Without them, we couldn't have got the job done."

Indeed. During an earlier interview held on the West Coast, a SEAL commander recalled watching an air force helicopter pilot rapidly preparing to leave the SEALs' combat search-and-rescue site after a SCUD attack. "I asked him where he was going, and he told me he was taking his Pave-Low farther inland where it was safer," the frogman remembered. "I reminded him it would take an additional hour for his aircraft to reach us if there was a pilot downed in the Gulf, but he didn't seem to care much about my opinion on the matter. Give me the guys from Task Force 160, any day. They just look at you and say 'When do you want to go?' They're not playing at special ops."

Colonel Fucci concluded our interview by saying ". . . we have perhaps a greater sense of urgency . . ." when it comes to supporting SOF personnel. As for the regiment's future needs, the colonel was precise. "We need to get more involved in aviation survival equipment. Radar, forward-looking infrared, chaff dispensers, early warning packages. We did quick modifications in the field during DESERT STORM, and they worked. But more emphasis is needed in these areas, and that means greater funding."

The 3d Bn, 160th, deployed to the Gulf early on. Roughly thirty days passed before the battalion received mission priorities, decided upon by SOCCENT. Combat Search and Rescue (CSAR) became the unit's number one priority because of the enormity of the planned air campaign. Foreign Internal Defense (FID) would be the 160th's other concern.

At SOFEX-91, a SpecWar convention held in November 1991 at Fort Bragg, USSOCOM commander in chief Gen. Carl Stiner offered his admiration for the tremendous achievement accomplished by SOA/SOF forces in undertaking the combat search-and-rescue mission. But his negative comments about its becoming a full-time mission for SOF were echoed by Colonel Fucci. "We don't want it [CSAR] and don't think we should have it. It's an air force mission, we're infiltration/exfiltration guys. We do practice internal CSAR, and we're quite good at it. Now if a higher authority gives us the mission formally, we'll do it to the best of our abilities, but [they'll have to] give us the means, as well."

SOCCENT turned the management of all aviation assets committed to CSAR over to Air Force Special Operations

Command Central (AFSOC). SOA aircraft, representing the army, navy, and air force, were to provide on-call rescue crews and airframes for downed pilots and crews and SOF forces. Aircrews and black operators conducting their missions in northern Iraq became the responsibility of special operations forces located in Turkey. In all, seven CSAR launch sites were made ready, five in Saudi Arabia and two in Turkey. Additional 160 missions included:

> Suppression of enemy air defenses
> Close air support
> Combat air support
> Location of penetration points
> Minimum risk routes

Training for CSAR began immediately. MH-60 Blackhawks and MH-47 Chinooks were utilized, their crews creating new tactics and maneuvers. "We began by planning how to avoid Iraqi SAM sites," offered one Chinook pilot. "Then we began flying practice missions of two hundred to four hundred miles. At night, we began by flying at three hundred feet, reducing that to one hundred feet at one hundred knots. During daylight hours, we'd fly at twenty-five to fifty feet off the deck." He went on to point out that the 160's MH-47s are easily the most sophisticated SOA airframes in service. "I've got eight years in this business, and I'm tired of hearing how great the air force is. The air force flies a piece of shit for an airplane, if you ask me. Their Pave-Lows seemed to lose engines every mission we flew. They can't do a rolling landing in brownout conditions, and I've watched them overfly landing points because their pilots rely totally on their instruments. We just wave good-bye and set our customers down where they're supposed to be."

Chinook crews from the 160th built security teams for CSAR operations using Green Berets, white SOF SEALs, AF combat controllers, and pararescue personnel. CSAR tactics included the infiltration of a rescue team and vehicle (Humm-V) up to two hundred miles behind the lines, with the 47 setting down while the mobile desert vehicle made the recovery. "We didn't have to fly right to the crash site," says another pilot. "Rather than alert the Iraqis—who were all over the place, anyhow—we could set down and let the ground operators go out and make the pickup. Everyone was using satellite navigational aids, which could tell to within a meter where you were standing, so getting lost wasn't a problem."

On February 17 at 2000 hours, a U.S. F-16 went down forty miles behind enemy lines. Two army SOA MH-60s, using night-vision devices, launched, accompanied by 2d Battalion, 5th Special Forces Group security teams armed with AT-4 handheld rocket launchers and M-16/203 assault rifles. The pilot was rescued even though frustrated Iraqis on the ground fired missiles after the retreating aircraft. Onboard jamming devices, coupled with emergency evasive action by the pilots, left the missiles far behind. This was the first and only CSAR mission conducted during the hours of darkness using night-vision guidance (NVG) capabilities under zero-illumination conditions.

On February 24 at 1400 hours, a three-man Special Forces reconnaissance team two hundred miles inside Iraq was compromised by civilian foot traffic. Making an immediate decision not to kill civilians despite having battlefield justification to do so, M.Sgt. Jeff Sims prepared for a fight. Taken under fire by Iraqi reaction forces sent out to capture them, the team requested a daylight "hot" extraction. AFSOC policy stated that daylight extractions were too dangerous for SOA rotary assets and that all infiltrations and extractions had to be conducted with two aircraft. The AFSOC commander made a gutsy decision, alerting the 160th to fly the mission anyhow.

Although reported by both the 160th and the media as a planned single-airframe rescue, in reality *two* MH-60 Blackhawks were scrambled. *Lady Godiva*, piloted by CWO Jim Crisafulli and CWO Randy Stephens, watched in horror as their sister ship's engine burst into flames while the two aircraft were still on the tarmac. "We knew they could cancel us right then," recalls Crisafulli, "but both Randy and I were praying they'd let us go." AFSOC did, launching *Lady Godiva* for a two-hundred-mile run through Iraqi air defenses in the middle of the day.

"We chose to fly almost directly to where the team was," Crisafulli remembers. "I knew these guys, having worked with them for several years when the SF aviation detachments were still around." Flying at twenty-five to fifty feet off the deck, the Blackhawk crew and its Special Forces security team watched as sunlight bounced off hundreds of vehicles' mirrors. "We didn't know if we were being fired at, or what. We just kept flying."

An F-16, called in by Sims to provide close air support, was relaying information to *Lady Godiva* as she flew through Iraq. "We never had direct commo with the team," the veteran helicopter pilot pointed out. "They'd lost their antenna, but were somehow communicating with the F-16, who relayed to us. He was dropping ordnance all around them, trying to keep the Iraqis off until we got there. Finally, I remember the pilot telling us if we weren't there in ten minutes, there'd be no team to recover."

Lady Godiva's crew put the pedal to the metal. Onboard, the crew chiefs were preparing the dual miniguns as the Green Beret security team readied its weapons. Finally, when the Blackhawk burst over the last ridge separating the Blackhawk from the aircrew, Crisafulli dropped the airframe into a dive as everyone attempted to spot the team's hiding place. "Someone yelled 'Missile!' " Jim recalls, "and we went into evasive action. It turned out later the team had popped a flare to attract our attention. I saw some huge steel towers, with power lines running between them, and headed for them, thinking the team was on the other side. Just as I was about to dive under the power lines, we spotted a third, smaller line." Crisafulli hauled back on the chopper's stick, rolling the straining aircraft over the power lines rather than underneath. "The crew chiefs were hanging on, the SF guys plastered up against the compartment's roof. Chief Crisafulli then discovered the team was on the *other* side of the lines when Master Sergeant Sims, using a VH-17 signal panel to attract the chopper's attention, caught their eye. "This all happened in split seconds," said Crisafulli. "I rolled the chopper back over the wires and set it down. All I could hear were the miniguns going off. One of the SF security team [Gordy Hopple] jumped off the bird and began firing his weapon from the hip. I remember Gordie's aim being very effective. People came running past where I was sitting in the cockpit. We were taking hits. Then I saw Jeff Sims [the team's leader] working his way toward me. He was hauling a rucksack full of gear they hadn't been able to destroy yet. He wasn't going to leave it behind. I watched him look up at me as he passed by, a big smile on his face. I thought to myself, Hey, you don't have time to smile. Get on board, we gotta get outta here!"

Crisafulli and Stephens were awarded Distinguished Flying Crosses for their heroic actions. Their crew received Bronze Stars with V devices. M.Sgt. Jeff Sims won the Silver Star, his two comrades awarded Bronze Stars with V devices. "You can say what you want about Rambo," offers Jim Crisafulli. "These guys [today's Green Berets] are the real thing. They make Rambo look like a pussy."

A fourth CSAR was made by the 160th, which was never made public. Little Birds—armed scout helicopters—from the unit were operating out in the Gulf one evening when one of the aircraft lost power and went down at sea. Under severe weather conditions, the second chopper dipped down assuming a hover just above the waves. As the frantically swimming pilot reached the lowered skid, he wrapped his arms and legs around it, signaling that he was okay. With that, the rescue ship transported its soggy "straphanger" to the shoreline of a small island, where rescue craft picked him up less than an hour later. In the meantime, the Little Bird flew cover for the grounded pilot until spotting the SEALs sent to pick him up. "It was a great bit of flying," said one pilot at the regiment's headquarters at Fort Campbell. "And one CSAR no one ever heard about."

At the conclusion of DESERT STORM, the 160th had accomplished the following:

No casualties (white SOA)
All missions flown to within thirty seconds of time-on-target
All missions 100 percent successful
First night CSAR flown
An operational readiness of 92 percent for MH-60s, 84 percent for MH-47s

But there had been casualties. Current special operations doctrine calls for no information to be released regarding black SOF/SOA missions. This includes POWs, MIAs, and those killed in action. Black SOF involves those units that are highly classified, units such as Delta and SEAL Team 6. Officially, USSOCOM gives USASOC casualties (KIA) as eight army SOF personnel. Four of those killed were from the 160th Special Operations Aviation Regiment. They were:

Capt. Charles W. Cooper
CWO 3 Michael F. Anderson
Sgt. Mario Vega-Velazquez
Sgt. Christopher J. Chapman

All four were killed when their MH-60 hit a sand dune while returning to a launch site. They were carrying Delta personnel involved in SCUD hunting missions. Three Delta operators, Sgt. Maj. Patrick R. Hurley, M.Sgt. Eloy A. Rodriguez, and M.Sgt. Otto S. Clark, were also killed in the crash.

As in every conflict, lessons are learned. The regiment found it needed better external security forces to secure its hangars and staging bases when deployed. More handheld antiaircraft weapons (Stingers) for base defense were needed. Command and control proved more than able to successfully manage mission requirements and priorities.

"What we need is a more active support base when it comes to giving the regiment the equipment and personnel we must have," commented a pilot involved in black SOF operations. "This unit did some incredible things over the desert, things no one will ever hear about. Missions no other SOA asset could fly. There are, in my opinion, no better SOF pilots and crews than those here with the 160th today. But we can only do so much with what we've got."

One thing the regiment needs is more helicopters. "We were supposed to get over fifty of the new MH-47 Echo models, but now we're being told we'll see about twenty-five. These are the most sophisticated penetrator rotary aircraft in the world, and we need all fifty!" Pilots and crews went on to say better management of SOA careers is needed, that more personnel were needed to take the strain off those already in the unit. Airframe survivability equipment is needed, radar detectors, chaff dispensers, antimissile systems, and improved on-board weaponry. Colonel Fucci believes his regiment's budget will be protected for at least another two years, but after that? "It's anyone's guess."

Perhaps the most qualified to vouch for this exceptionally professional and highly dedicated unit are their "customers." "If the 160th puts you on the ground, they'll be back to get you," says one decorated operator. "No one can touch us when we fly at night," offers a veteran Night Stalker. "At night, we rule the air. You have to have special people for this job, special people with special talents. We're here to take care of the guys on the ground. That's our job, that's what they pay us for."

Task Force 160 was recognized as a unit on October 16, 1981. They became known as the "Night Stalkers," due to their unique ability to navigate in total darkness, flying just above the deck. The Night Stalkers were capable of striking anywhere in the world.

Their first combat deployment was OPERATION URGENT FURY, in Grenada. In June 1988, the task force once again answered the call of the National Command Authority, flying a classified mission (OPERATION MOUNT HOPE III) under the most demanding circumstances faced by army aviators. During OPERATION PRIME CHANCE, the force supported a joint task force in yet another classified mission. This time, the Night Stalkers participated in the first ever neutralization of an enemy threat while using night-vision goggles and forward-looking infrared devices.

During OPERATION JUST CAUSE, the 160th provided daring air support for the Rangers and other black and white SOF assets. Their skills allowed them to rule the night, often chasing Panama's dictator as he attempted to evade U.S. security forces.

Today, the 160th SOAR is a proud regiment tasked with the management and training of the finest special operations pilots and crews in the world. The regiment's motto, "Night Stalkers Don't Quit," announces the unit's commitment to those it serves. The unit logo is a winged horse, symbolizing aviation. Behind the horse sits the moon, representing night. The stars flowing behind the horse represent night vision, and the sword held above the rider's head demonstrates the desire to strike quickly and with accuracy. The rider, of course, is Death.

"Death Waits In the Dark—Night Stalkers"
160th Special Operations Aviation Regiment

CHAPTER NINETEEN

A new chapter in coalition warfare was written by every 5th Special Forces Group and ARSOTF soldier. New military relationships were forged and a country freed as a direct result of their dedication and call to duty in serving their nation. This is the hallmark of the Quiet Professionals, this is the essence of Special Forces. *DE OPPRESSO LIBER!*

COL. JAMES KRAUS, Commander
5th Special Forces Group (A)

Activated on September 21, 1961, the 5th Special Forces Group (Airborne) has been assigned an impressive military heritage dating back to 1942. Although a history to be proud of, it is a heritage granted by the conventional army, which, after their deactivation, had nothing better to do with the lineage of the units involved. Originally called Headquarters and Headquarters Detachment, 1st Battalion, Third Regiment, 1st Special Service Force, this lineage traces America's earliest commandos, who were a part of the joint Canadian-American conventional warfare effort, which fought the Germans in Europe. Although disbanded in 1945, its colors were reconstituted on April 15, 1960, and consolidated with those of Headquarters and Headquarters Company, 5th Ranger Infantry Battalion. This link with the Rangers dated back to 1943, when Ranger battalions were formed to fight in the European and Pacific campaigns.

Personnel from the 7th Special Forces Group and Special Warfare Training Center made up the initial manning roster of the 5th. Special Forces had been involved in Vietnam since 1957, with teams from the 7th and the 1st Groups working closely with Republic of Vietnam (ARVN) forces. By 1964, the entire 5th Group was deployed to Vietnam, and would take over or initiate a number of projects, including support of the Civilian Irregular Defense Group (CIDG) and, in 1966, the MACV Recondo School. Special projects such as Sigma and Omega would have 5th Group involvement until they were turned over to MACV-SOG in 1967. The group's efforts would provide division corps, and army-level combat reconnaissance to those commanders undertaking campaigns against the Viet Cong and North Vietnamese army. The 5th also served as a clandestine personnel pipeline for Special Forces operators volunteering for duty with the MACV-SOG projects.

Throughout the war in Southeast Asia, the 5th's distinctive "flash" would be the Special Forces insignia most frequently seen. The Department of the Army originally approved an all-black flash for the 5th Group. In 1964, a white "mourning" border, reflecting the 5th's respect for slain president John F. Kennedy, was authorized by the U.S. Army Special Forces, Vietnam (Provisional). The flash evolved further when a yellow and red bar pattern was superimposed diagonally across the insignia's black background, representing the operational teams provided to Vietnam by the 1st (Yellow), 7th (Red), and 5th (Black) Special Forces Groups. Coincidentally, red and yellow were the national colors of the Republic of Vietnam. This flash was approved by the Department of the Army through a request submitted by Col. John H. Spears.*

*In 1984, Col. James A. Guest, then commander of the 5th Group, was successful in his bid to change the 5th's flash back to a solid black shield with white border. Guest reasoned that the colors of a foreign flag should not be incorporated in U.S. Army insignia, pointing out the Republic of Vietnam no longer existed and that the 5th's mission orientation was no longer toward Southeast Asia. Approved by the Institute of Heraldry on January 16, 1985, the return of the original flash brought an end to twenty years' worth of military history as established by the 5th. Unofficially, it is said that Guest wanted to remove the "stigma" of Vietnam from the 5th's present activities. True or not, the decision was highly unpopular among the 5th's troops. This effort would impact upon several other SF flashes, to include the 10th's single battalion in Germany and "Det K" in Korea. The only other unauthorized flash which has become a part of Special Forces history is the 7th's "El Salvador" flash, which offered blue and white bars imposed against a red background. The first such flashes were created and handed out to members of ODAs 13 and 2, 3d Battalion, 7th Special Forces Group (Panama) during the establishment of the National Training Base in La Union, El Salvador, in 1984, and were designed and seen fabricated by the author.

By the end of the war in Vietnam, 5th Group soldiers had earned 17 Medals of Honor, 60 Distinguished Service Crosses, 814 Silver Stars, 13,234 Bronze Stars, and more than 14,000 other awards. After returning to Fort Bragg, North Carolina, the group continued to train and deploy mobile training teams throughout its new area of interest, the Middle East. Ordered to move its entire command to Fort Campbell, Kentucky, in the late 1980s, the 5th formally took over its new compound on June 16, 1988.

In August 1990, the 5th received word that it should begin preparing to deploy operational detachments to Southwest Asia. Iraq's invasion of Kuwait demanded the unique talents of Green Berets whose region of responsibility was the Middle East. Within seventy-two hours, elements from the 5th were at their staging areas on Fort Campbell. "It was hectic, even confused at times," one team sergeant recalls. "First only one battalion was going, then a second battalion was alerted. Finally, all three battalions were given the go-ahead despite the fact that 3d Battalion was lacking the bulk of its equipment and nearly all its personal weapons!" By August 30, the 5th was fully operational and beginning to launch its teams on any available aircraft leaving Fort Campbell. Many of the SF elements were "melted in" with units from the 101st Airborne, which had also been ordered to deploy to the Gulf. A total of 106 special operations teams took part in OPERATIONS DESERT SHIELD and DESERT STORM, the bulk of them coming from the 5th Group, which completed its deployment to Saudi Arabia on September 21.

Organized as Special Forces Operational Base 50 (SFOB 50), the group subdivided its forces into three forward operational bases (FOBs 51, 52, and 53). Combined with assets from the 160th SOAR (Night Stalkers), 112th Special Operations Signal Battalion, and support from the 528th Special Operations Support Battalion, the SFOB was redesignated the Army Special Operations Task Force (ARSOTF) in November 1990. Headquartered at King Khalid Military City, a forward command-and-control element supported FOBs 52, 53, the 3/ 160th SOAR (white SOF operations), and other additional elements necessary to oversee operations in the Joint Forces Command (North) sector. At King Fahd International Airport, the ARSOTF headquarters, FOB 51, and primary elements from the 528th SOSB oversaw those operations planned for Joint Forces Command (East). Commanding the 5th was Col.

James W. Kraus, whose operations center was established at the King Fahd International Airport. His staffs would oversee the special reconnaissance combined headquarters, and the special operations coordination teams (SOCOORDs) assigned to major operational commands throughout theater. In addition, the operations center was responsible for control and coordination of the group with Special Operations Command Central (SOCCENT), headed by Col. Jesse Johnson. "Colonel Kraus was the primary and most influential SF commander in Saudi Arabia," says one of his battalion commanders. "Without his foresight and his ability to properly use the 5th Group's assets, we would have seen far less success in the field and, in fact, could have been misused."

One of the first missions assigned the 5th went to its 1st Battalion. The defense of Saudi Arabia was of exceptional importance, and SOF units were some of the first to arrive in country. According to senior SF officers who served in the Gulf, the Saudis had adopted a "no aggression" stance with Iraq, pulling back all of its military units some twenty miles from the Saudi-Kuwaiti frontier. "No one at Central Command (CENTCOM) was truly aware of how vulnerable Saudi Arabia was to an invasion by the Iraqis until our initial reconnaissance teams began driving up along the frontier," one officer remembers. What these teams found were small groups of border guards manning outposts overlooking the occupied sands of Kuwait. They also found outposts that had been occupied by small Iraqi patrols. "Saudi Arabia was totally unprotected, and U.S. forces were completely without a warning system. The Saudis believed that, if they abandoned the frontier, the Iraqi government would interpret their absence as an acceptance of the invasion of Kuwait. They couldn't have cared less about the country [Kuwait] being occupied. Why the Iraqis didn't roll across the border and continue their drive into Saudi Arabia in those early days, we'll probably never know."

Reported by the 5th's motorized reconnaissance elements, the situation was corrected when a Saudi prince who'd attended the Special Forces officers' course at Fort Bragg met with Saudi King Fahd. The prince's grasp of what needed to be done was supported by Colonel Kraus's staff, and in the end, the 5th was permitted to deploy early warning teams along the frontier in order to provide static and mobile reconnaissance of the frontier.

What would have happened if the Iraqis had come across in

the first phase of DESERT STORM? "The border surveillance guys would have been gone, period," said one Gulf War veteran. "The 82d Airborne would have been mere 'speed bumps' for the Iraqi armor, and that would have been it."

The 1st Battalion's teams took part in the border surveillance missions, which was DESERT SHIELD's only combined forces operation, which continued until the end of the war. With its FOB at King Fahd International Airport, the 1st deployed three advanced operational bases. These were AOBs 510, 520, and 530. Operational detachments (ODAs) began training their counterparts in a wide variety of subjects, logging over four thousand hours of instructional time during DESERT SHIELD alone. With the AOBs working at brigade level, the ODAs were assigned battalions for which they were responsible. These units included forces from Saudi Arabia, Kuwait, United Arab Emirates, Qater, Oman, and Bahrain. Special Forces advisers assisted and advised at every level, often becoming responsible for providing forward air control (FAC) and close air support (CAS) to their Coalition counterparts.

With the onset of DESERT STORM, the 1st Battalion deployed several special reconnaissance teams (ODAs 525 and 532, for example) deep inside Iraq to support the intelligence needs of the XVIII Airborne Corps. Attached to Joint Forces Command East (JFCE), the battalion also fought alongside its counterparts all the way to Kuwait City. In all, 1st Battalion could claim entering combat with twenty-one Coalition battalions, preventing any exchanges of friendly fire between the JFCE and the Marines, which were located on their left flank.

Second Battalion found itself at King Khalid Military City. For three months, they were among the most isolated forward-deployed U.S. military elements in theater. The battalion was located along the Saudi/Kuwaiti/Iraqi tri-border area, a wasteland of sand dunes and roving Arab nomads. One SF trooper recalls being visited early on by Col. Jesse Johnson, the SOCCENT commander. "When the colonel arrived, we asked him where the front was in conjunction with our position at KKMC. He kinda smiled, then told us we were at the front, that Iraqi forces were less than an hour away by road!" Lt. Col. Bill Davis, 2d Battalion's commander, said that from then on his troops trained in contingency plans "that bore a resemblance to Custer's last stand."

Davis organized his battalion into four AOBs in order to meet Coalition warfare requirements. His men would ride alongside one of the first Egyptian divisions to breach enemy obstacle belts during DESERT STORM. Second Battalion teams would attack Al-Jahra City, supporting the reserve Syrian division during the combined Saudi-Kuwaiti attack on Kuwait City. "The Syrians only became active players in DESERT STORM once it became clear the Iraqis were putting up little to no resistance," Davis said. "They were not inclined to accept our advisers until it became obvious they wouldn't receive air support unless my people called it in. Up until the final minutes of the berms' being breached, the Syrians were contemplating what their involvement would be. They finally joined the effort, taking part in the victory by simply tagging along." All total, the 2d Battalion could claim responsibility for directly coordinating the combat actions of three and a half divisions and aiding in the capture of over 8,700 POWs. Supporting combat search-and-rescue operations (CSAR), a 2d Battalion security team was successful in locating and rescuing one American F-16 pilot shot down behind enemy lines. "In my opinion, our greatest accomplishment may have been the passage-of-lines operation, conducted in the dead of night, which saw the 1st Cavalry Division (Armor) relieve the Syrian armored division," Davis said. ODAs 543 and 544 ensured the successful transition between the two forces, with no casualties incurred despite the Syrians' use of Soviet armor, which would have made it easy to mistake them for Iraqi forces. "It was very nerve-racking," one operator remembers. "Our guys were being moved up to assume a frontline position against a possible Iraqi threat, and the Syrians were all operating Soviet tanks and personnel carriers—just like the Iraqis were using. If anyone had misread a signal, or gotten the wrong word, it could have been a disaster. Luckily for everyone, we pulled it off despite some fairly interesting problems along the way."

While Company A of the 2d Battalion was performing search-and-rescue missions and close-air-support training, Company B teams worked along the border as surveillance units and trained the Egyptian infantry division located northwest of Hafir Al-Batin. As DESERT STORM loomed closer, four detachments were tasked to become forward-air-control (FAC) teams, providing terminal guidance for close air support during the assault to liberate Kuwait. On February 24, the Egyptians joined the attack against an estimated five Iraqi divisions. The division's primary goal was the Al-Abraq army barracks, which was to be captured by February 28. Along with its Special Forces advisers, the Egyptian division succeeded in capturing the barracks on the February 26, two full days earlier than demanded by Schwarzkopf. Leaping toward the Ali As-Salem airfield on the outskirts of Kuwait City, the Egyptians and their attached SF teams secured the airfield, their final goal of the campaign. Company C teams conducted desert mobility operations, also working alongside the Syrian regiment during close-air-support operations. At the onset of the ground war, the company's teams were relocated with the Egyptian armor division, for which they provided both close-air-support and "ground-truth" services.

Third Battalion's deployment was as surprising to its troops as it must have been to the group commander. The newest battalion to be brought on-line, the 3d lacked team equipment and its complete inventory of weaponry. Many of its enlisted and commissioned personnel were newly arrived from the training grounds of Fort Bragg, some having appeared just forty-eight hours prior to the 5th's being ordered to begin loading for Saudi Arabia. "The rumor was, we were getting 1st Battalion's mission because they'd had problems with their Saudi counterparts," one senior NCO commented. "In the end, we pulled a few special reconnaissance missions, retrained the Kuwaiti army, worked alongside the Saudi Brigades, and trained with the French Foreign Legion." At the onset of the ground war, the 3d Battalion's teams were farmed out to Coalition ground units moving into Kuwait and Iraq. These teams would fight their way into Kuwait City alongside the Kuwaiti army, staying with the liberation forces until ordered to pull out well after the end of the war.

"We never stopped training," one NCO said. "If you weren't on a mission, then you were training for the next one. It made us better soldiers, and I think it helped us to survive." Indeed, Colonel Kraus demanded that his teams adhere to strict training programs, which revolved around their assigned missions. Because of their military backgrounds, the advisers' innovative approaches to training overcame obstacles, which seemed to arise as quickly as the desert's sand storms. Classes in chemical weapons, desert survival, antitank warfare, close air support, combat search and rescue, small-unit tactics, weapons, land navigation, and Arab-American relations continued until the ground war began. "I can't begin to say how proud I am of not only my men, but the entire 5th Group," Lieutenant Colonel Davis said. "Our teams were scattered all over the desert, conducting a multitude of mission taskings, working with nearly every Coalition nation in Saudi Arabia. Despite incredible challenges and frustrations—and there were more than a few—they accomplished the mission exactly as it was laid out."

Indeed, the 5th's already impressive array of combat decorations would see an additional two Silver Stars, two Distinguished Flying Crosses, two Soldier's Medals, and seventy Bronze Stars with valor devices. Sadly, the Group would see Sgt. Leonard A. Russ listed as KIA, the 5th's only casualty during the war.

There was an additional facet of the war that attributed to the 5th's success, that of the support seen back home in the United States. "We were overpowered by everything we heard about support of the troops," recalls one adviser decorated for valor. "Letters, packages, gifts—you name it, and we saw it arrive. I don't think anyone can measure how much that kind of thing means to the individual soldier, not to mention to the unit as a whole. It made a major difference in how we went about our jobs because you knew the entire country was behind you, counting on you, and supporting you. I'd like to say 'thanks' to everyone who said even a prayer . . ."

Teams from the 5th began redeploying to Fort Campbell in March 1991. Because its presence was necessary during the cleanup of Kuwait City once the war was over, Company B, 3d Battalion, was one of the last elements to come home. The group's accomplishments were many, and impressive. Its teams trained thousands of Coalition soldiers, spending many hours in the field with them under the most austere of conditions. Gen. Norman Schwarzkopf would say, "Special Forces were the eyes and ears on the ground." Not only was the CENTCOM commander speaking of the highly dangerous missions conducted in occupied Kuwait and fortified Iraq, he was also referring to the ground-truth teams, a concept developed and executed by Colonel Kraus. "Ground truth was simply being able to accurately and quickly tell the commander exactly where his units were and what they were doing," one SF officer explained. "Colonel Kraus saw to it that every American and Coalition battalion had SF personnel attached as ground-truth assets. General Schwarzkopf's staff could pinpoint exactly what was going on with his forces simply by making a call. It was a brilliant manner of utilizing Special Forces on the air-land battlefield, and the first time such a concept was implemented with the assistance of Special Forces."

Today the 5th is once again hard at work training, its teams deploying on mobile training missions in the new awareness that they have been battle-tested and found not wanting. "There was a lot of hard feelings about the [changes to the] old beret flash, because there was so much history behind it and so many guys died wearing it," said one soon-to-retire sergeant major. "But perhaps the group's performance in the Gulf overshadows all of that. It's a new Special Forces today, with new goals and new objectives. It doesn't matter which flash we wear, only that we wear it proudly and in the knowledge that we're the best there is."

CHAPTER TWENTY

Early on we briefed the Kuwaiti soldiers on the Geneva Convention and the treatment they would be expected to give POWs once Kuwait was retaken. They told us not to worry about prisoners . . . because there wouldn't be any. They wanted to waste everybody. In the end we got through to maybe 95 percent of them. But it was that remaining 5 percent that caused most of the problems.

Lieutenant Colonel BROWNLEE, Operations
5th Special Forces Group

On August 2, 1990, a Kuwaiti balloon-borne radar system detected large numbers of vehicles approaching the Iraq-Kuwait border from the north. Although it was not learned until later, the vehicles represented three Republican Guard divisions assigned objectives inside oil-rich Kuwait. Fleeing the country minutes ahead of an Iraqi heliborne assault on his palace, Sheik Jabar al-Ahmad al-Sabah managed to avoid capture. His armed forces put up stiff resistance for the next ninety-six hours, retreating into Saudi Arabia only when their fuel and ammunition ran out. A small band of Kuwaiti soldiers elected to stay behind, forming the country's armed resistance movement. The Kuwaiti army had just two armored and a mechanized infantry brigade prior to the invasion, and the 25th and the 15th Brigades left most of their equipment behind as the Iraqis mopped up. The 35th Armored Brigade did somewhat better, both in terms of inflicting casualties on the Iraqis and in slipping into Saudi Arabia with many of its tanks and weapons systems. Nevertheless, the Kuwaiti army had been destroyed as an effective fighting force, and many of its senior officers had fled to Saudi Arabia, Egypt, Europe, and the United States.

Activated on September 21, 1961, the 5th Special Forces Group was responsible for the bulk of all Special Forces missions conducted in the Republic of Vietnam. On June 16, 1988, the group relocated from its home at Fort Bragg, North Carolina, to Fort Campbell, Kentucky. At the time of the invasion of Kuwait, the 5th had two battalions on line, with a third barely stood up. "We were alerted on either the second or the third of August," recalls a Special Forces team leader, "to be prepared to deploy to Saudi Arabia. The 3d Battalion was brand-new, we didn't have much of our authorized equipment, including our personal weapons. Many of us, including myself, had just reported in to the 5th for duty. As the situation became more serious, we began believing we'd actually be deployed despite our organizational shortcomings."

By September 24, the 5th was fully operational. The 3d Battalion had seen a flood of needed equipment arrive, including their M-16s, 203s (grenade launchers), and side arms. The deployment had not been without its drawbacks. A lack of sufficient aircraft, along with shifting priorities for troop deployment, resulted in many false starts. "We'd say good-bye to the families, leave for the planes, then return home when the movement would be canceled," one operator remembers. "It created a lot of tension. Very hard on the married guys, especially." Adding to the stress of on-again, off-again flight schedules was the lack of hard intelligence concerning the 3d's mission. Told that the 1st Battalion would be training coalition forces in foreign internal defense (FID), the 3d believed they would receive direct-action missions to be carried out against Iraqi command-and-control sites. It wasn't until they arrived at King Khalid Military City (KKMC) that the 3d's command structure would discover what they would be tasked to accomplish during DESERT SHIELD.

"The 1st Battalion originally began foreign-internal-defense training, but we heard they came on too strong and pissed off the Saudis. That's how we inherited their mission," laughs an SF NCO. Stunned by the 120-degree heat and not sure of where they'd been landed, the first teams to arrive in Saudi Arabia were to hole up at King Khalid Military City. They spent two days in an aircraft hangar while arrangements were made for them to move into the city. "It was like a college campus," said one interviewed trooper. "We had to set up for the rest of the battalion, which meant each team got one room for personnel and equipment. We were told by Colonel Johnson [the SOCCENT commander] that we were 'at the front,' that Iraqi forces were less than an hour away if they came over the border." KKMC became home to the 2d and 3d Battalions' forward operational bases (FOBs), as well as to the 3/160th Special Operations Aviation Regiment (SOAR) and parts of the 528th Special Operations Support Battalion.

In the meantime, the fate of a reconstituted Kuwaiti military force had to be decided. With portions of its decimated army in Egypt and Saudi Arabia, it appeared the Kuwaitis would be left to wait out the war while Coalition forces reconquered their country. "They had a camp across from us at KKMC," remembers one Green Beret. "All sorts of [Kuwaitis] were showing up—police officers, air force personnel, even Kuwaitis from America arrived. Probably 50 percent of those we trained were civilians with no military background. They all wanted to do something to get their country back." But with no organization or equipment, there was little that could be done except to wait. Finally, Maj. Mark Phelan, the commanding officer for B Company, 5th Special Forces, came up with a plan.

"It is Major Phelan who deserves the credit for rebuilding the Kuwaiti army," said one of his team leaders. "He saw the potential sitting there in the desert. Mark realized it was the classic unconventional warfare mission [UW], only with a conventional twist. He wrote the program, staffed it, presented it to Colonel Johnson at SOCCENT, and sold it as a Bravo Company tasking." Originally directed to train a Kuwaiti commando battalion, the mission was later altered to completely reorganize, equip, and train several mechanized infantry brigades. A newly formed A-team found itself tasked to create a program of instruction meant to turn out a combat-ready force in time for the coming ground war.

From the beginning, SF advisers were faced with challenges they'd only heard about while attending the qualification course at Fort Bragg. "The Kuwaiti officers were very arrogant," says one of this team. "There was no NCO corps; the officers [were] responsible for everything. In addition, the Kuwaiti army didn't have an effective personnel accountability system. If a soldier didn't show up for morning formation, it wasn't a big deal as to where he might be, or what he might be doing." As training began, it became apparent that the Kuwaiti officer corps would become dependent upon their advisers for direction. Used to a military life of simply giving orders and having someone else carry them out, the command structure was frozen when faced with having to act on its own. "They were lost without us, for a variety of reasons," offers one senior NCO. "Their military culture and philosophy is totally different from ours, and a number of the officers at KKMC were 'young turks' in the Kuwaiti armed forces. They were committed to freeing Kuwait, but they were ill equipped to do so on their own."

As training began at KKMC, obtaining equipment became a priority. Phelan's teams were given almost total autonomy over their program since higher headquarters saw a Kuwaiti military force as a political consideration rather than as a factor on the impending battlefield. SF team leaders turned to their teams, drawing on the years of conventional military skills possessed by the Special Forces soldiers. Seventy-five percent of those assigned to Phelan's command had just earned their berets; only a few of the experienced advisers had actual foreign-internal-defense (FID) experience. "It was classic SF doctrine," explains one senior NCO serving as a team sergeant. "All of today's operators are second-term soldiers, meaning they've served at least one enlistment in the conventional army. You might not have known a guy was qualified in antiaircraft defense until the class came up and he volunteered to teach it." This NCO, himself a former Ranger and mountaineering instructor, went on. "Nearly everyone has a basic infantry background, and that's what saved the day for us. Good, solid SF skills and a high level of conventional skills brought to the teams by the new guys."

Broken down into committees, the advisers prepared their classes, scouted and built ranges, and scrounged equipment wherever they could find it. "We blamed everyone for the lack of gear," recounts one trainer. "But we later found out it was the emir who intentionally held back everything we needed to get his army outfitted." As he feared the revolutionary potential of the Kuwaiti resistance, the emir also feared that a well-equipped and trained army might overthrow him once the capital had been reoccupied, and he refused to sign the necessary paperwork to release to his stranded brigades thousands of tons of equipment waiting on the docks of America and Saudi Arabia. "Once he [the emir] was back in Kuwait City, the paperwork was signed and stuff started rolling in like you wouldn't believe," says a senior SF officer. "But by then, senior officers loyal to the al-Sabah family were back in country and were retaking control of the military to avoid any chance of a coup."

To fight the war, the Kuwaiti brigades were forced to rely on M-84 tanks, Soviet BMP "infantry fighting vehicles," Chevy pickup trucks armed with .50-caliber machine guns, what small arms and munitions could be arranged for—and guts. One trainer remembers the only "uniform" provided the infantry were British chemical suits, one per man. Within days, many of those were worn out and exchanged for whatever other clothing might be available. "Had the Iraqis used chemical weapons during the first hours of the ground war, the Kuwaitis would have been slaughtered," says a 5th Group adviser.

Phelan's men were broken down so that two SF NCOs were assigned per Kuwaiti company. From then on, the Green Berets ran the show, seldom interfered with as they slowly developed their charges' small-unit skills as a mechanized infantry force. Moved thirty kilometers into the desert the day after Christmas, the Kuwaitis could no longer utilize the single mock city for training in urban warfare. The need for the move was questioned by SF trainers, who knew their counterparts might be expected to fight block-for-block inside Kuwait City. "The Kuwaitis were the bastard children of the Arab Coalition," one adviser points out. "The Saudis had no use for them and had to be fought with time and again to obtain the hard intelligence the Kuwaitis could use. It became very frustrating to us because they [the Kuwaitis] were so intent on being a part of the overall effort to win the war."

On February 24, 1991, the ground war began, and Special Forces trainers became advisers. They'd been working feverishly, briefing their Kuwaiti field commanders and coordinating air support for the actual breaching of the berm. In addition to call signs, radio frequencies, and order-of-movement briefings, SOF forces were also told to cut their hair, trim their mustaches, and to remove any and all personal flags or symbols from Kuwaiti armored vehicles. Moving only three hundred meters on the first day of the campaign, the brigades "belonging" to B Company were sandwiched between the Saudis and Syrians, everyone trying to get positioned for the assault through the berm separating Saudi Arabia from occupied Kuwait. Hundreds of vehicles were stretched out in long columns, the desert littered with units attempting to take their position in the order decreed by the berm-breaching plan.

"When we finally got through [the berm], the Arabs became euphoric," recalls one adviser. "They were shooting their weapons into the air and acting as if we'd already recaptured Kuwait City. Our vehicles were bumper-to-bumper in the lane, minefields on either side of the column. Tactically, it was very unsound. The Saudis were firing rockets over the berm; some of them were reported to be hitting their own people." Ten kilometers inside of Kuwait, the column ground to a halt. Up front, the brigade commander was posing for pictures with two of his battalion commanders alongside an abandoned Iraqi mortar. A terse SF captain issued some strongly worded "advice" to the Kuwaiti officer, noting that his antics were stalling the brigade's advance toward the capital. Souvenir hunting would have to wait. The celebration gunfire was becoming so prevalent, SOF officers threatened to pull their teams away from the Kuwaitis if it wasn't brought under control. All around the stalled convoy were unlit fire trenches, heavily fortified bunker systems, minefields, and scores of booby traps. Made nervous by the Saudi's rocket mishaps, the "green hats" wanted to get moving. In addition, the advisers worried about the Iraqis counterattacking.

Due to the Arab Coalition's slow first day, the Kuwaitis were forced by CENTCOM to make a night movement. Not having been allowed to rehearse such actions during DESERT SHIELD, U.S. advisers took control of the column and executed a near-perfect march across the desert, arriving at their objective by 0600 the next morning. "The Kuwaitis were afraid of the dark, so we couldn't train at night," pointed out one SOF operator. "During the movement, the Kuwaitis stopped to pray several times, which caused a real commotion as we were trying to make linkup at the appointed hour." At CENTCOM, General Schwarzkopf was angry. The American units were too far forward of their Arab counterparts and were offering their badly exposed flanks to possible Iraqi attack. The combined Arab force had yet to reach its first objective, a military barracks located at a major road intersection. Schwarzkopf ordered his SOF advisers to "get the lead out."

The Arab force pulled up short of the barracks by nearly fifteen hundred meters. This would be their first trial under fire since Saudi and Omani forces had retaken Khafji early in the conflict. Green Berets had fought alongside their Arab counterparts during that encounter, directing the battle from inside Coalition armored vehicles and calling close air support onto Iraqi positions inside the town. It is not widely known that the Iraqis mounted a parallel attack, through the Wafrah oilfields, while moving against Khafji. "Saddam knew he'd lose a division, but his intent was to bloody the nose of the Arab Coalition. He didn't believe they'd fight, and wanted to show the Allies they couldn't count on the Saudis in particular," said one operator. But the Iraqis at Wafrah were spotted by SOF border watchers, who began calling in air strikes and gunship support. It was there that an air force AC-130 was shot down and all fourteen crew members killed. In all, Special Forces teams directly aided in the destruction of nearly half an Iraqi division. "The story never made the news because the Iraqis didn't get across the border," offers one SOF officer. "They were stopped cold at the oilfields, the push into Khafji blunted by the Arab forces and their SOF advisers." MARCENT, whose Marines had ignored the early warnings about Iraqi troop movement toward their positions at the border town, would later apologize to both CENTCOM and SOCCENT for failing to heed red flags raised by the Special Forces. As a result of their error, the Marines had been pushed out of Khafji, which was then retaken by the Arabs.

After a short period of time, the Iraqi commander of the Kuwaiti barracks offered to surrender. But he felt obligated to fire some shots to preserve his men's honor. So, taking an armed Humm-V to within five hundred meters of the facility, an SF major ordered rounds from the vehicle's Mk-19 automatic grenade launcher to be fired at the barracks. Machine-gun fire from vehicle-mounted .50-caliber machine guns soon followed. The Iraqis then fired a mortar, offering some return machine-gun fire as well. One Green Beret was struck in his flak vest by shrapnel. He was able to pluck it free with his fingers. Finally the white flag was raised. Moving forward, Major Shaw from the 5th Special Forces Group accepted the Iraqi commander's surrender. In all, the major and his Humm-V crew are credited with the capture of over five hundred Iraqi POWs.

"The Egyptians and Kuwaitis went crazy," remembers Lieutenant Colonel Brownlee. "All they wanted to do was celebrate. But CENTCOM wanted them at their second objective before nightfall, and they were dragged back into the war by Colonel Kraus." Having "won" a victory with no losses, the Arabs weren't excited about pressing their luck. Moving onward, JFC-North reached the airbase at Ali As-Salem, but they encountered no resistance. By then, Kuwait City was nearly surrounded. The Marines had sealed off the 6th Ring Road, and the VII and XVIII Corps were making a sweep to cut off Iraqi forces trying to escape back into Iraq.

Reaching a second Kuwaiti military barracks, SOF advisers were informed they would be detached from the brigades because General Schwarzkopf had ordered that "no Americans would go past the 6th Ring Road outside of Kuwait City." The order was not well received by the advisers or the Kuwaiti officers.

"It was not a popular decision, and it reminded many of us of the Bay of Pigs, Vietnam, and other places where we earned our allies' trust and then abandoned them to fight on their own," points out one SF officer. "We were pulled away from the Kuwaitis a total of four times during the ground war. After each time, they'd link us back up once the decision was reversed. The Kuwaitis finally refused to go any farther unless we were alongside them. Perhaps that's what turned the trick." Perhaps, but another factor was intelligence. U.S. and Coalition forces had captured every objective but Kuwait City. Central Command (Schwarzkopf) needed hard information on what was going on inside the capital's city limits, intelligence which could only be provided by American eyes and ears. It was then that the Kuwaiti resistance, having served its purpose, begun to be excommunicated from the occupation effort. The advisers were ordered to proceed with their Kuwaiti companies. All other Arab forces were held in place as the liberation of the capital began in earnest.

Entering the city, the Kuwaitis began firing their weapons in celebration. This caused major problems as sporadic Iraqi resistance attempted to engage Kuwaiti patrols and convoys. Each Kuwaiti company was given a sector of the city to clear, some of them containing over 250,000 inhabitants. "It became very difficult to tell what fire was friendly and what was hostile," says one senior captain. "My team received permission to link back up with our battalion, the 10th. When we reached their position, we found them clearing buildings, collecting weapons and ammunition, and questioning prisoners." One of this officer's team found a huge stockpile of ammunition stored in a school building, the markings on the boxes showing that the munitions came from Jordan.

Once in the city, SF advisers began directing the clearing operation. Although wildly enthusiastic, the Kuwaitis' training was still rudimentary, and their supplies were limited. Many SF advisers were of the opinion that had the Iraqis put up stiff resistance, the Kuwaiti forces would have been wiped out. One veteran operator said, "Their officers would not move without us and were not adept at urban street fighting. They had limited supplies and no support they could call on effectively. Half the time they were celebrating, the other half seeking revenge against Iraqi troops and collaborators. If we hadn't been there during the early stages of retaking the city, who knows what might have happened?"

Working alongside the Kuwaiti troops, SOF advisers began providing their higher command elements with intelligence about Kuwait City and the Iraqi occupation. They soon found themselves intervening in vengeance acts taken by the army against Iraqi and suspected civilian supporters of Saddam Hussein. At one point, a Kuwaiti brigade commander was convinced to remove his pistol's barrel from the mouth of a POW. "We tried to stop as many beatings and shootings as possible," recalls a Special Forces NCO. "Sometimes you'd stand right next to the soldier or officer, telling him you'd have to take your people and leave if they didn't knock it off. Most of the time that would work; sometimes, we simply had to leave." Says an officer about the same situation, "They [the Kuwaitis] had pretty good intelligence as to who was a collaborator and who wasn't. It's pretty hard to apply our standards to their culture, especially when you hear that the offender is responsible for an atrocity or murder or rape of one of your counterpart's family members. Many of our counterparts went back to their homes and found the Iraqis had given the dwellings to collaborators, who were still living in them."

"We pretty much lost control of the situation once the city was secured," points out another adviser. "The Kuwaiti army became the Kuwaiti martial law police once they were back on their home turf. The city was divided into sectors, and the Kuwaiti army began administering these sectors, we were politely pushed to the side. That's when our higher-higher wisely pulled us out." In truth, the 5th Group's advisers told CENTCOM that they were no longer able to control their counterparts. Hammered by the international press for their inability to stop beatings of "innocent" civilians, the Green Berets knew they needed to be pulled out. "The media didn't want to understand that the occupation was not a U.S. operation," explains one senior SF NCO. "As advisers, we could only offer advice and could intervene only to a certain extent. First they [the media] would be critical of us for doing too much, then they would blast us for doing too little. We couldn't win in that kind of environment."

No longer directly involved in army operations, SOF personnel from the 5th began searching for ammunition dumps and weapons caches. Before leaving the city, Saddam's forces had trained and armed many non-Kuwaiti collaborators, depositing thousands of rounds and hundreds of crates of weapons all over the city. Intelligence reports gathered from captured Iraqis pointed to an attempt by Hussein to turn Kuwait City into another Beirut. In addition to weapons searches, 5th Group medics visited local hospitals to provide what medical support they could. SF engineers marked unexploded bombs and mines, while their comrades reconned the city. One such team of advisers discovered a pile of priceless gems and gold jewelry in an apartment vacated by Iraqi troops. "There must have been hundreds of thousands of dollars laying on the floor," remembers one of the operators. "But we left it where we found it. We weren't there to loot or benefit from the Kuwaitis' misfortunes."

The 5th would be asked to remain in Kuwait City for an additional three weeks after the war's end. B Company, 3/5th, would redeploy from King Khalid Military City after Christmas, its job with the Kuwaiti army finished. Overall, the 3d Battalion's teams completed foreign internal defense training missions with the Saudis and Kuwaitis, Companies A and C assisting in explosive ordnance disposal, PSYOP/civil affairs activities, and urban security measures in Kuwait City. "Despite the frustrations, the setbacks, the obstacles, and the challenges, they did a damn fine job where the Kuwaiti army was concerned," offers a 5th Group officer. "That the Kuwaitis were able to field a liberation force is directly due to the involvement of Major Phelan's teams. It was a classic SF mission, and it proved our worth as a credible element within the conventional commander's overall war plan."

But SOF forces had accomplished much more than that. They were directly responsible for pushing the Arab Coalition into Kuwait, often leading the combined forces in person until their objectives were reached. Without both the two joint-force commands, the ground war would have been a strictly Allied effort, with American and NATO troops taking all the risks. It was an impressive showing on the conventional battlefield.

CHAPTER
TWENTY-ONE

The Scout must learn to crawl noiselessly, slowly, and interminably. He must be infallible in his orientation at all times. He must be as ingenious in the use of cover as a Comanche Indian. He must have the ruthlessness of a knife-killer, the persistence of a fanatic, the endurance of a martyr, and above all, the patience of a saint.

Lt. Col. JAMES W. BELLAH
The Infantry Journal, 1943

What is special reconnaissance (SR)? Today, these operations cover a broad scope of actions and activities, including surveillance, reconnaissance, target acquisition, and bomb-damage assessment. SR provides combat information to tactical field commanders, and SR patrols are the battlefield's primary source of human intelligence. By providing accurate and timely intelligence about the enemy, the weather, and the terrain to be fought on, SR becomes an integral facet of battle.

In the Gulf, General Schwarzkopf and his staff were seeking to set the terms of the battle by their actions. CENTCOM had to think and act faster than the Iraqi military, then coordinate its resources and forces to defeat Hussein in combat. The huge distances involved demanded accurate and timely intelligence in order to accomplish this coordination. The information necessary had to be specified, then collected and processed, with the final stage having to do with getting the finished product to the right people in time so they could use it.

DESERT SHIELD/DESERT STORM demonstrated the extraordinary advances technology has made in terms of intelligence gathering. CENTCOM was able to rely upon its technology far more than any other combat command in the history of warfare.

Even so, weather and terrain often interfered with collection activities at the most inopportune times. In addition, sophisticated equipment demands careful attention to keep functioning, and there, too, problems arose that hindered the gathering of good intelligence.

SR personnel are organized, trained, and equipped to enter enemy areas and to observe and report on enemy dispositions, movements, and activities. They also record the battlefield's condition. Missions, targets, and objectives are based upon intelligence requirements of the tactical field commander. For a number of reasons, special reconnaissance teams avoid contact with the enemy and civilians. Primarily this is because the purpose of a reconnaissance team is to get into an area and out again without anyone knowing it's been there. SR teams rely on both attended and unattended sensors and other special-purpose listening and viewing equipment to perform their missions. Such teams can perform either static or mobile reconnaissance, depending upon mission requirements and available equipment.

SR operators must be experts in both attended and unattended infiltration and exfiltration methods. They must possess strong survival instincts and excellent fieldcraft. In addition, reconnaissance troops must be experts in a wide variety of communications systems and information-gathering skills. They must train constantly on the enemy's tactics, organization, and equipment.

Such teams operate within the area of interest of their commander. Specific areas are assigned for each SR mission. These areas can be free-fire zones or restricted-fire areas, so the team must be prepared to react properly to its tactical environment. SpecRecon teams may be tasked to provide linkup between advancing and/or friendly forces.

Historically, the successful execution of SR has demanded that such teams have self-supporting operations areas. This held true in the Gulf, where specific command elements ensured SR personnel were provided with a communications staff, predeployment isolation area, and security. Combat-support aviation was provided by the 160th SOAR and the air force's 1st Special Operations Wing, whose personnel were well qualified to fly SpecRecon operations. The selection of team and individual equipment was generally guided by standard operating procedures, service regulations, operational needs, and the environment.

Unlike division reconnaissance companies, which generally conduct their operations within the range of field artillery, SR teams can at best rely upon fixed-wing aircraft support, which may or may not have all-weather strike capabilities. Such aerial support is dependent upon the battlefield conditions presented the team. For example, an AC-130 gunship offers a variety of superb fire support but cannot be deployed over a team's area of operations (AO) if the enemy has anything other than minimal or degraded antiaircraft defense systems available. Helicopter support can consist of antitank guided missiles, 2.75-inch rockets, 20mm cannon, and 40mm grenade launchers. Such support is accurate and responsive and is restricted only by the equipment available and experience of the crews flying it. Armed helicopter escorts were often used during the Gulf War, SR teams being infiltrated and exfiltrated by MH-60 Blackhawks armed with six-barrel miniguns capable of inflicting extensive damage. In some cases, such as missions conducted by the SEALs, naval gunfire can play an important part in the protection of an SR team's defense.

The employment of SpecRecon assets is greatly affected by adverse weather and terrain conditions. Gulf operations were made difficult by the lack of water, scarcity of vegetation, extensive sand areas that hampered movement, extreme temperatures, and brilliant sunlight. Movement was restricted to the hours of darkness unless a team was compromised, with observation carried out day and night. On the positive side, SR teams normally experienced excellent radio communications in the desert and had superb field of observation. The introduction and heavy use of global positioning systems made land navigation accurate and easy as the teams were able to pinpoint their locations anywhere in the theater of operations to within ten meters.

The conduct of battlefield reconnaissance revolves around standard infantry patrolling tactics and techniques. Because their missions are always beyond conventional fire support and sustainment, a deep knowledge of and ability to conduct such patrolling is required of SR personnel. The canny use of stealth is one trait of the successful SpecRecon operator. Deception is another. It is common practice for SpecRecon teams to dress in uniforms and/or clothing that is not U.S. issue, and to carry and operate sterilized—nontraceable—equipment. In most cases, battlefield reconnaissance includes surveillance, which may be of a facility, roadway, or troop concentration.

Another aspect of SpecRecon has to do with the clandestine collection of intelligence. In this area, SOF operators will often work alongside intelligence agency personnel, using equipment and techniques unique to the U.S. intelligence community. This was often the case during the Gulf War where black SOF operations were conducted in support of national and theater commands. When the ground war began, a small number of SF teams were inserted into Iraq to monitor road traffic along that country's main highway leading into Kuwait. In those cases, CENTCOM and the commander in chief wanted immediate and continuing intelligence regardless of weather or terrain conditions that might affect other information-gathering means.

The scope of such operations was limited because of General Schwarzkopf's concern about putting U.S. personnel on the ground deep within Hussein's area of control. Using fewer teams to gather intelligence translated into better odds against their capture. So targets were carefully chosen and were assigned based upon their immediate impact upon the war's first few hours.

While single teams are able to effectively cover single targets, many SR missions conducted during DESERT STORM used multiple teams to effectively monitor Iraqi troop movements. To do this, an SR forward operating base (FOB) was established. The FOB would establish and title areas of interest, assigning SR teams according to the size of the area to be covered and the troops' estimated movement rates into (and out of) Kuwait. After being informed of their intelligence requirements, the teams would then pick surveillance sites within the assigned area of interest.

Normally, SpecRecon intelligence needs are broken down as follows:

Priority Intelligence. Those requirements for which the commander has an anticipated and stated priority in his planning and decision making

Information. Items of information regarding the enemy and his environment

Specific Information. Basic questions which need answers or confirmation of unsupported answers already given

SR teams depend upon a wide variety of communications equipment to monitor and report. During DESERT STORM, CENTCOM needed near-real-time information to support units in the field heading for Kuwait City. SpecRecon teams always planned their communications requirements around redundant radio systems, so each team carried up to three separate systems to the field. One was usually a satellite communications (SATCOM) system, which was the primary means of communication. A UHF system served as a means of voice backup (a PRC-70 or 74, depending upon which was available). The third system might be UHF or HF. It was packed as either an emergency radio or for escape and evasion. The PRC-90 was favored by individual operators who could get hold of them.

Essentially, SpecRecon missions revolve around the following taskings:

Meteorologic, geographic, or hydrographic reconnaissance to support specific land or maritime operations
Location and surveillance of POW or hostage facilities
Collection of military order-of-battle information
Target acquisition and surveillance of hostile troop concentrations, deep-strike weapons, or military targets of strategic or operational importance
Bomb damage assessments

"The most important SR mission of the war was the border-surveillance operation," stated one 5th Group officer. Not only was this the first special reconnaissance mission conducted by U.S. ground forces in Saudi Arabia during DESERT SHIELD, it was also the only joint reconnaissance mission run for the duration of the conflict. Saudi Special Forces troops worked closely with U.S. SpecWar operators to reoccupy, and in some cases retake, Saudi border stations on the Kuwait/Saudi frontier. During the hours of daylight, these small outposts would conduct static reconnaissance, using optical equipment such as binoculars and range spotting scopes. At night, mobile patrols operated between posts, covering assigned areas of responsibility. Armed with night-vision devices, including rifle scopes, the patrols searched for Iraqi reconnaissance patrols and infiltrators.

Of significance are the two critical combat employments the border surveillance participated in. Although covered previously, it is important to note that both the armed incursion at Khafji and the attempted border crossing at the Wafrah oilfields were detected, reported, and then engaged by SOF border watchers. Air strikes, naval gunfire, and a determined ground attack broke the Iraqi army's back at Khafji. At the same time, border surveillance personnel engaged numerous Iraqi probes all along the frontier with artillery fire and, sometimes, sniper fire. Those duels in the desert went largely unreported but served to keep the Iraqis off guard. Had Hussein mounted a major offensive during the early stages of DESERT SHIELD, it would have been up to the surveillance teams monitoring his most likely avenues of approach to alert CENTCOM. "It was mostly long, hot, boring work," says one operator who was on the border. "But it was a crucial mission because we were the early warning system for all our people in the rear areas."

In support of the conventional battlefield, SOF personnel responded to a request by the commander of VII Corps for special reconnaissance to be conducted on his behalf. Assigned by Schwarzkopf to take part in the coming "Hail Mary" sweep through western Iraq, the Corps's mission would demand moving its men and machines over vast tracts of desert. The condition of the proposed route was of primary concern. Would the soil allow for heavy track traffic, or would the tanks and armored personnel carriers become bogged down on their way toward the final objective? To find out, Special Forces soldiers were flown to different locations along the route. Once on the ground, the Green Berets collected soil samples, using probes and shovels, bagging and tagging each sample. Because of their efforts, a final route was selected that would hold up under the combined weight of hundreds of military vehicles on the move. "Without the route's being reconned by Special Forces well ahead of the ground war, General Schwarzkopf's daring plan may not have seen the light of day," commented one Green Beret at Fort Campbell.

Delta's special reconnaissance missions remain officially classified, although its SCUD hunting forays are common knowledge. Unique about these missions was the use of handheld laser devices, which allowed an operator to "paint" a confirmed SCUD site so it could be engaged by roving Coalition fighters. To accomplish this task, the Delta operator would prearrange his laser's frequency with the air force element assigned to support him. Once a target was located and confirmed, the operator would contact his aircraft, giving his own coordinates and those of the SCUD. Several minutes before the plane's estimated time on target, the SOF soldier would activate his laser, aiming its beam toward the enemy site. Inside the aircraft's cockpit its pilot would dial in the laser, using a sophisticated piece of equipment mounted on his instrument panel. While making his bomb or rocket run, the pilot would release his ordnance, which would then home in on the target painted by the operator. The result would be another destroyed SCUD, with no losses suffered by the clandestine spotter and his team.

Even the 5th's ground-truth efforts were considered a kind of special reconnaissance. "The goal was to keep CENTCOM informed as to what its subordinate commands were up to. In addition, Colonel Kraus ordered the information to be passed laterally as well as upward so those commanders on the right and left of each other were equally aware of the most immediate ground situation. This required observing, reporting, and doing so in a manner that was as unobtrusive as possible," offers an SOF officer.

Of the still-classified SR missions run by Special Forces, the three most important may have taken place on February 23, 1991. Ordered to infiltrate the Euphrates River valley and to take up hide sites along Highway 8, the three SR teams were responsible for providing near-real-time intelligence on military traffic moving toward Kuwait from military installations located in and around Baghdad. At least one Iraqi chemical weapons facility was located along that route, which was considered a high-speed avenue of approach by CENTCOM. Most worrisome to Schwarzkopf's staff would be the movement of reinforcements from Hussein's Republican Guard units, of which an impressive number of units had been held in reserve around the capital and in northern Iraq.

Training in special reconnaissance had been taking place since early October, after the 5th Group's deployment to Saudi Arabia. At King Fahd International Airport the group's operations center had a Special Reconnaissance Combined Headquarters, whose targeting team consisted of CWO Fritz Campbell and Sgt. Sam Brander. The center was responsible for the control and coordination of the group itself as well as further coordination with SOCCENT and the other major operational commands.

Meanwhile, Green Berets were experimenting with their tactics and techniques out in the desert. SR training was conducted around Kfia and King Khalid Military City, with hide sites the men's primary concern. Due to the barren terrain in which they would be operating, the teams would have to rely on underground observation posts dug rapidly during darkness. The problems soon became obvious. Where did they put the dirt and sand once it was excavated? What could they cover the hide with once it was near completion? What materials made for the best viewing ports? In the end, all of these problems would be solved. Empty sandbags would be carried in to build internal walls, using the sand taken from the hole. An umbrellalike frame of lightweight pipe covered with sand-colored canvas would shield the hide from the sun and prying eyes. Square portals of wood made for viewing ports that wouldn't cave in. Each team developed its own construction plan, gathering the necessary materials and training until they could erect a site within hours.

Then came the hands-on portion. Conducting mock infiltrations, the SR teams dug hide sites into the earth. By first light, they needed to be in position, ready to observe and record. Friendly conventional forces were used to conduct activities in the teams' areas, activities which included searching for the SF soldiers hidden underground. Sometimes they were found right away; other times they escaped notice and completed their mission. As DESERT STORM loomed closer, the teams became more proficient. Hole configurations were decided upon, based on trial and error. Individual tasks for hide construction were assigned to speed up the process. Construction materials were divided among team members. Food, water, ammunition, weapons, observation equipment, and redundant radio systems were selected, weighed, and readied. By February, the teams were ready for whatever General Schwarzkopf had in mind.

A small number of teams were deployed along the Tigris and Euphrates river valleys during the ground war. These were primarily static observation positions, which covered main supply routes leading from confirmed military sites in and around the Baghdad area. Team size ran from three men to as many as eight, depending upon location and mission. The larger teams normally split into smaller subunits to cover several different positions. The headquarters for SR operations was positioned at the small Saudi town of Al-Ruqi, a few short kilometers from the Saudi-Iraq-Kuwaiti border. In addition to those teams flown into Iraq, a number of SR teams operated as mobile reconnaissance teams using Humm-Vs. The mobile effort's area of operations centered around Kuwait itself. Living conditions at Al-Ruqi were spartan, the canvas tents, which served as the men's living quarters, crowded. Outdoors, the perimeter was dotted with sandbagged fighting positions, with .50-caliber machine guns and Mk-19 grenade launchers as protection against a surprise Iraqi attack. Most of the teams would actually launch from King Khalid Military City, flown into Iraq by aircrews from the 160th SOAR.

On February 23, three teams were launched. Their aircraft flew from King Khalid Military City to a refueling base at Rhafa airfield on the Saudi-Kuwaiti border. The teams were to provide near-real-time information to the units tasked with sweeping into western Iraq toward the valley. This fast-moving force consisted of the 101st Airborne Division, 82d Airborne Division, the 3d Armored Cavalry, and 24th Infantry Division. A head-on collision with Iraqi armor/infantry units was not considered to be in the best interests of the invading force, so special reconnaissance far forward was deemed imperative.

All three teams needed to be on the ground in Iraq by 2200 hours. They would be inserted more than two hundred miles behind the lines, one team less than a half-hour's drive from Baghdad. Two three-man teams would cover the northern portion of Highway 8, with a larger eight-man team responsible for the southern portion of the highway. Roughly fifty miles separated the hide sites from each other.

Onboard the MH-60s, the teams checked their equipment for the final time. They would be expected to remain on the ground for at least four days. Exfiltration could be by Blackhawk, or by linkup with elements of the VII and XVIII Corps as they assumed their forward positions in the valley. Rucksacks were heavy. Every man was carrying a double combat load of ammunition for the M-16, which translated into 420 rounds per man. In addition there were hand and smoke grenades, claymore antipersonnel mines, and extra rounds for their 9mm Beretta pistols. Some had elected to draw silenced MP-5 submachine guns rather than assault rifles. These would be used against curious animals and roving Iraqi soldiers, should either stray too close to the hide site.

Food was broken down into individual packets made up primarily of proteins and carbohydrates. An average of ten quarts of water was carried by each man. Also packed into their rucks were the hide construction materials. Radios, batteries, emergency medical equipment, including IVs and painkillers were all neatly wrapped and packed into the olive drab backpacks. Each load averaged 165 pounds. Some Green Berets would be carrying their own body weight into Iraq. "We're used to packing a heavy rucksack," explains one SF soldier. "What you're going to live off of and fight with is going in with you, so it's just a matter of being strong enough to hump a ruck."

M.Sgt. Jeff Sims and his two-man team crossed the border at 2100 hours. Sims was the team sergeant for ODA 532, Company C, 1st Battalion. It was a clear night, the Blackhawks flying ten feet off the deck at over one hundred miles per hour. Sims and his men had to be at their insertion point by 2200 hours, as did the other SR teams being sent in. From there, he would move to his final hide position, located near the Iraqi village of Qasam al-Hamash just outside of Baghdad. They'd have roughly five hours to prepare the hide. Master Sergeant Sims wanted to be under wraps prior to first light to avoid being compromised by early risers who might be out on the road.

Flying the infiltration corridor with Sims's Blackhawk was a second Night Stalker. Its three-man team would take up position just south of Sims. Fifty miles out from their infiltration points, the two helicopters split up. From there on out, the Green Berets were on their own.

Farther south, another team was preparing to leave the safety of its aircraft. Commanded by CWO Richard Balwanz, ODA 525 was one of Company B, 1st Battalion's teams. The 1st Battalion had been heavily involved with the border surveillance mission and was providing several SR teams in support of the corps's sweeping into western Iraq. Detachment 525 was a "heavy" team, its eight men to be inserted near the village of Suwayqiyh-Ghazi, located on a tributary of the Euphrates River. Their mission was to monitor traffic moving along Highway 8 from Baghdad to An-Nasiriyah.

ODA 532's men jumped off their helicopter and were greeted by the eerie and unwanted sound of dogs barking from somewhere nearby, and the team wasn't happy. Forming a tiny defensive perimeter, the team waited to see if their landing would be investigated by anyone. The Blackhawk would stand by for several minutes, ready to pull an emergency extraction should Sims call for one. He didn't. No one owning the dogs was apparently interested in their midnight howling. The team began moving toward its objective. They faced a five-hour "hump" before reaching the hide site. Once there, the team had just four hours to dig the position, camouflage it, and crawl inside.

Farther south, ODA 525 was having problems of its own. En route to its infiltration point, the team's Blackhawk was ordered to abort the mission. Its crew confirmed the abort order and swung around to head back toward the Saudi border. Refueling at Rahfa, the team was then ordered to continue its mission. Once again crossing over the border, Chief Balwanz noted he was nearly an hour behind schedule, but he knew his team could make the time up on the ground once they started moving. Of more concern was the satellite time reserved for their use. Balwanz needed the "eye in the sky" for his global positioning fix during insertion. Only so much time was allotted to anyone on the system, and ODA 525's was running out. Lining up for the final approach, the team leader winced as the pilot informed him they'd be dropped off "somewhere near" where they were supposed to be. It wasn't a great way to start the ground war.

By first light, Master Sergeant Sims and his fellow operators were in position. They'd been surprised by their surroundings, which were made up of rich farmland rather than the dry and dusty sands of King Khalid Military City. As well as a view of the highway, ODA 532 was also watching scores of Iraqi civilians making their way to work in the fields surrounding the hide site. For the next eight hours the team sweated out discovery as people passed by their position. No one had expected so much foot traffic, which either didn't notice or didn't care about the team's clandestine construction.

At roughly 1400 hours their luck went from bad to worse. A small child and her grandfather walking passed the hide suddenly stopped. The girl, curious about something she'd seen, sat. She was joined by her grandfather, and the two Iraqis stared intently at the strange "thing" just inches from their own position. Inside the hide, Sims turned to SFC Ronald Torbett and whispered a few words. As one, the men threw back the canvas top of their observation post, grabbing the girl and her grandfather and dragging the two startled civilians down into the earth with them. S.Sgt. Roy Tabron, the third member of the team, was already in contact with Lt. Col. Roger Watson at XVIII Airborne Corps. Watson was their SF liaison. Sims wanted a "hot" extract. They'd been compromised, and there was no reason to hang around any longer.

Sims attempted to calm down everyone in the overcrowded hole. The Green Berets weren't about to kill an old man and a child, and all the SR team leader wanted to do was get both the Iraqis and his men out of the ground and headed in their separate directions. By then, curious as to what was going on beneath the ground, a crowd had gathered around the hide site. They soon found out as the team whipped the canvas ceiling back, weapons at the ready. Jumping out of the hole the team moved quickly away from the assembled crowd, but there was no cover available to them. No place to run, no place to hide. While the operators sought cover, from somewhere nearby the old man had retrieved a hunting rifle, and began shooting at the Americans. By then Sims and his men had been able to move only five hundred meters from the hide site, and the SF sergeant realized they'd simply have to find another hole from which to make a stand.

Selecting a small ditch, the SR team made ready to do battle. Within thirty minutes Iraqi troops began arriving by truck along the highway. The team began sniping the enemy soldiers, knocking them down one by one. Then two busloads of soldiers arrived, increasing the odds against the team's survival. Overhead an F-16 came on station and began dropping cluster bombs on the Iraqi highway. The pilot managed to kill at least a platoon's worth of enemy soldiers. Still the Iraqis kept coming. Each Green Beret maintained his calm, selecting the next man to die and pulling the trigger once at a time. Their ammunition limited, the team knew it had to hold out until dark if the Night Stalkers were going to come in to extract them. Sims, noting one Iraqi leader on top of a building over five hundred meters away, killed the man with a single shot. Still, the Iraqis kept charging over the open field toward the team's position.

ODA 532 was rescued by *Lady Godiva*, a single MH-60 flown by CWO Randy Stephens and CWO Jim Crisafulli. It was the only daylight hot extraction carried out during DESERT STORM, with over 240 nautical miles covered by the 160th SOAR crew across enemy territory in broad daylight. Using the aircraft as a shield, Stephens was able to get Sims and his people onboard despite murderous fire raking the Blackhawk's flank. As the helicopter's security crew laid down a wall of steel to cover the SR team's rush for its open doors, Iraqi soldiers pressed forward until some were within feet of the madly firing Special Forces soldiers. Minigun fire made short work of their courageous final assault.

After landing at King Khalid Military City, the team and aircrew celebrated their safe return. By then, the Marines were in sight of Kuwait City, and the army task force sweeping into Iraq was moving forward at a brisk pace. For Sims, getting his people home safely and in one piece was the greatest reward. The army would add to that accomplishment by awarding him the Silver Star, this country's third highest award for bravery. Tabron and Torbett received Bronze Stars with V devices for their courage and daring at the battle of Qasam al-Hamash.

Chief Balwanz's mission had run into similar problems. Once on the ground, ODA 525's team leader had discovered they'd been dropped nearly fifteen hundred meters off their target. The team had humped hard to make up both distance and time, arriving at their objective with just enough time to get two hides dug in. By morning, their area of observation was also covered by civilian traffic, including a multitude of small children playing near the hide sites.

Suddenly one of the children peered through a viewing port and discovered the Green Berets inside. Shocked at what must have looked like green-faced monsters hiding in the earth, the Iraqi kids scattered, yelling at the top of their lungs. Balwanz at once ordered an extraction via the SATCOM radio and sent one of his men to inform the other hide site of the compromise. Moving away from their position, the team hunkered down and waited for the storm. But unlike Sims's situation, the Iraqi civilians appeared not to have noticed their children's warnings or to have taken them seriously. Balwanz took a chance and canceled the Blackhawks. He informed XVIII Airborne Corps that he'd continue the mission, but to stand by just in case.

Just after the lunch hour, the team was again compromised, this time by older children whose alarm would be taken seriously. Soon people began edging closer to where the team was hiding. The operators of ODA 525 knew that their time was up and began pulling farther back from the highway, knowing the Iraqi military would use it once the word was passed that intruders were in the area. Eventually several larger trucks arrived at the scene, Balwanz estimating at least one company, about 150 soldiers, was now in pursuit of his detachment. Once again a hot extraction call was sent out. But at midday with over 250 miles separating them from the Blackhawks, chances of rescue were dim.

Ordering most of their radios and all other sensitive items to be thrown into one rucksack, Balwanz ensured the team would be able to destroy the equipment before they were overrun. An explosive charge was rigged and set, its one-minute fuse lit. The team then threw their remaining rucks on top of the commo ruck, tampering the charge to ensure the most powerful blast possible when the block of C-4 blew. They would fight with what they were carrying on their combat harnesses. By then, several platoon-size elements of Iraqi soldiers were worming their way toward the Americans.

The Iraqis opened fire just as the C-4 charge exploded, destroying the team's gear. Balwanz found a bend in a canal and placed his men into position. Like Sims's team, each man made every shot count. With over half of the detachment trained as SOF snipers, the body count began rising as the Iraqis reverted to human wave assaults over the open fields separating them from the Green Berets. Despite their heavy losses the enemy kept trying to overrun the team, causing two of Balwanz's team members to wave good-bye to each other as they locked eyes from their individual fighting positions.

Suddenly a flight of four F-16s appeared. Using a PRC-90 emergency radio, SFC Robert Degroff contacted the aircraft and began directing air strikes against the advancing Iraqis. Cluster bombs were dropped on a line of trucks stopping to reinforce those Iraqis already engaged in the battle, and over fifty enemy soldiers were killed. Despite the pleas to stop from their comrades still alive, a second convoy sped past, apparently not interested in testing the skills of the pilots already lining up for another run. Closer to the team, Degroff directed fire onto a group of Iraqis hidden behind a dirt mound so close to the Green Berets that each group could have exchanged verbal greetings. Hugging the ground, the SR team was pounded by the resounding explosions as more cluster bombs tore through the packed Iraqi mass. By now the Green Berets were charged up, knowing if they could hold out until dark the 160th could get to them.

Balwanz, taking one man with him, ran down the ditch where he believed some Iraqis might have survived the cluster bomb onslaught. Turning a corner, the two soldiers came face-to-face with three armed Iraqis whom the Green Berets cut down with automatic-weapons fire. Moving forward, they checked the area where the rucksacks had been destroyed. The sight which met them was gruesome. Bits and pieces of dead Iraqi soldiers littered the killing area. Gathering up some abandoned enemy weapons and ammunition for their own use, the men returned to the main party.

Balwanz ordered small teams of soldiers to pull farther back, each escape group covering the next team's withdrawal with accurate fire. If the extraction choppers were to get to them in time, they'd need a place to land. ODA 525 was going to find one for them. By dark the Blackhawks were on station. Degroff, using his invaluable PRC-90 as a beacon, was able to guide the rescue ships in to the encircled SR team's position. No enemy fire was taken as the Iraqis had been shot, bombed, and beaten into silence. Despite the fury of the daylong firefight, not one member of Balwanz's team was wounded or killed.

Chief Richard Balwanz would also be awarded the Silver Star. Each member of his team would receive a Bronze Star with V device for his actions at An-Nasiriyah. Each pilot who flew the hot extractions for both ODAs would be awarded Distinguished Flying Crosses for their heroism. Together, ODAs 532 and 525 accounted for an estimated 250 to 300 enemy dead and wounded.

In March 1992, air force major Jay Lindell was awarded the Silver Star for his efforts in saving the lives of Balwanz's men. Major Lindell was a student at the Command and General Staff College in Fort Leavenworth, Kansas, at the time of the ceremony. Also in attendance were the members of ODA 525 who were still stationed at Fort Campbell. Col. Kenneth Bowra, commander of the 5th Group, had made special arrangements to have the men present for the medal's awarding. Bowra, who'd served with CCN in Vietnam, wanted his men to meet the man most responsible for saving their lives out in the desert. It was the first time such a ceremony had ever been conducted between Special Forces and the air force. One month later, Bowra hosted Major Lindell at Fort Campbell, where the 5th Group made the pilot an honorary Green Beret and life member of the 5th Special Forces Group.

Other special reconnaissance missions conducted in support of the ground war remain classified, but they were not as dramatic as Sims's and Balwanz's mission. "All the other teams involved got in without a fuss, dug their hides, and counted vehicles and soldiers," comments an SOF officer. Like beach reconnaissance, SR is most often tedious—and undiscovered by its subjects. Of the direct-action (DA) missions conducted by SOF forces, no details are available. Nearly all of those were black operations, having to do primarily with the destruction of

Iraqi command-and-control sites, as well as selective target interdiction.

Unlike the previous conflicts discussed, special reconnaissance in the Gulf was restricted to specific taskings, which, in nearly every case, supported the ground commander's needs. Forays into Iraq were limited and confined to surveillance missions along major highway systems. General Schwarzkopf's concern for POWs meant that each SR mission had to meet specific criteria, i.e., it had to be important to the conduct of the war. By the beginning of the ground phase, Schwarzkopf had been convinced that his special operations forces were capable, willing, and prepared to support whatever request he could make of them. That newfound respect between the man and the organization he'd been critical of in the past demonstrated Schwarzkopf's unusual ability to maintain an open mind and SOF's dedication to becoming an integral and respected force to be used as a resource by the conventional commanders.

CHAPTER
TWENTY-TWO

I shouldn't forget our [Special] Forces. We put them deep
into the enemy territory. They went out on strategic reconnaissance for us, and they let us know what was going on
out there. They were our eyes, and it's very important I not
forget those folks.

GEN. NORMAN SCHWARZKOPF
Riyadh, February 27, 1991

SOF forces met the demands made of them, delivering impressive results across the entire theater of operations. Whether
it was Coalition training, close air support, ground truth, chemical warfare training, direct action, or special reconnaissance
behind the lines, their small teams of highly motivated professionals delivered the goods. But how did special operations
make itself heard by General Schwarzkopf? The answer to this
question is one of the most impressive operations carried out
by SOF during the conflict.

"By mid-December," recalls Lieutenant Colonel Brownlee,
"CENTCOM and ARCENT had special operations right where
they wanted us. They had reliable reporting—good information
and assessments—about what was going on at the division
level and below." In short, the army's Special Forces and the
navy's SEALs had been effectively leashed by Central Command and Army Central to a set of missions which would allow SOF a war role yet keep their operations in line and under
strong conventional control. But ARCENT was having problems of its own.

Under the command of Lieutenant General Yeosock,
ARCENT was and continues to be a peacetime command,
based in Atlanta, Georgia. In case of war, the command is ac-

tivated and "plussed up," given those forces deemed necessary to participate in the conflict. Many times these units require crash training programs in order to bring them up to the level of proficiency demanded by the battlefield environment. ARCENT is essentially a skeleton command, which is augmented by other staffs in time of war.

Upon ARCENT's arrival in the Gulf, it was quickly discovered that little actual control could be exercised by the command over others in theater. These included the U.S. Third Army (XVIII and VII Corps), MARCENT, CENTAF, SOCCENT, NAVCENT, and the Joint Forces Commands. This was due to the fact that, with the exception of SOCCENT, no one command outranked the other. In every case, ARCENT's three-star was met by a three-star representing one of the above commands except for SOCCENT's commander, Jesse Johnson, who was a full colonel. "ARCENT could only nominally exercise control over the other commands," says Brownlee, "but in reality they could only render advice as to what they thought should be done."

SOCCENT was the one exception. Commanded by a colonel, SOF forces did not enjoy the influence held by its peers. To many in the special operations community, it seemed that arrangement was intentional. "It ensured we were kept under strict control by anyone and everyone involved," explains one SOF officer. "A colonel cannot compete with a table full of three-stars when final decisions are made about how his forces are to be used."

Still, ARCENT lacked a cohesive command-and-control architecture linking the five major ground commands. Running an administrative "Hail Mary" of its own, ARCENT recommended the formation of "Project Five" to the Joint Chiefs of Staff. Project Five would allow ARCENT to infiltrate the ground commands with individual eight-man command-and-control cells to be directly responsible to ARCENT's chain of command. Happily, the JCS signed off on the project, and recruiting began immediately.

As the air-land battle formula was going to be instituted, ARCENT searched out this doctrine's most talented minds that had not already been deployed to the Gulf. They would come from the Pentagon, Europe, and elsewhere, a think tank meant to devise war plans and to exercise control and coordination between the forces. Each cell would be self-contained, possessing robust and redundant communications systems. They would mirror the command-and-staff structure of a U.S. brigade, a full colonel commanding each individual cell, which in turn was made up of lieutenant colonels and majors.

Besides their hidden agenda to strengthen and support ARCENT, each cell had the ability to step in and establish a new command structure should an entire brigade's staff have been wiped out in battle. In fact, every battalion commander in theater possessed several emergency backups should he have become a casualty. This was also true for major SOF commanders, who had designated replacements waiting in the wings ready to assume control in case of sickness, injury, or death.

With Project Five in place, planning from the divisional level upward could begin. At the same time, each cell recognized it couldn't be effective unless it knew what was going on at division and below. There was no such information loop available as each command was only interested in its own "turf" and, therefore, could provide only that information which applied to itself. Each Project Five cell could write war plans and act as a link to ARCENT/CENTCOM, but unless it knew what exactly was going on below division level, no reliable tactical input could be incorporated into any plans sent forward. By then SOCCENT had been effectively cut out of the ground war, relegated to reporting to the Arab Joint Forces Command, where SOF forces were primarily concentrated. "We didn't call up General Schwarzkopf at CENTCOM and tell him what was going on," recalls Brownlee. "What we did was contact that 06 colonel at JFC in Riyadh, who in turn passed along what we had to say to both his Arab three-star and to the other project cells colocated with their commands."

It wasn't too long before Project Five determined that Special Forces could provide the missing intelligence link so necessary for the project's success. With Green Berets scattered throughout the theater and attached to every major command on the ground, their information-gathering efforts gave an accurate picture of the overall tactical situation and those assets available to carry out specific plans. Soon Project Five was feeding off the SOF structure, encouraging it to establish close ties with the cells in order to be heard at both ARCENT and CENTCOM. In return, Special Forces commanders were eager to exploit this new relationship as it allowed their input to be presented by a three-star rather than SOCCENT's bird colonel. In essence, Project Five ended up acting as the front man for

SOF, which was working quietly in the background to support the urgent needs of ARCENT/CENTCOM. "The cell colocated with JFC was our [Special Forces] link to the four-star level," says Brownlee. "Where Project Five got the credit for presenting what was going on at the tactical level, the fact was they didn't have the faintest idea until we began providing the information to them." In short, without SOF's input forwarded by ground operators who were conducting ground-truth and special reconnaissance during DESERT SHIELD/DESERT STORM, General Schwarzkopf's staff would have been hard-pressed to effectively carry out its war plans despite ARCENT's special project.

General Schwarzkopf was right about his Special Forces. They were his eyes on the ground, as well as his ears. Relying on its philosophy of remaining the "Quiet Professionals," SOF understood that it would better serve CENTCOM if it allowed others to take the credit for its efforts in support of the overall campaign. It was perhaps the most effective covert special reconnaissance mission of the war.

CHAPTER
TWENTY-THREE

They can produce results that far outweigh their numbers. You can demand anything of them ... anything you can name, and you can demand it with impunity, without any hesitation. But it takes good leaders, good training, people who know their business.

COL. ARTHUR "BULL" SIMONS

Special Forces and the operations they are asked to conduct have never fit well into the conventional military system, and they never will. This is a fact of our military history which can be traced from conflict to conflict—as is shown throughout this book. SOF warfare is tolerated only as long as it produces results deemed unobtainable by other, more conventional, means. SOF personnel will be tolerated as long as they carry out the difficult missions and are protected by congressional support for the concept of a united special operations command. Sadly, such a command can quickly be stripped of its influence and power if it does not continue to receive adequate funding and oversight.

But SOF faces its own internal challenges. The events of the past have illuminated the need for employment of only the proper force to accomplish a given mission. The spectacular success of the navy's SEALs in the Gulf War are overshadowed by their commander's singular victory in bringing all 105 operators home alive and uninjured. SEALs will no longer accept multiplatoon missions—the tragedy of Paitilla is an argument that cannot be challenged. Special Forces, learning from the navy's mistakes, has elected to ensure that its forces will not undertake missions requiring more than a twelve-man operational detachment. Anything larger becomes a Ranger mission, and correctly so. As for the Rangers, of which only Company B, 1st Battalion, 75th Rangers was deployed to the Gulf as an immediate strike force for General Schwarzkopf, they, too, have their restrictions. As superb light infantrymen, the Rangers were left out of the Gulf because their primary mission is to seize airfields. There were none in Kuwait important enough to demand this SOF unit's unique capabilities in this area. Rather than waste them as potential speed bumps for Iraqi armored forces, the Rangers were allowed a presence but not a role. In turn, the air force was content to deploy its superlative pararescue force (PJs) to augment the critical combat search-and-rescue mission, while combat-control personnel (CCT) participated in a sophisticated air-asset control mission. Finally, the war-fighting role of Delta was verified and confirmed for the first time since the unit's inception. In short, for the first time in modern American military history, a strong SOF command ensured the best use of its most specialized forces in support of the conventional commander.

Internally there are additional concerns and challenges that lie ahead.

In their zeal to conform to the conventional mind-set and to maintain a role on the modern battlefield, some SOF commanders are inclined toward creating super Rangers out of forces never meant to reflect the Ranger imprint. This is a path much traveled in times past, and its destination is always the same. Green Berets are not Rangers, as Rangers are not Green Berets. Individuals who volunteer for those exceptional units are inclined toward the philosophy and mission orientation of the unit in question. Rangers who have turned in their black berets for a tour with Special Forces have eagerly returned to the regiment, many expressing disappointment in their experience. The same holds true on the other side of the house. If the army wants Rangers, it must allow that certain personalities will naturally gravitate to that superconventional SOF force. In return, the unique talents and abilities required of a Special Forces soldier cannot be regulated out of the system without driving a substantial number of quality SF soldiers from the organization.

Recently a "new" SF philosophy has been encouraged within the ranks. It calls for maturity, responsibility, multiple talents, and exceptionally high levels of professionalism. Although valid, this philosophy is not new to Special Forces as the same thoughts were originally prescribed for the organization in 1952, under the careful study and direction of Col. Aaron Bank. These traits have always been at the core of Special Forces and have never been improved upon. Today, however, far too many exceptional SF operators are being involuntarily discharged from the army because of a perceived failure on their parts to uphold the new philosophy. In one instance, a senior NCO with the 1st Special Forces Group was recently discharged because of a letter of reprimand placed in his personnel file several years previously. After that lone incident, the soldier's record was never again marred. He took part in OPERATION JUST CAUSE as a senior jumpmaster, whose responsibility it was to lead his plane's stick out the door at 480 feet above the ground while under intense enemy fire. But somewhere along the line, based upon one letter of reprimand, it was determined that he was not SOF material.

In another, more recent, instance, a group sergeant major announced that "we are going to get rid of all you liars, thieves, cheats, and troublemakers—this isn't the old Special Forces anymore!" If this attitude is the norm as promoted by the army, then the conventional side of the house deserves equal attention. Those with conventional experience know full well that there are far more "liars, thieves, cheats, and troublemakers" not wearing berets than wearing them. The very nature of special operations demands a level of worldliness perhaps frowned upon by more conventional commanders, but even the Ranger Creed offers "You can lie all you please when you tell other folks about the Rangers, but don't never lie to a Ranger or officers." SOF is losing too many good operators to the administrative whims of a downgrade mentality, which sees an opportunity to flush out the ranks in the name of cutbacks. This agenda should be recognized for what it is, and brought to a halt. Today's real-world obligations already outstrip current Special Forces' personnel resources. With fewer volunteers seeking careers in a field with little civilian application, special operations must rely on and develop those already within the system in order to remain a strong force.

USSOCOM must also assess its use of its Special Forces reserve components. Originally established to form a manpower pool of qualified civilian-soldier operators, there are four SF reserve organizations, or groups. During OPERATION DESERT SHIELD, USSOCOM ordered the activation of "the most combat-ready reserve group available, to be utilized for worldwide deployment." The 20th Special Forces Group (Airborne) was selected, a National Guard organization with elements scattered across more than five states.

Brought to Fort Bragg, the 20th required more than ninety days' assessment and training to upgrade its combat readiness to a state where its personnel could be considered ready for deployment. In addition, a full battalion from the 7th Special Forces Group (Airborne) was pulled from real-world commitments in order to conduct the 20th's training. In the end, only half of the 20th's teams could have been deployed as fully certified twelve-man detachments, and those would have had to be composite detachments.

Contrary to that performance was the deployment to DESERT SHIELD/DESERT STORM of twenty-nine selected SF operators from the 11th and 12th Active Army Reserve Groups (AAR). For the active reserves, as little as fifteen hours was necessary to activate the operators and prepare their orders; special permission was required from each governor whose National Guard controlled a Special Forces organization before such a selection and activation could be made. In addition, SF reserve personnel handlers in St. Louis reported more than two hundred qualified AAR Special Forces volunteers requesting to be immediately assigned to active duty at the onset of DESERT SHIELD. Clearly the Active Army Reserve program deserves strong attention from USSOCOM as it can provide fully qualified personnel on a moment's notice to augment active duty teams scheduled for deployment. Some voices within the reserve/active components offer that there is no need for National Guard Special Forces groups, and that the funds, personnel, and equipment devoted to them would be better utilized within the Active Army Reserve system to more fully prepare those groups already in existence, or to reactivate an additional Active Army Reserve Group.

The navy faces similar challenges. But in the SEAL's case, the incorporation of the early Scout Swimmers and UDT programs in support of the fleet has always created a kinship between naval special operations and the conventional navy. This does not mean no one in the navy wouldn't be pleased to see SEALs disappear in favor of a new battleship, but it does allow for a generally more tolerant attitude about SEALs and their applications. The challenge for naval special warfare will be to maintain the high standards required of its SEAL candidates and to upgrade its already proven capabilities as a maritime and riverine SpecWar force. The creation and support of a naval special operations aviation group similar to that of the army's 160th SOAR will be of critical value to NAVSPECWAR's ability to carry out its missions.

On the heels of DESERT STORM, the SOF community also faces a unique set of mission challenges. Many of the men I interviewed for this book expressed concern that roles are being confused within USSOCOM itself. They point out the Rangers' proposal to practice small-boat insertions from far out at sea. What are the SEALs for if the Rangers are going to conduct small-boat operations? Why are SEALs becoming involved in force multiplication if that is what the army's Special Forces excel at? Why are the Marines creating their own SOF while refusing to assign Marine assets to the unified special operations command structure? These are all questions which must be resolved if USSOCOM is to be successful. Indeed, the resolution of such questions is one of the reasons that USSOCOM was established. Despite their contribution to the constrained victory of DESERT STORM, Special Forces and their operations continue to face the challenge of being considered part of the overall military force. Though General Schwarzkopf was pleased with their performance, it is unlikely he has become an avid supporter of the SOF community. Those conventional force commanders who witnessed firsthand the contributions of SpecWar in the desert are bound to speak highly of them, but perhaps not as loudly as is needed to continue the bonding between conventional and unconventional lines of thought. Therefore the challenge to successfully integrate conventional forces and SOF remains, and it is hoped senior SOF commanders will be astute enough to realize that it will be performance that ensures acceptance as opposed to the compromising of their troops' unique identity and character traits.

Today the threat of Saddam Hussein is nearly as strong as it was when he ordered the invasion of Kuwait. Should it be determined that Iraq's leadership must be changed in order for peace and stability to return in the Gulf, SOF forces will lend their talents toward the realization of the goal. In other parts of the world special operations forces are carrying out both humanitarian and military missions, including the bitter war against drugs, which is being fought in Latin America and Southeast Asia. Like the war in El Salvador, such conflicts may not see campaign medals or Combat Infantry Badges formally authorized to combat veterans, but they remain wars nonetheless. If they are to be won on the ground, it will be by SOF soldiers from all the services, working together as a combined force.

AREA STUDY—KUWAIT

National Trade Data Bank - The Export Connection (R)
ITEM ID : CI WOFACT 126
DATE   : Dec 28, 1991

AGENCY   : Central Intelligence Agency
PROGRAM : WORLD FACTBOOK
TITLE   : Vital Statistics - KUWAIT

Updated sched: ANNUAL
Data type : TEXT
Country : 126   I KUWAIT
End year : 1991

KUWAIT
GEOGRAPHY
Total area: 17,820 km2; land area: 17,820 km2

Comparative area: slightly smaller than New Jersey

Land boundaries: 462 km total; Iraq 240 km, Saudi Arabia 222
km

Coastline: 499 km

Maritime claims:

Continental shelf: not specific

Territorial sea: 12nm

Disputes: Iraqi forces invaded and occupied Kuwait from 2 August 1990 until 27 February 1991; in April 1991 official Iraqi acceptance of UN Security Council Resolution 687, which demands that Iraq accept its internationally recognized border with Kuwait, ended earlier claims to Bubiyan and Warbah Islands or to all of Kuwait; ownership of Qaruh and Umm al Maradim Islands disputed by Saudi Arabia

Climate: dry desert; intensely hot summers; short, cool winters

Terrain: flat to slightly undulating desert plain

Natural resources: petroleum, fish, shrimp, natural gas

Land use: arable land NEGL%; permanent crops 0%; meadows and pastures 8%; forest and woodland NEGL%; other 92%; includes irrigated NEGL%

Environment: some of world's largest and most sophisticated desalination facilities provide most of water; air and water pollution; desertification

Note: strategic location at head of Persian Gulf

PEOPLE
Population: 2,204,400 (July 1991), growth rate 3.6% (1991)

Birth rate: 29 births/1,000 population (1991)

Death rate: 2 deaths/1,000 population (1991)

Net migration rate: 10 migrants/1,000 population (1991)

Infant mortality rate: 15 deaths/1,000 live births (1991)

Life expectancy at birth: 72 years male, 76 years female (1991)

Total fertility rate: 3.7 children born/woman (1991)

Nationality: noun-Kuwaiti(s); adjective—Kuwaiti

Ethnic divisions: Kuwaiti 27.9%, other Arab 39%, South Asian 9%, Iranian 4%, other 20.1%

Religion:
Muslim 85% (Shia 30%, Sunni 45%, other 10%), Christian, Hindu, Parsi, and other 15%

Language: Arabic (official); English widely spoken

Literacy: 74% (male 78%, female 69%) age 15 and over can read and write (1985)

Labor force: 566,000 (1986); services 45.0%, construction 20.0%, trade 12.0%, manufacturing 8.6%, finance and real estate 2.6%, agriculture 1.9%, power and water 1.7%, mining and quarrying 1.4%; 70% of labor force was non-Kuwaiti

Organized labor: labor unions exist in oil industry and among government personnel

GOVERNMENT
Long-form name: State of Kuwait

Type: nominal constitutional monarchy

Capital: Kuwait

Administrative divisions: 4 governorates (muhafazat, singular—muhafazah); Al Ahmadi, Al Jahrah, Al Kuwayt, Hawalli; note—there may be a new governorate of Farwaniyyah

Independence: 19 June 1961 (from UK)

Constitution: 16 November 1962 (some provisions suspended since 29 August 1962)

Legal system: civil law system with Islamic law significant in personal matters; has not accepted compulsory ICJ jurisdiction

National holiday: National Day, 25 February

Executive branch: amir, prime minister, deputy prime minister, Council of Ministers (cabinet)

Legislative branch: National Assembly (Majlis al Umma) dissolved 3 July 1986

Judicial branch: High Court of Appeal

Leaders:

Chief of State—Amir Shaykh Jabir al-Ahmad al-Jabir al-SABAH (since 31 December 1977)

Head of Government—Prime Minister and Crown Prince Sad al-Abdallah al-Salim al-SABAH (since 8 February 1978); Deputy Prime Minister Salim al-Sabah al-Salim al-SABAH

Political parties and leaders: none

Suffrage: adult males who resided in Kuwait before 1920 and their male descendants at age 21; note—out of all citizens, only 8.3% are eligible to vote and only 3.5% actually vote

Elections:

National Assembly—dissolved 3 July 1986; new elections are scheduled for October 1992

Communists: insignificant

Other political or pressure groups: large (150,000) Palestinian community; several small, clandestine leftist and Shia fundamentalist groups are active; prodemocracy opposition

Member of: ABEDA, AfDB, AFESD, AL, AMF, BDEAC, CAEU, ESCWA, FAO, G-77, GATT, GCC, IAEA, IBRD, ICAO, ICC, IDA, IDB, IFAD, IFC, ILO, IMF, IMO, INMARSAT, INTELSAT, INTERPOL, IOC, ISO (correspondent), ITU, LORCS, NAM, OAPEC, OIC, OPEC, UN, UNCTAD, UNESCO, UNIDO, UPU, WFTU, WHO, WMO, WTO

Diplomatic representation: Ambassador Shaykh Saud Nasir al-SABAH; Chancery at 2940 Tilden Street NW, Washington DC 20008; telephone (202) 966-0702

US—Ambassador Edward (Skip) GNEHM; Embassy at Bneid al-Gar (opposite the Hilton Hotel), Kuwait City (mailing address is P.O. Box 77 Safat, 13001 Safat, Kuwait City); telephone 965 242-4151 through 4159

Flag: three equal horizontal bands of green (top), white, and red with a black trapezoid based on the hoist side

ECONOMY

Overview: Up to the invasion by Iraq in August 1990, the oil sector had dominated the economy. Kuwait has the third largest oil reserves in the world after Saudi Arabia and Iraq. Earnings from hydrocarbons generated over 90% of both export and government revenues and contributed about 40% to GDP. Most of the nonoil sector has traditionally been dependent upon oil-derived government revenues. Iraq's destruction of Kuwait's oil industry during the Gulf War has devastated the economy. Iraq destroyed or damaged more than 80% of Kuwait's 950 operating oil wells, as well as sabotaging key surface facilities. Western firefighters had brought about 140 of the 600 oil well fires and blowouts under control as of early June 1991. It could take two to three years to restore Kuwait's oil production to its prewar level of about 2.0 million barrels per day.

GDP: $19.8 billion, per capita $9,700; real growth rate 3.5% (1989)

Inflation rate (consumer prices): 3.3% (1989)

Unemployment rate: 0% (1989)

Budget: revenues $7.1 billion; expenditures $10.5 billion, including capital expenditures of $3.1 billion (FY88)

Exports: 11.5 billion (f.o.b., 1989);

commodities—oil 90%;

partners—Japan, Italy, FRG, US

Imports: $6.3 billion (f.o.b., 1989);

commodities—food, construction materials, vehicles and parts, clothing;

partners—Japan, US, FRG, UK

External debt: $7.2 billion (December 1989 est.)

Industrial production: growth rate 3% (1988); accounts for 52% of GDP

Electricity: 8,280,000 kW capacity; 10,000 million kWh produced, 5,000 kWh per capita (1989)

Industries: petroleum, petrochemicals, desalination, food processing, salt, construction

Agriculture: virtually none; dependent on imports for food; about 75% of potable water must be distilled or imported

Economic aid: donor—pledged $18.3 billion in bilateral aid to less developed countries (1979–89)

Currency: Kuwaiti dinar (plural—dinars);
1 Kuwaiti dinar (KD) = 1,000 fils

Exchange rates: Kuwaiti dinars (KD) per US$1—0.2915 (January 1990), 0.2937 (1989), 0.2790 (1988), 0.2786 (1987), 0.2919 (1986), 0.3007 (1985)

Fiscal year: 1 July–30 June

COMMUNICATIONS
Highways: 3,000 km total; 2,500 km bituminous; 500 km earth, sand, light gravel

Pipelines: crude oil, 877 km; refined products, 40 km; natural gas, 165 km

Ports: Ash Shuaybah, Ash Shuwaykh, Mina al Ahmadi

Merchant marine: 31 ships (1,000 GRT or over), totaling 1,332,159 GRT/2,099,303 DWT; includes 1 cargo, 4 livestock carrier, 20 petroleum, oils, and lubricants (POL) tanker, 5 liquefied gas, 1 bulk; note—all Kuwaiti ships greater than 1,000 GRT were outside Kuwaiti waters at the time of the Iraqi invasion; many of these ships transferred to the Liberian flag or to the flags of other Persian Gulf states; Kuwaiti tankers are currently managed from London and Kuwaiti cargo and container ships are managed from Dubai

Civil air: 19 major transport aircraft

Airports: 7 total, 4 usable; 4 with permanent-surface runways; none with runways over 3,659 m; 4 with runways 2,440–3,659 m; none with runways 1,220–2,439 m

Telecommunications: excellent international, adequate domestic facilities; 258,000 telephones; stations—3 AM, 2 FM, 3 TV; satellite earth stations—1 Indian Ocean INTELSAT, and 2 Atlantic Ocean INTELSAT; 1 INMARSAT, 1 ARABSAT; coaxial cable and radio relay to Iraq and Saudi Arabia

DEFENSE FORCES
Branches: Army, Navy, Air Force, National Police Force, National Guard

Manpower availability: males 15–49, 738,812; 441,611 fit for military service; 19,452 reach military age (18) annually

Defense expenditures: $1.1 billion, 4.8% of GDP (1990)

AREA STUDY—IRAQ

National Trade Data Bank - The Export Connection (R)
ITEM ID : CI WOFACT 107
DATE   : Dec 28, 1991

AGENCY   : Central Intelligence Agency
PROGRAM : WORLD FACTBOOK
TITLE   : Vital Statistics - IRAQ

Update sched: ANNUAL
Data type : TEXT
Country : 107 | IRAQ
End year : 1991

IRAQ
GEOGRAPHY
Total area: 434,920 km2; land area: 433,970 km2

Comparative area: slightly more than twice the size of Idaho

Land boundaries: 3,454 km total; Iran 1,458 km, Iraq - Saudi
Arabia Neutral Zone 191 km, Jordan 134 km, Kuwait 240 km,
Saudi Arabia 495 km, Syria 605 km, Turkey 331 km

Coastline: 58 km

Maritime claims:

Continental shelf: not specific

Territorial sea: 12nm

Disputes: Iran and Iraq restored diplomatic relations on 14 October 1990 following the end of the war that began on 22 September 1980; progress had been made on the major issues of contention—troop withdrawal, prisoner-of-war exchanges, demarcation of the border, freedom of navigation, and sovereignty over the Shatt al Arab waterway—but written agreements had yet to be drawn up when frictions reemerged in March 1991 in the wake of Shia and Kurdish revolts in Iraq that Baghdad accused Tehran of supporting; Kurdish question among Iran, Iraq, Syria, Turkey, and the USSR; shares Neutral Zone with Saudi Arabia—in December 1981, Iraq and Saudi Arabia signed a boundary agreement that divides the zone between them, but the agreement must be ratified before it becomes effective; Iraqi forces invaded and occupied Kuwait from 2 August 1990 until 27 February 1991; in April 1991 official Iraqi acceptance of UN Security Council Resolution 687, which demands that Iraq accept its internationally recognized border with Kuwait, ended earlier claims to Bubiyan and Warbah Islands or to all of Kuwait; periodic disputes with upstream riparian Syria over Euphrates water rights; potential dispute over water development plans by Turkey for the Tigris and Euphrates Rivers

Climate: desert; mild to cool winters with dry, hot, cloudless summers

Terrain: mostly broad plains; reedy marshes in southeast; mountains along borders with Iran and Turkey

Natural resources: crude oil, natural gas, phosphates, sulfur

Land use: arable land 12%; permanent crops 1%; meadows and pastures 9%; forest and woodland 3%; other 75%; includes irrigated 4%

Environment: development of Tigris-Euphrates river systems contingent upon agreements with upstream riparians (Syria, Turkey); air and water pollution; soil degradation (salinization) and erosion; desertification

PEOPLE
Population: 19,524,718 (July 1991), growth rate 3.9% (1991)

Birth rate: 46 births/1,000 population (1991)

Death rate: 7 deaths/1,000 population (1991)

Net migration rate: 0 migrants/1,000 population (1991)

Infant mortality rate: 66 deaths/1,000 live births (1991)

Life expectancy at birth: 66 years male, 68 years female (1991)

Total fertility rate: 7.2 children born/woman (1991)

Nationality: noun—Iraqi(s); adjective—Iraqi

Ethnic divisions: Arab 75–80%, Kurdish 15–20%, Turkoman, Assyrian, or other 5%

Religion: Muslim 97% (Shia 60–65%, Sunni 32–37%), Christian or other 3%

Language: Arabic (official), Kurdish (official in Kurdish regions), Assyrian, Armenian

Literacy: 60% (male 70%, female 49%) age 15 and over can read and write (1990 est.)

Labor force: 4,400,000 (1989); services 48%, agriculture 30%, industry 22%, severe labor shortage; expatriate labor force about 1,600,000 (July 1990)

Organized labor: less than 10% of the labor force

GOVERNMENT
Long-form name: Republic of Iraq

Type: republic

Capital: Baghdad

Administrative divisions: 18 provinces (muhafazat, singular—muhafazah); Al Anbar, Al Basrah, Al Muthanna, Al Qadisiyah, An Najaf, Arbil, As Sulaymaniyah, At Tamim, Babil, Baghdad, Dahuk, Dhi Qar, Diyala, Karbala, Maysan, Ninawa, Salah ad Din, Wasit

Independence: 3 October 1932 (from League of Nations mandate under British administration)

Constitution: 22 September 1968, effective 16 July 1970 (interim constitution); new constitution drafted in 1990 but not adopted

Legal system: based on Islamic law in special religious courts, civil law system elsewhere; has not accepted compulsory ICJ jurisdiction

National holiday: Anniversary of the Revolution, 17 July (1968)

Executive branch: president, vice president, chairman of the Revolutionary Command Council, vice chairman of the Revolutionary Command Council, prime minister, first deputy prime minister, Council of Ministers

Legislative branch: unicameral National Assembly (Majlis Watani)

Judicial branch: Court of Cassation

Leaders:

Chief of State—President Saddam Hussein (since 16 July 1979); Vice President Taha Muhyi al-Din MARUF (since 21 April 1974); Vice President Taha Yasin RAMADAN (since 23 March 1991)

Head of Government—Prime Minister Sadun HAMMADI (since 27 March 1991); Deputy Prime Minster Tariq AZIZ (since NA 1979); Deputy Prime Minister Muhammad Hamza al-ZUBAYDI (since 27 March 1991)

Political parties: National Progressive Front is a coalition of the Arab Bath Socialist Party, Kurdistan Democratic Party, and Kurdistan Revolutionary Party

Suffrage: universal adult at age 18

Elections:

National Assembly—last held on 1 April 1989 (next to be held NA); results—Sunni Arabs 53%, Shia Arabs 30%, Kurds 15%,

Christians 2% est.; seats—(250 total) number of seats by party NA

Communists: about 1,500 hardcore members

Other political or pressure groups: political parties and activity severely restricted; possibly some opposition to regime from disaffected members of the regime, army officers, and religious and ethnic dissidents

Member of: ABEDA, ACC, AFESD, AL, AMF, CAEU, ESCWA, FAO, G-19, G-77, IAEA, IBRD, ICAO, IDA, IDB, IFAD, IFC, ILO, IMF, IMO, INMARSAT, INTELSAT, INTERPOL, IOC, ISO, ITU, LORCS, NAM, OAPEC, OIC, OPEC, PCA, UN, UNCTAD, UNESCO, UNIDO, UPU, WFTU, WHO, WIPO, WMO, WTO

Diplomatic representation: no Iraqi representative in Washington; Chancery at 1801 P Street NW, Washington DC 20036; telephone (202) 483-7500

US—no US representative in Baghdad since mid-January 1991; Embassy in Masbah Quarter (opposite the Foreign Ministry Club), Baghdad (mailing address is P. O. Box 2447 Alwiyah, Baghdad); telephone 964 (1) 719-6138 or 719-6139, 718-1840, 719-3791

Flag: three equal horizontal bands of red (top), white, and black with three green five-pointed stars in a horizontal line centered in the white band: the phrase Allahu Akbar (God Is Great) in green Arabic script—Allahu to the right of the middle star and Akbar to the left of the middle star—was added in January 1991 during the Persian Gulf crisis; similar to the flag of Syria that has two stars but no script and the flag of Yemen that has a plain white band; also similar to the flag of Egypt that has a symbolic eagle centered in the white band

ECONOMY
Overview: The Bathist regime engages in extensive central planning and management of industrial production and foreign trade while leaving some small-scale industry and services and most agriculture to private enterprise. The economy has been dominated by the oil sector, which has provided about 95% of foreign ex-

change earnings. In the 1980s financial problems, caused by massive expenditures in the eight-year war with Iran and damage to oil export facilities by Iran, led the government to implement austerity measures and to borrow heavily and later reschedule foreign debt payments. After the end of hostilities in 1988, oil exports gradually increased with the construction of new pipelines and restoration of damaged facilities. Agricultural development remained hampered by labor shortages, salinization, and dislocations caused by previous land reform and collectivization programs. The industrial sector, although accorded high priority by the government, was also under financial constraints. Iraq's seizure of Kuwait in August 1990, subsequent international economic embargoes, and military actions by an international coalition beginning in January 1991 drastically changed the economic picture. Oil exports were cut to near zero, and industrial and transportation facilities severely damaged.

GNP: $35 billion, per capita $1,940; real growth rate 5% (1989 est.)

Inflation rate (consumer prices): 30–40% (1989 est.)

Unemployment rate: less than 5% (1989 est.)

Budget: revenues $NA billion; expenditures $35 billion, including capital expenditures of NA (1989)

Exports: $12.1 billion (f.o.b., 1989);

commodities—crude oil and refined products, fertilizer, sulfur;

partners—US, Brazil, Turkey, Japan, France, Italy, USSR (1989)

Imports: $10.3 billion (c.i.f., 1989);

commodities—manufactures, food;

partners—US, FRG, Turkey, UK, Romania, Japan, France (1989)

External debt: $40 billion (1989 est.), excluding debt to Arab Gulf states

Industrial production: NA%; manufacturing accounts for 10% of GDP (1987)

Electricity: 9,902,000 kW capacity; 20,000 million kWh produced, 1,110 kWh per capita (1989)

Industries: petroleum, chemicals, textiles, construction materials, food processing

Agriculture: accounts for 11% of GNP but 30% of labor force; principal products—wheat, barley, rice, vegetables, dates, other fruit, cotton, wool; livestock—cattle, sheep; not self-sufficient in food output

Economic aid: US commitments, including Ex-Im (FY70–80), $3 million; Western (non-US) countries, ODA and OOF bilateral commitments (1970–88), $627 million; OPEC bilateral aid (1980–90), more than $30 billion; Communist countries (1970–89), $3.9 billion

Currency: Iraqi dinar (plural—dinars); 1 Iraqi Dinar (ID) = 1,000 fils

Exchange rates: Iraqi dinars (ID) per US$1—0.3109 (fixed rate since 1982)

Fiscal year: calendar year

COMMUNICATIONS

Railroads: 2,962 km total; 2,457 km 1.435-meter standard gauge, 505 km 1.000-meter gauge

Highways: 25,479 km total; 8,290 km paved, 5,534 km improved earth, 11,655 km unimproved earth

Inland waterways: 1,015 km; Shatt al Arab usually navigable by maritime traffic for about 130 km, but closed since September 1980 because of Iran-Iraq war; Tigris and Euphrates navigable by shallow-draft steamers (of little importance); Shatt al Basrah canal navigable in sections by shallow-draft vessels

Ports: Umm Qasr, Khawr as Zubayr, Al Basrah

Merchant marine: 43 ships (1,000 GRT or over) totaling 944,253 GRT/1,691,368 DWT; includes 1 passenger, 1 passenger-cargo, 17 cargo, 1 refrigerated cargo, 3 roll-on/roll-off cargo, 19 petroleum, oils, and lubricants (POL) tanker, 1 chemical tanker; note—since the 2 August 1990 invasion of Kuwait by Iraqi forces, Iraq has sought to register at least part of its merchant fleet under convenience flags; none of the Iraqi flag merchant fleet was trading internationally as of 1 January 1991

Pipelines: crude oil, 4,350 km; 725 km refined products; 1,360 km natural gas

Civil air: 64 major transport aircraft (including 30 IL-76s used by the Iraq Air Force)

Airports: 111 total, 102 usable; 73 with permanent-surface runways; 9 with runways over 3,659 m; 52 with runways 2,440–3,659 m; 15 with runways 1,220–2,439 m

Telecommunications: good network consists of coaxial cables, radio relay links, and radiocommunication stations; 632,000 telephones; stations—9 AM, 1 FM, 81 TV; satellite earth stations—1 Atlantic Ocean INTELSAT, 1 Indian Ocean INTELSAT, 1 GORIZONT Atlantic Ocean in the Intersputnik system; coaxial cable and radio relay to Kuwait, Jordan, Syria, and Turkey

DEFENSE FORCES
Branches: Army and Republican Guard, Navy, Air Force, Border Guard Force, Internal Security Forces

Manpower availability: males 15–49, 4,270,592; 2,380,439 fit for military service; 228,277 reach military age (18) annually

Defense expenditures: $NA, NA% of GDP

BIBLIOGRAPHY

Primary Sources

Adams, James. *Secret Armies*. New York: Atlantic Monthly, 1988.

Bacevich, A. J., et al. [Bacevich, Hallums, White, Young] *American Military Policy in Small Wars: The Case of El Salvador*. Massachusetts: Macmillan, 1988.

Bank, Aaron. *From OSS to Green Berets*. California: Presidio Press, 1986.

Donnely, Thomas, et al. [Donnely, Roth, Baker] *Operation Just Cause*. New York: Free Press, 1991.

*Emerson, Steven. *Secret Warriors*. New York, 1988.

Klare, Michael, and Peter Kornbluh. *Low Intensity Warfare*. New York: Pantheon, 1988.

*Kyle, James. *The Guts to Try*. New York: 1990.

Marcinko, Richard, and John Weisman. *Rogue Warrior*. Edited by Judith Regan and Paul McCarthy. New York: PB Co., 1992.

McConnell, Malcolm. *Just Cause*. New York: St. Martin's Press, 1991.

Moon, Tom. *This Grim and Savage Game*. California: Burning Gate Press, 1991.

Newman, John M. *JFK and Vietnam*. New York: Warner Books, 1992.

*Paddock, Alfred. *U.S. Army Special Warfare: Its Origins*. Washington, D.C.

Pyle, Richard. *Schwarzkopf in His Own Words*. New York: NAL-Dutton, 1991.

Schemmer, Benjamin. *The Raid*. New York: Harper & Row, 1976.

Stanton, Shelby L. *Green Berets at War*. California: Presidio Press, 1985.

Stanton, Shelby L. *Special Forces at War*. Edited by Kathleen D. Valenzi. Virginia: Howell Press, 1990.

Sutherland, Ian. *Special Forces of the United States Army*. California: Bender Pub., 1990.

Watson, Bruce W., et al. [Watson, George, Tsouras, Cyr]. *Military Lessons of the Gulf War*. California: Presidio Press, 1991.

Secondary Sources

*Kirkbride, Wayne. *Special Forces in Latin America*. North Carolina, 1991.

*Chapter #38, SFA, FIFTH SPECIAL FORCES GROUP (AIRBORNE) IN DESERT SHIELD AND DESERT STORM, Tennessee, 1991.

The New Face of War, Special Forces and Missions. Virginia: Time-Life Books, 1990.

Manning, Robert, ed., *War in the Shadows*. Boston: Boston Publishing Company, 1988.

*Montrem, Alfred. *The Role of the Air Force in the Assault on the POW Camp at Son Tay*. Alabama, 1978.

Walker, Greg. "The Montagnard Rebellion." *Gung-Ho* (January/February 1983).

Walker, Greg. "Salvadoran Insights." *Gung-Ho* (November 1983).

*Walker, Greg. "On the Ground in El Salvador." *Gung-Ho* (November 1983).

*Walker, Greg. "Killer Dune Buggy." *Gung-Ho* (June 1984).

Walker, Greg, and Tom Halliwell. "Vietnam's Recon Commandos." *Gung-Ho* (February 1985).

*Walker, Greg. "Special Forces—the Real Story." *Gung-Ho* (January 1983).

Walker, Greg. "Special Forces in Central America." *Gung-Ho* (December 1983).

*Walker, Greg. "Rangers." *Gung-Ho* (May 1982).

*Walker, Greg. "The Snipers of El Salvador." *Gung-Ho* (January 1987).

*Walker, Greg. "Target America." *Gung-Ho* (May 1983).

*Walker, Greg. "Commando." *Gung-Ho* (June 1984).

*Walker, Greg. "Base Camps." *Gung-Ho* (June 1982).

*Walker, Greg. "Military Kidnapping." *Gung-Ho* (July 1982).

*Walker, Greg. "The Art of Ambushing." *Gung-Ho* (April 1988).

*Walker, Greg. "Techniques of Patrolling." *Gung-Ho* (November 1981).

Walker, Greg. "The Real Peace Corps." *Eagle* (April 1986).

*Walker, Greg. "Airborne Splashdown." *Soldier of Fortune* (January 1987).

Walker, Greg. "Booby Traps." *Soldier of Fortune* (May 1985).

Walker, Greg. "Blending with the Bush." *Soldier of Fortune* (June 1985).

Walker, Greg. "Night Stalkers Don't Quit." *Soldier of Fortune* (March 1992).

Walker, Greg. "SEALing Saddam's Fate." *Soldier of Fortune* (February 1992).

Walker, Greg. "Blue Badges of Honor." *Soldier of Fortune* (February 1992).

Walker, Greg. "From Refugees to Liberators." *Soldier of Fortune* (June 1992).

Walker, Greg. "Special Operations—the Cutting Edge." *Fighting Knives* (Winter 1990).

Walker, Greg. "USAF Parajumpers." *International Combat Arms* (September 1989).

Walker, Greg. "Eyes in the Dark." *International Combat Arms* (July 1989).

Walker, Greg. "The Army's New M-24 Sniper Rifle." *International Combat Arms* (March 1989).

Walker, Greg. "Elite SEAL Units, Navy's Silent Warriors." *International Combat Arms* (November 1989).

Note: Those sources by the author which have been annotated with an * were published under one of several pen names used by the author.